Developing C# Windows Software

Jason Bell
Benny B Johansen
Matthew Reynolds
Thiru Thangarathinam
Neil Whitlow

Wrox Press Ltd. ®

Developing C# Windows Software

© 2002 Wrox Press

Printing History
First published   July 2002

Published by Wrox Press Ltd,
Arden House, 1102 Warwick Road, Acocks Green,
Birmingham, B27 6BH, UK
Printed in the United States
ISBN 1-86100-737-X

Trademark Acknowledgements

Credits

Authors
Jason Bell
Benny B Johansen
Matthew Reynolds
Thiru Thangarathinam
Neil Whitlow

Commissioning Editor
Daniel Kent

Technical Editors
Christian Peak
Robert FE Shaw

Managing Editor
Louay Fatoohi

Project Manager
Christianne Bailey

Author Agent
Charlotte Smith

Index
Martin Brooks

Technical Reviewers
Chris Crane
Mitch Denny
Damien Foggon
Brian Hickey
Vic Honnaya
Mark Horner
Phil Powers de George
Larry Schoeneman
Gavin Smyth

Production Project Coordinator
Abbie Forletta

Illustrations
Abbie Forletta

Cover
Natalie O'Donnell

Proof Reader
Chris Smith

About the Authors

Jason Bell

After eight years of developing software for the U.S. Air Force, Jason Bell is now an MCSD working as a consultant for Stroudwater NHG, a Microsoft Certified Partner located in Portland, Maine.

Benny B Johansen

Benny B Johansen is V. P. of Software Development at Sound ID, a Palo Alto based startup using innovative technology to 'enhance the appreciation of sound'. He has a B.Sc. in Computer Science, an MBA in Corporate Strategy, and most importantly of course an MCSD.

When not cracking the whip at Sound ID, or teaching ASP.NET at UC Berkeley Extension, he enjoys running, cooking, and trying to improve his piano playing. He can be reached at bjohansen@soundid.com or bennynet@etvoila.com.

I would like to thank my wife Dorthe and my two daughters Michelle and Nicole for filling my life with joy and delight.

Matthew Reynolds

After working with Wrox Press on a number of projects since 1999, Matthew is now an in-house author for Wrox Press writing about and working with virtually all aspects of Microsoft .NET. He's also a regular contributor to Wrox's ASPToday and C#Today, and Web Services Architect. He lives and works in North London, Great Britain, and can be reached on matthewr@wrox.com.

Thiru Thangarathinam

Thiru works as a Consultant at Spherion Technology Architects, an international technology consulting company, in Phoenix, Arizona. He is an MCSD. During the last two years, he has been developing Distributed N-Tier architecture solutions for various companies using latest technologies such as VB, ASP, XML, XSL, COM+, and SQL Server. He can be reached via e-mail at ThiruThangarathinam@spherion.com.

I would like to dedicate this book to my family and friends who have been providing constant motivation and help all these years. Also special thanks to Charlotte Smith and Daniel Kent for their excellent support and encouragement throughout this project.

Neil Whitlow

Neil Whitlow is currently working as a Senior Systems Analyst developing software for pen-based computers with a large insurance company in Nashville, Tennessee.

Table of Contents

Table of Contents

Table of Contents

Table of Contents

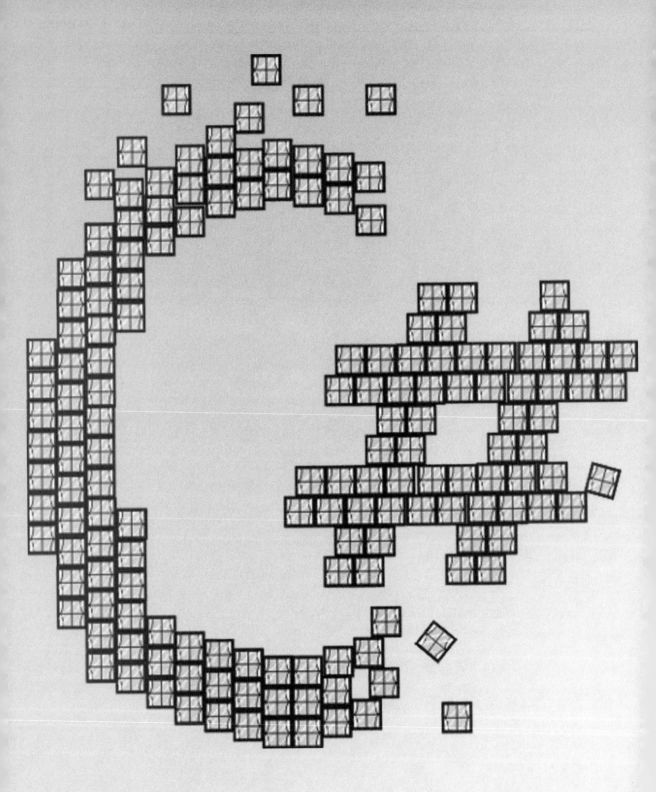

Introduction

The power of the C# language, coupled to the simplicity of developing Windows Forms in Visual Studio .NET, makes real-world Windows application development faster and easier than ever before.

Developing C# Windows Software teaches you how to design, implement, and deploy powerful Windows applications based upon Windows Forms and C#. We will show you how to make the most effective use of the Microsoft .NET Framework classes in your applications, and guide you around the Visual Studio .NET IDE – the development tool of choice for Windows applications. In each chapter we will discuss important aspects of Window application design, and illustrate their use by building up practical, real-world sample applications. In no time at all you will become a skilled Windows application developer.

Who is this Book For?

This book is for developers who want to learn how to create powerful, robust, user-friendly Windows applications based upon Windows Forms. You will need to have some basic C# programming skills, and some familiarity with the concepts of databases. Some experience in the use of the Visual Studio .NET IDE and Windows Forms is helpful, although not required.

What does this Book Cover?

Chapter 1 – Basic Windows Programming. We start here by looking at building our first Windows application using C# and the main user interface components used when developing Windows applications.

Chapter 2, **Chapter 3**, and **Chapter 4**. These chapters look at using the controls in the Visual Studio .NET toolbox to create User Interfaces.

Chapter 5 – Using Graphics. This chapter gives you an overview of using graphics and GDI+ in Windows applications.

Chapter 6 – Printing. This chapter will look at how to "print enable" our applications so that as well as sending their output to the screen, users can send their output to a printer either attached to the local machine, or attached somewhere on the network.

Chapter 7 – Linking to a Database. This chapter will look at how to connect to a DBMS from our .NET applications, how to manipulate data in the database from our code, and how to retrieve and display database data.

Chapter 8 – File and Registry Operations. This chapter will look at two alternative places to store data: the file system and the Registry. We will explore the classes used to read and write data, especially text, to the file system. We will look at how we can navigate the file system. We will demonstrate how to serialize object state into XML. We will discuss how the Registry is structured, and which classes can be used to access it.

Chapter 9 – Using the Document/View Model. In this chapter we will look at dealing with more than one document at the same time. We will show you how to design and implement a Windows application that can handle multiple documents at once.

Chapter 10 – Providing Help. We will teach you design guidelines for creating help systems, following that with an examination of the different help authoring tools available. The chapter will also cover the support provided by the .NET Framework for linking external help systems to Windows applications.

Chapter 11 – Distributing Windows Applications. This chapter discusses the support provided by the .NET Framework in deploying Windows applications to the end user's machine. We will also cover different types of deployment options provided by the .NET Framework

What do you Need to use This Book?

There are software and knowledge requirements for successful progress through this book.

Software

❏   Microsoft Windows 2000 or XP

❏   Visual Studio .NET, either the full version or the Visual C# Standard package version

Knowledge

❏   Some knowledge of the C# language is assumed

Conventions

We've used a number of different styles of text and layout in this book to help differentiate between different kinds of information. Here are examples of the styles we used and an explanation of what they mean.

Code has several styles. If it's a word that we're talking about in the text – for example, when discussing a `for` loop, it's in this font. If it's a block of code that can be typed as a program and run, then it's also in a gray box:

```
<asp:Textbox id="MyTextBox" runat="server"/>
```

Sometimes we'll see code in a mixture of styles, like this:

```
private void MyButton_Click(object sender, System.EventArgs e){
    //Incredibly useful code here...
    Response.Write(MyButton.Text);
}
```

In cases like this, the code with a white background is code we are already familiar with; the line highlighted in gray is a new addition to the code since we last looked at it.

Advice, hints, and background information comes in this type of font.

> **Important pieces of information come in boxes like this.**

Bullets appear indented, with each new bullet marked as follows:

- ❑ **Important Words** are in a bold type font
- ❑ Words that appear on the screen, or in menus like the Open or Close, are in a similar font to the one you would see on a Windows desktop
- ❑ Keys that you press on the keyboard like *Ctrl* and *Enter*, are in italics

Customer Support

We always value hearing from our readers, and we want to know what you think about this book: what you liked, what you didn't like, and what you think we can do better next time. You can send us your comments, either by returning the reply card in the back of the book, or by e-mail to feedback@wrox.com. Please be sure to mention the book title in your message.

How to Download the Sample Code for the Book

When you visit the Wrox site, http://www.wrox.com/, simply locate the title through our Search facility or by using one of the title lists. Click on Download in the Code column, or on Download Code on the book's details page.

When you click to download the code for this book, you are presented with a page with three options:

- ❏ If you are already a member of the Wrox Developer Community (if you have already registered on ASPToday, C#Today or Wroxbase), you can log in with your usual username and password combination to receive your code.

- ❏ If you are not already a member, you are asked if you would like to register for free code downloads. In addition you will also be able to download several free articles from Wrox Press. Registering will allow us to keep you informed about updates and new editions of this book.

- ❏ The third option is to bypass registration completely and simply download the code.

Registration for code download is not mandatory for this book, but should you wish to register for your code download, your details will not be passed to any third party. For more details, you may wish to view our terms and conditions, which are linked from the download page.

Once you reach the code download section, you will find that the files that are available for download from our site have been archived using WinZip. When you have saved the files to a folder on your hard drive, you will need to extract the files using a de-compression program such as WinZip or PKUnzip. When you extract the files, the code is usually extracted into chapter folders. When you start the extraction process, ensure your software (WinZip, PKUnzip, etc.) is set to use folder names.

Errata

We've made every effort to make sure that there are no errors in the text or in the code. However, no one is perfect and mistakes do occur. If you find an error in one of our books, like a spelling mistake or a faulty piece of code, we would be very grateful for feedback. By sending in errata you may save another reader hours of frustration, and of course, you will be helping us provide even higher quality information. Simply e-mail the information to support@wrox.com; your information will be checked and if correct, posted to the errata page for that title, or used in subsequent editions of the book.

To find errata on the web site, go to http://www.wrox.com/, and simply locate the title through our Advanced Search or title list. Click on the Book Errata link, which is below the cover graphic on the book's detail page.

E-mail Support

If you wish to directly query a problem in the book with an expert who knows the book in detail then e-mail support@wrox.com, with the title of the book and the last four numbers of the ISBN in the subject field of the e-mail. A typical e-mail should include the following things:

- ❏ The **title of the book**, **last four digits of the ISBN (737X)**, and **page number** of the problem in the Subject field.

- ❏ Your **name**, **contact information**, and the **problem** in the body of the message.

We won't send you junk mail. We need the details to save your time and ours. When you send an e-mail message, it will go through the following chain of support:

- ❏ Customer Support – Your message is delivered to our customer support staff, who are the first people to read it. They have files on most frequently asked questions and will answer anything general about the book or the web site immediately.

❏ Editorial – Deeper queries are forwarded to the technical editor responsible for that book. They have experience with the programming language or particular product, and are able to answer detailed technical questions on the subject.

❏ The Authors – Finally, in the unlikely event that the editor cannot answer your problem, they will forward the request to the author. We do try to protect the author from any distractions to their writing; however, we are quite happy to forward specific requests to them. All Wrox authors help with the support on their books. They will e-mail the customer and the editor with their response, and again all readers should benefit.

The Wrox Support process can only offer support to issues that are directly pertinent to the content of our published title. Support for questions that fall outside the scope of normal book support, is provided via the community lists of our http://p2p.wrox.com/ forum.

p2p.wrox.com

For author and peer discussion join the P2P mailing lists. Our unique system provides **programmer to programmer™** contact on mailing lists, forums, and newsgroups, all in addition to our one-to-one e-mail support system. If you post a query to P2P, you can be confident that it is being examined by the many Wrox authors and other industry experts who are present on our mailing lists. At p2p.wrox.com you will find a number of different lists that will help you, not only while you read this book, but also as you develop your own applications. Particularly appropriate to this book are the beginning_c_sharp, dotnet_windows_app_design and the pro_windows_forms lists.

To subscribe to a mailing list just follow these steps:

1. Go to http://p2p.wrox.com/.

2. Choose the appropriate category from the left menu bar.

3. Click on the mailing list you wish to join.

4. Follow the instructions to subscribe and fill in your e-mail address and password.

5. Reply to the confirmation e-mail you receive.

6. Use the subscription manager to join more lists and set your e-mail preferences.

Why this System Offers the Best Support

You can choose to join the mailing lists or you can receive them as a weekly digest. If you don't have the time, or facility, to receive the mailing list, then you can search our online archives. Junk and spam mails are deleted, and your own e-mail address is protected by the unique Lyris system. Queries about joining or leaving lists, and any other general queries about lists, should be sent to listsupport@p2p.wrox.com.

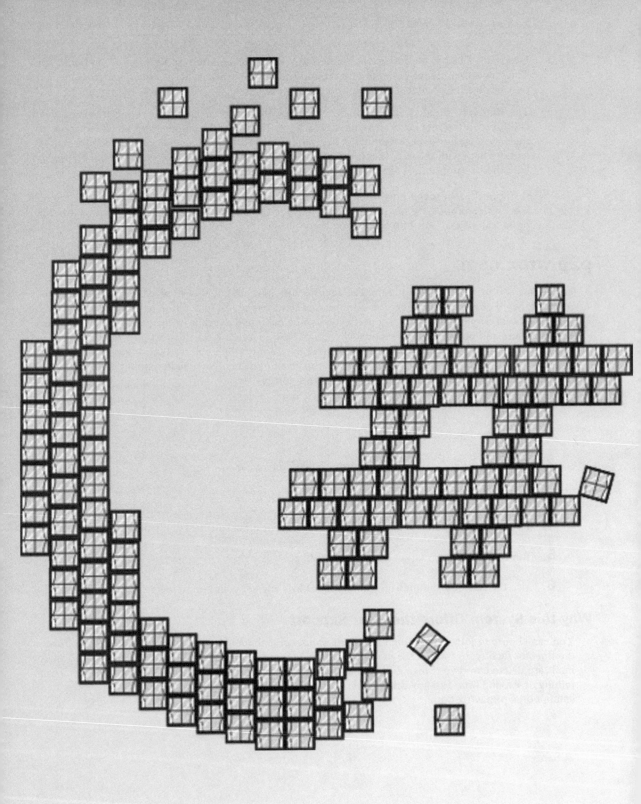

Basic Windows Programming

With the release of .NET and the C# language, Microsoft has provided us with a very efficient and powerful set of tools for building a variety of applications, including interactive web applications and XML-based web services. However, our focus for this book is the development of desktop Windows applications. Even though it may not get as much press as some of the web-related technologies, desktop application development has also undergone significant changes with the arrival of .NET. By the end of this book, you should be starting to feel comfortable with developing Windows applications using Visual Studio .NET and the C# language.

In this first chapter, we will work our way through the building of our first Windows application using C#. Along the way, we'll cover a variety of topics and form a foundation for future chapters that will each add more sophisticated functionality to your applications. By the end of this chapter, you will have learned about:

- ❑ The main User Interface components used when developing Windows applications
- ❑ The Visual Studio .NET IDE and what it provides for Windows developers
- ❑ How to start a new Windows Form-based application project
- ❑ How to respond to user events like the clicking of a button
- ❑ How to display a message box to a user

Windows and Forms

In .NET, you will often see the terms **window** and **form** used interchangeably. This is because there has been a change in terminology in this area with .NET. Up until now, you would refer to an object with a title bar on your screen as a window. Well, these are now more properly referred to as forms. In any event, what we're going to look at now is what will be the main element of every visual Windows application you will ever build – a Windows Form.

What is a Windows Form?

A Windows Form is a window you can use to present information to the user and to accept input from the user – in other words you create a user interface using a form. Forms can be standard windows, multiple document interface (MDI) windows, dialog boxes, or display surfaces for graphical routines. You will normally create a Windows Form-based application using the Visual Studio .NET IDE, which we will discuss in the next section.

As with all objects in the .NET Framework, forms are instances of classes. The form you create with the Visual Studio .NET Designer is a class, and when you display an instance of the form at run time, this class is the template used to create the form. Forms are objects, exposing properties that define their appearance, methods that define their behavior, and events that define their interaction with the user. By setting the properties of the form and writing code to respond to its events, you customize the object to meet the requirements of your application.

The Framework also allows you to inherit from existing forms to add functionality or modify existing behavior. When you add a form to your project, you can choose whether it inherits directly from the `System.Windows.Forms.Form` class provided by the Framework, or from a form you have previously created. For more information about the `Form` class (or any other class in the Framework), you can refer to the MSDN library at http://msdn.microsoft.com/library/.

Controls

Controls are objects that either display information to the user, or respond to user input. They are contained within `Form` objects. Each type of control has its own set of properties, methods, and events that make it suitable for a particular purpose. By combining different sets of controls and your own code, you can get information from the user and respond to it, work with existing stores of data, and query and write back to the file system and Registry on the user's local computer. You can manipulate controls on a form in the Visual Studio. NET Designer, and even write code to add controls dynamically at run time. We will be looking more closely at the most commonly used controls over the next few chapters.

Finally, you should note that forms are controls too, because they inherit from the `System.Windows.Forms.Control` class.

Menus and Toolbars

Menus are an easy way to allow a user to gain access to the main functions and utilities of our applications, for example, opening files, creating new files, and saving files. Toolbars are frequently used as an alternative way to access the main function of our applications: think of a "save" button in a toolbar. We will go into greater depth about menus and toolbars in Chapter 4.

The System.Windows.Forms Namespace

You may already have learned that the heart and soul of .NET from a developer's perspective is the .NET Framework class library. This is what provides access to all of the public classes and interfaces in .NET and is the foundation upon which all applications, components, and controls are built. Related classes and interfaces are grouped together into **namespaces**.

Of these, the namespace we'll be most concerned with as we develop Windows applications based upon Windows Forms is `System.Windows.Forms`. Within this namespace are all of the classes for creating Windows-based applications, including forms, controls, components (like menus) and common dialog boxes (open, save, font, and print). This namespace contains nearly 200 classes. However, most of these will either be used behind the scenes by other classes, or will be manipulated visually in the Visual Studio IDE.

One common misconception about the `System.Windows.Forms` namespace is that it replaces the Win32 API (Application Programming Interface). In fact, Windows Forms can just be thought of on a basic level as a wrapper, or more developer-friendly way, of using the same set of OS functions that pre-.NET development tools used. The idea is to package everything in such a way that developers can focus less on understanding the machinery of Windows and more on building great applications, so that's exactly what we're going to do. If you do happen to be interested in leaning more about the aspects of .NET "under the hood", you should take a look at a number of other books currently available on the topic including *Professional .NET Framework* (ISBN 1-86100-556-3), also from Wrox Press.

A Brief Tour of the Visual Studio .NET IDE

The Visual Studio IDE family has been around in a variety of guises for quite some time now. While much of it will look very familiar to those that have worked with previous versions, the .NET version of Visual Studio does bring with it some significant improvements and additions. There has been consolidation of many separate applications into one development environment. For example, InterDev is not a separate application, as it was in Visual Studio 6, and forms part of the IDE; also, SQL Server has been integrated into the IDE via the Server Explorer. We can also add to our solutions several different types of projects, for example, VB.NET and C# (Windows, ASP.NET, or Class Library projects, and so on). Microsoft has done a fine job of making Visual Studio .NET as intuitive as possible, so we'll just go over a few of the basics first and then pick up the rest as we go along.

> Some readers may not be using the full Professional version of Visual Studio .NET, just the standard Visual C# IDE (which is essentially a stripped down version of Visual Studio .NET that is intended for application development in C# only). Rest assured that all examples that we cover in this book will work on both IDEs.

Solutions and Projects

In Visual Studio .NET, all of your work is organized into solutions and projects. A **project** can consist of a single Windows application (`.exe`), a class library (`.dll`), or even a web site. A **solution** is simply a collection of projects, which could be a mix of Windows applications, web applications, and web services. For example, you can have your application's executable and all of its related `.dll`s in one solution. You should notice that when you create a new project and don't specifically say to add it to a current solution, Visual Studio .NET will create a new solution file for you. Because of the way that solutions and projects are created in the directory structure it is a good idea to create a solution folder and subfolders to contain the individual projects (it gets confusing when you have a solution file and a project file in the same directory).

Solution files are always given the file extension .sln, while the extension of a project file depends on the type of project involved. In the case of a C# project, the extension is .csproj.

Obviously the best way to learn about Visual Studio .NET is to open it up and take a look. So let's do that.

Try It Out – Creating a New Windows Application Project

In this, our first Try It Out example, we are going to start simple, and just open up a new Windows application project in Visual Studio .NET so that we can have a look at the development environment available to us.

1. Start Visual Studio .NET. The Start page will then be visible, you can use the New Project button there to create a new project, or you can use the File | New Project... menu command to bring up the following dialog.

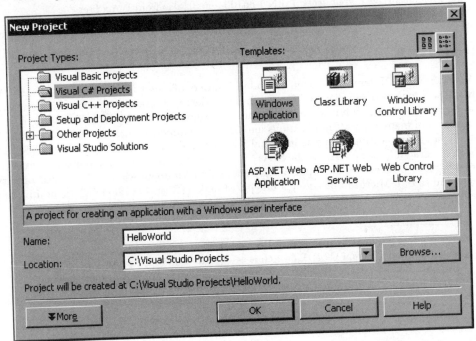

2. Select the Visual C# Projects folder and then choose the Windows Application template. You can name the project anything you like; we have called ours HelloWorld. You can also choose a location to save the solution and project.

One thing to notice is that Visual Studio .NET will use the location you supply as a base directory, and then create a subfolder under that location with the same name as your project. All of your project's files will normally reside inside this directory, including the project (.csproj) and solution (.sln) files themselves. If you click on the More button you can create an initial solution directory that will then contain the project files in their own sub folders. This is normally used for solutions that will contain multiple projects.

10

We'll be sticking pretty much to the Windows application type projects in this book but will be taking a look at setup and deployment projects in Chapter 11.

3. Once you've created your new project, you should be looking at the Visual Studio .NET IDE in all of its glory.

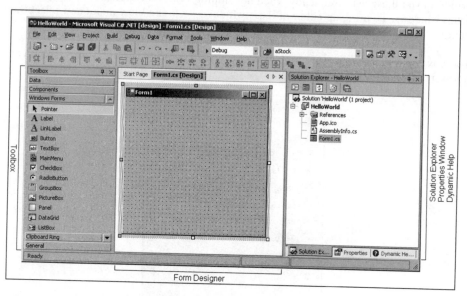
Form Designer

You should notice that the IDE is divided up into several panels, mainly: the **Toolbox**, the **Form Designer**, and a panel that contains the **Solution Explorer**, the **Class View**, the **Properties** window, and the **Dynamic Help** window. The Designer allows you to drag and drop controls stored in the Toolbox onto the form. Double-clicking on the form in the Designer will cause the **Code Editor** window to pop up; the IDE automatically generates the form class skeleton for you. The Solution Explorer window allows you to quickly access the contents of the solution:

Let's now take a closer look at the panels and windows of the IDE that we'll be using most frequently.

The Toolbox and Properties Windows

Two windows you'll use very frequently when developing Windows applications are the Toolbox and Properties windows. To bring up either of these windows go to the View menu and select the windows you want to see.

The Toolbox contains a dynamically updated collection of controls and components that you can add to your form. For a Windows Form the Toolbox should look like the following:

As you can see from the screenshot, the controls in the Toolbox are separated into different categories according to what they might be used for. If more controls are available than can be displayed then you can scroll through the full list by using the black arrows or by using your mouse's scroll wheel. If you drag a control from the Toolbox to the form and then switch to the code for the form you will see that the appropriate code for the control has been generated automatically.

Some controls are designed for data entry within the application, such as the TextBox and ComboBox controls. Other controls display application data, such as Label and ListView. The System.Windows.Forms namespace also provides controls for invoking commands within the application, such as Button and ToolBar. In addition, the PropertyGrid control can be used to create your own Windows Forms designer that displays the designer-visible properties of the controls.

Like the Toolbox, the Properties window allows you to change the code behind a form without having to write a line of code. The Properties window is most useful when working in the Designer document window; the window automatically updates itself with a list of properties (or events) for the element of the page currently selected in the Designer – form, control, image, and so on.

There is a great deal of information contained in the Properties window, so let's see what is displayed starting from the top.

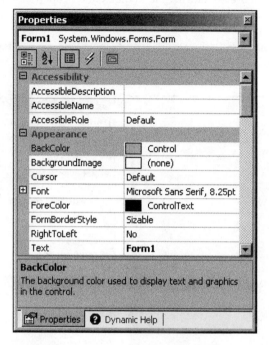

The drop-down list at the top of the window contains a list of all the items currently in the Designer that can be accessed and altered. These are listed alphabetically by name and have their .NET object type listed next to them. As you drag controls from the Toolbox to the form more entries will appear here.

The icons underneath this list allow you to choose what to see and how to see it. From left to right, the icons allow you to group an item's events or properties by category, or alphabetically. The next two switch between views of the item's properties and its events. The last item will give you access to a project's Property pages when selected in the Solution Explorer or Class view.

The main area of the Properties window displays the item's properties/events/messages and their current values, if any. It is here that you can change the values for the various properties.

The last area of the Properties window is the textbox under the property selection area. This box gives a user-friendly description of the property selected.

You will soon find that the Properties window is one of your best friends in Visual Studio .NET as everything in the IDE has a property pane. This saves the developer huge amounts of time by being able to configure much of the user interface at design time without having to write a single line of code.

Try It Out – Using the Properties Window and the Toolbox

Now that we know a little more about what the Toolbox and Properties windows are for, let's get our feet wet and play around with our blank form.

1. Click on the blank form in the Designer and you should see a default Properties window for the form appear:

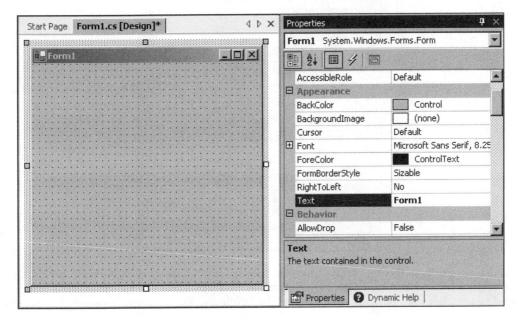

2. In the Properties window change the Text property to Main Form.

3. Now change the StartPosition property from WindowsDefaultLocation to CenterScreen. This will cause the application to appear in the center of the screen.

4. Even though we do have a working application at this point, it's not very interesting. Now add a Button to the form by dragging one from the Toolbox. You will see that if the button is selected, the Properties window changes dynamically to include the properties of the button. Change its Text property from button1 to Hello Form.

Your form should then look something like the following:

This is a bit more interesting, but what we really want to do is have something happen when the user clicks the Hello Form button – pop up a message box, for instance. However, before writing the code to do this, we will need to briefly take a look at how to respond to user actions and how to get the system to display our message box, so we will put this off until later in the chapter.

The Dynamic Help Window

Dynamic Help is a very useful feature in Visual Studio .NET that some developers who are starting out overlook. Much like the Properties window displays the properties of the currently selected UI element, the Dynamic Help window will display links to relevant help topics for the selected element. For example, if you were to click on the dynamic help tab with the Design View of the form visible, you would see something like the following:

You can see that not only does this offer you help about using forms, but also about using the Form Designer itself, and it provides a link to some samples. You should use this feature often while working though the examples in this book to find out more information about a specific topic.

The Class View

By default the Class View window is the second tab of the window displaying the Solution Explorer. We said "by default" because Visual Studio is very flexible in allowing you to position windows in the way you feel most comfortable with; it's just a matter of dragging the tab to where you like it. You can have the window as a separate floating window, or as an additional tab of a different panel. The screenshot below shows the class view for our new project in its default position.

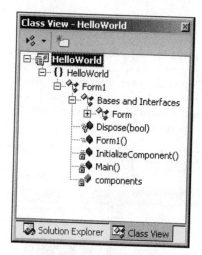

As you might expect, instead of a file-based view of your project, the Class View displays the classes contained in your project in hierarchical form. You can use this window to navigate through your code, or perform a variety of functions using a wizard-driven interface. The screenshot below shows the context-sensitive menu displayed through the use of a right-click for the Form1 object in this case.

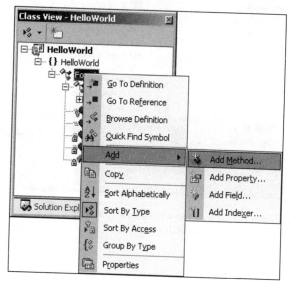

The Object Browser

An invaluable tool, especially when learning .NET, is something that looks like a bigger, meaner version of the Class View window, and it basically is. It's the **Object Browser**, and you can bring it up using View I Other Windows I Object Browser; alternatively you can use the keyboard shortcut *Ctrl-Alt-J*. What this allows you to do is not only browse your project but also browse the class library itself. For example, the screenshot below is the result of digging down into System.Windows.Forms and taking a look at the CancelButton property of the Form class.

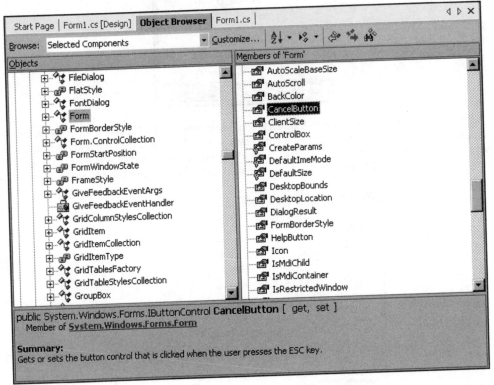

As you can see, not only does the object browser allow you to see what properties and methods belong to an individual class but it also gives you a description of each item. This can be a great complement to the help system.

The Code Editor

The Code Editor is where we can enter, display, and edit either code or text. The Editor supports the language of the project, with features like IntelliSense and early binding of objects. We can add all of our handwritten code to the IDE-generated code that is created using the Designer. To bring up the code editor for a file, either select Code from the View menu or press *F7* when on the file you wish to see. Alternatively you can get access to the code from the Solution Explorer by right-clicking on the file of interest, and in the pop-up context menu selecting View Code. Finally, you can also invoke the Editor by double-clicking on the form in the Designer.

Auto-Generated Code

We mentioned earlier that the Visual Studio .NET IDE automatically generates the skeleton of the class representing our form for us. Open up the Editor for our **HelloWorld** example by double-clicking on the `Button` in the Designer. If you look above the `button1_Click()` method, you should see several other methods defined, as well as a "folded" section of code given the title of **Windows Form Designer generated code**. This is exactly what it sounds like: code that has been generated for you because of things you've done in the IDE (for example, setting properties of the form). Before expanding this region, you should take a moment to look at the rest of the code. This includes a series of `using` statements, a constructor, and a `Dispose()` method. These are probably already familiar to you, but Visual Studio .NET does include a number of helpful comments in the code it generates too.

Let's take a look at what's in the folded region of code by expanding it with the + button in the right margin of the code window. The code you see should resemble the following:

```
#region Windows Form Designer generated code
    /// <summary>
    /// Required method for Designer support - do not modify
    /// the contents of this method with the code editor.
    // </summary>
    private void InitializeComponent()
    {
        this.button1 = new System.Windows.Forms.Button();
        this.SuspendLayout();
        //
        // button1
        //
        this.button1.Location = new System.Drawing.Point(104, 112);
        this.button1.Name = "button1";
        this.button1.TabIndex = 0;
        this.button1.Text = "Hello Form";
        this.button1.Click += new System.EventHandler(this.button1_Click);
        //
        // Form1
        //
        this.AutoScaleBaseSize = new System.Drawing.Size(5, 13);
        this.ClientSize = new System.Drawing.Size(292, 266);
        this.Controls.AddRange(new System.Windows.Forms.Control[] {this.button1});
        this.Name = "Form1";
        this.StartPosition = System.Windows.Forms.FormStartPosition.CenterScreen;
        this.Text = "Main Form";
        this.ResumeLayout(false);
    }
#endregion
```

As you can see, the very first lines in this region of code give you a warning not to modify the contents of this method with the Editor. This is good advice. This portion of code allows Visual Studio .NET to maintain a link between the code and the visual tools in the IDE. For example, if you were to remove the button from your form in the visual form view, Visual Studio .NET would be able to keep things nice and tidy by removing the section of code related to that button. Of course, this only applies to this region and you would have to remove any other references you have to the button elsewhere in code.

If there are some other initialization tasks you would like to do in code, you can do so in the constructor. Once again there's a comment telling you just where this is:

```
public Form1()
{
    //
    // Required for Windows Form Designer support
    //
    InitializeComponent();
    //
    // TODO: Add any constructor code after InitializeComponent call
    //
}
```

Now that we've toured around the Visual Studio .NET IDE, let's delve behind the scenes of Windows applications a little.

Handling Events

Earlier we stated that before we could make our sample HelloWorld application pop up a message box, we'd need to understand how our Windows applications respond to user actions. Fundamental to this is the concept of an **event**. Let's take a closer look at what this means.

A GUI-based application spends most of its time waiting around for the user to do something. Once the user performs an action (for example, clicking the mouse) the system determines which application the click was intended for and delivers a notification object (an event) to a queue for that application. It is then up to the application to pull events off of its queue and handle them. Luckily, with Windows programming in .NET, we need to worry very little about this process. We just need to decide which events we're interested in and write code for those events. There are a good number of events that have default event handlers provided by the system, meaning that we don't have to code for every little eventuality.

This is where we come into contact with a second aspect of the Properties window. For not only does it display all of the properties for a selected object, but it also can display all of the events that can be associated with the object. You can see this by clicking the Events toolbar button (the one that has a lightning flash on it) at the top of the Properties window. Go ahead and make sure your new button has the focus and clink the Events button to display a list that looks something like the following:

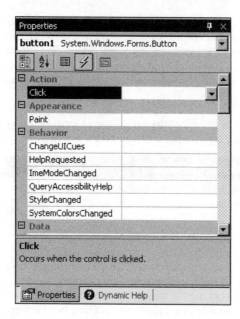

If you scroll down in this window, you'll see a pretty extensive list of events that you can respond to. This provides a great deal of flexibility in building your applications. Find the event named Click. The space next to each event name is the name of the function that will be called when the event occurs. As you can see, all of the events are blank right now since we haven't added any handlers yet.

Using Message Boxes

Even if you haven't used them in your own applications, you're exposed to message boxes all the time by other applications, and by Windows itself. They are pop-up dialog windows used to get the user's undivided attention, and are *modal* in nature – the user must dismiss a message box before the user can continue working with the application. They can be informational in nature, or display a warning or error of some sort. They also can request the user to make a choice presented as a series of buttons. For example, the following shows a screenshot of a message box displayed by Visual Studio .NET when I try to delete a file in the Solution Explorer.

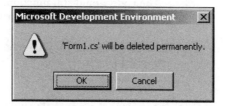

It's important not to overuse message boxes, since their appearance does have the effect of interrupting the user's work flow. However, there are times when that's what you want to do. For example, in the case of the message box above, this action is not one the user can undo so it's important to confirm that that's what the user really wants. It's also a good practice to be as descriptive as possible with your message to the user. Form1.cs will be deleted permanently is much better than Are you sure?

Message boxes can also be useful for debugging and testing. They provide an easy way to pause the execution of your application and output some values for you to inspect. We often use this technique before firing up the debugger to get information about what's happening in an application.

It is worth noting that the message box is a property of the form – we can't use it in a console application, for example.

Now that we understand about the event-driven nature of form-based applications, let's enhance our sample application by making it pop up a message box when the user clicks the button.

Try It Out – Displaying a Message Box

In this Try It Out we're going to modify our HelloWorld application so that it displays a welcome message when we click the button.

1. Open the HelloWorld project we created at the start of the chapter.

2. We need an event handler for the event fired when the button is clicked. There are two ways of doing this. You may have used the first way already if you took a look at the auto-generated code earlier: double-clicking on the button on the form (this works for just about any other control too). The other way is to select the Button on the form and then click the Events toolbar button (the one that has a lightning flash on it) at the top of the Properties window, then double-click the event name (Click). Either way, you'll produce an empty click event handler method:

```
private void button1_Click(object sender, System.EventArgs e)
{

}
```

Note the name Visual Studio .NET chose for your new method: the control element's name (button1), followed by an underscore, and then followed by the event name (Click). This is generally a pretty good convention to use and there is really no good reason for us to change it. One thing you need to be aware of here is that even though the method name was generated based on the name of the button, there is no link maintained here. For example, if you were to now change the name of the button to HiButton, the method name would still remain as button1_Click(). The code would still function, but to maintain consistency in your code, you might want to correct the method names afterward.

3. Now add a line of code that will display a simple message box. Add the following highlighted line to the button1_Click() method where shown:

```
private void button1_Click(object sender, System.EventArgs e)
{
    MessageBox.Show("Hello Windows application user!", "Hello User");
}
```

Now that our application can actually do something, let's go ahead and run it for the first time, after saving all the files (which is a habit you should get into if you don't already).

4. Before you run the application, you will need to build (compile) the solution. Go to the **Build** menu and selecting **Build Solution**. This will create the `Helloworld.exe` file.

5. Now either choose **Start** from the **Debug** menu, or click the button that looks like a play button, or press *F5*. If all goes well, you should see a form that looks very much like it does in the Designer with our **Hello Form** button. Click the button. You should see this:

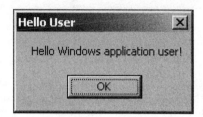

How It Works

This is the first example where we've actually modified code directly in the Editor, so let's review what we did. We added the following line to the `Button`'s `Click` event handler, which resulted in a message box popping up:

```
MessageBox.Show("Hello Windows application user!", "Hello User");
```

As you can see, the first parameter of the `MessageBox` class' `Show()` method is the actual message, while the second parameter is what will appear in the title bar of the message box.

There are actually many different versions of the `Show()` method based on the number and type of parameters we provide. For example, we could have omitted the title bar text and it just would have been displayed with a blank title bar. We also omitted what buttons we'd like, meaning that we get the default: an **OK** button. We also omitted an icon value for the message box, meaning that we don't have an icon appear. We could therefore change our `Show()` method to something a little more professional-looking. If you want, stop the application by either dismissing the message box and closing the main form, or clicking the **Stop** button on the toolbar, and then change the line of code above to the following:

```
    if (MessageBox.Show("This will cause the application to quit",
                        "Hello User",
                        MessageBoxButtons.OKCancel,
                        MessageBoxIcon.Exclamation) == DialogResult.OK)
    {
        Application.Exit();
    }
```

In this case, we've changed the parameters that have been added to the method; this time we added the buttons that will be on the message box and the icon that will show in the message box.

Run the application again, and click the button to see the new message box. Then choose to quit the application after checking that the Cancel button works properly.

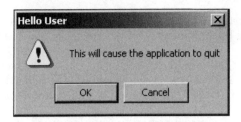

Using IntelliSense

This is a good time to point out something that Visual Studio .NET provides that you may have seen when typing in the code up to this point – **IntelliSense**. This is a feature of the code editor in Visual Studio .NET that can be a big help. You may already be familiar with this feature if you have used a previous version of Visual Studio but basically it pops up a list of choices when appropriate to your code. For example, in the last version of the message box's Show() method, when typing the period after DialogResult, you may have seen a list pop up with all of the available options, with OK being one of them. More interesting, though, is the help you get when typing the comma after each parameter in the Show() method. The screenshot below is an example.

```
if (MessageBox.Show("This will cause the application to quit",
    "H[▲7 of 12 ▼] System.Windows.Forms.DialogResult MessageBox.Show (string text)
    Me[Displays a message box with specified text.]
    MessageBoxIcon.Exclamation) == DialogResult.OK)
{
```

As you can see, this is one serious tool tip. It provides a scrollable list of all the various versions of the Show() method and lists out the parameters for each. For instance, for the MessageBoxButtons parameter, we can use any of the following:

❑   AbortRetryIgnore

❑   OK

❑   OKCancel

❑   RetryCancel

❑   YesNo

❑   YesNoCancel

The name of each value should give you a pretty good idea of when to use each.

Summary

In this chapter, you've been introduced to the `System.Windows.Forms` namespace and Windows application development in .NET. With Windows Forms development, you can think of a form as being a blank canvas upon which you design the interface through which your users will communicate with the application. What you use to actually build this UI is the collection of controls available to you. These controls are available from the Toolbox in the Visual Studio .NET IDE, and you've already used one of them – `Button`. You got a taste of developing form-based applications with Visual Studio .NET by building a simple application and learning about the `MessageBox` object.

However, what we've done so far is still a long way from being a useful "real-world" application. So, in the next few chapters, we'll be steadily working through most of the controls available in the VS.NET toolbox. You'll soon be well on your way to having the skills needed to build an effective, attractive interface for your .NET Windows applications.

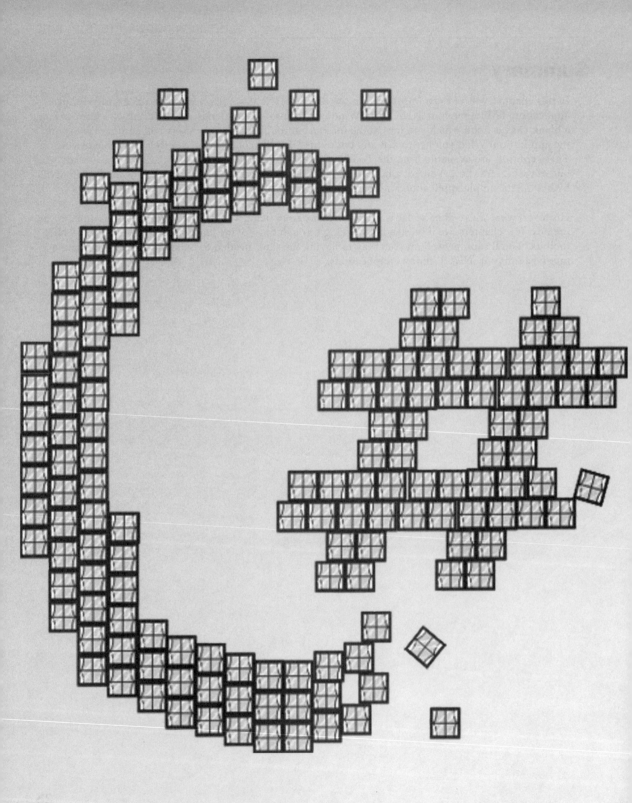

Simple User Interface Controls

In the first chapter, we looked at the steps needed to create a simple Windows Application with Visual Studio .NET and C#. However, the focus of this book is to equip you with the knowledge and skills necessary for building "real-world" Windows Applications. Perhaps the most valuable asset you need as you pursue this goal is a strong familiarity with the user interface components that are available to you.

In this chapter, we'll look at the simplest controls made available to you from the Visual Studio .NET toolbox, including:

❑ Button-based controls

❑ Textboxes

❑ List controls

❑ Labels

❑ Pictureboxes

❑ Groupboxes

In the next chapter we'll discuss most of the other toolbox controls. We'll work through the controls one at a time, so as well as providing a useful tutorial in the use of them, these chapters can also be used later as a control reference guide when building your own applications.

That said, we are not going to attempt to cover every single property and method for each control. However, those that we don't cover will either be rarely needed when building applications, or they will be too advanced in nature for scope of this book. We'll point out when this is the case and mention where you can go to explore these elements further.

User Interface Design Considerations

Before starting to look at the individual controls available to you, there are a few general issues to keep in mind when designing a UI for a Windows Application. It's often said that a good piece of software with a great UI will outsell a great piece of software with a good UI every time. In other words, the key to a winning application is to make things as easy and intuitive as possible for the user.

One of the best ways to make your application intuitive is to make it behave in a way that they are already accustomed to. For example, many users would probably expect to use the *Tab* key to move between fields when entering some data on a form. In many cases, Visual Studio .NET and the controls themselves will take you a good part of the way. However, when designing how the controls are arranged and how they interact, you probably already have much of the experience you need – your experience of other Windows software and the OS itself. You can look to applications like Microsoft Office and see how they present features and interact with the user.

So it's a good idea to make your applications behave in a similar way to other common applications that users will have encountered before. However, this doesn't mean that you should just copy the UI design of your favorite application. Although there are some things that really should be the same for all applications – for example, having the Help menu listed last in the menu bar, or having the *Tab* and *Esc* keys behave in a consistent manner, there is still a lot of room for creativity and originality in designing a user interface. An original approach may be the one thing that can most easily set your application apart from the rest. The key is to work toward that balance of familiarity and uniqueness that makes an application both easy and fun to use.

We as developers need to understand the psychology of the users of the application, and the respective use modes. There are some use modes where speed is essential, for example, a user enquiry – our user maybe handling an urgent enquiry on behalf of a hospital casualty department and a quick response is vital. Or maybe speed is not so important, such as for a routine update of a customer's change of address details. To a user the user interface is the system, and to a developer a user interface is one of our best guides of how the logic and data of our system will be used.

> *Microsoft does have a program to help software makers to produce applications that "deliver a high-quality computing experience". This program is referred to as the "Microsoft Windows Logo Program". Benefits include the right to display the "Designed for Windows" logo on your product and inclusion in Microsoft's Windows Catalog. Accordingly, there are some steps to take and requirements to follow. These are all provided on Microsoft's web site at http://www.microsoft.com/winlogo.*

A Tour of Simple User Interface Controls

Obviously the best way to learn how different controls are used is to illustrate their use in an application. So, over the course of this chapter we'll demonstrate the use of basic controls by creating a simple user interface for a hypothetical audio player application called MyPlayer. Since we'll only be demonstrating basic controls in this chapter, it means that in some cases we won't always be creating elements that adhere to contemporary "best practices". While this is, of course, necessary and beneficial to ease us into the world of controls while still providing relevant examples, we will try to point out circumstances where more advanced controls covered in later chapters might serve better. Two examples that immediately come to mind are drop down menus and tab controls. If you're familiar with modern Windows applications at all, you'll realize that the absence of these two current mainstays will mean our sample application in this chapter will already be a little "non-standard".

All of the controls that we will encounter in this chapter can be found in the `System.Windows.Forms` namespace, and are derived from the base `System.Windows.Forms.Control` class.

PictureBoxes

The `System.Windows.Forms.PictureBox` control is used as a container for an image. We can set the `Image` property of a `PictureBox` to a bitmap, icon, metafile, JPEG, GIF, or PNG image file, and it will display that image. We can set the `Image` property at either design time time or run time. We can also control the border of the `PictureBox` using the `BorderStyle` property. The `BorderStyle` property defaults to no border, but you can specify a regular flat, single line style or even a three dimensional border.

Try It Out – Adding a PictureBox Control

We'll start out very simply by using a `PictureBox` to display a logo for our sample application.

1. Let's begin by creating a new C# Windows Application project. Call it MyPlayer.

2. Change the `Text` property of the form (`Form1.cs`) in the project to `MyPlayer`. Now it's time to start placing some controls.

3. Select a `PictureBox` control from the Toolbox, drag it over to the empty form in our project and drop it in the top right corner.

4. Now, set the `Image` property of the control to the `PlayerLogo.bmp` file supplied with the chapter code download.

5. Set the `BorderStyle` property to `Fixed3D` to give the image a sunken, 3D feel.

6. For our convenience, let's set the Anchor property of this control to Top and Right. This means the logo image will stay in the top-right corner as we stretch the form to accommodate more controls later. The Anchor property is a handy feature inherited from the System.Windows.Forms.Control base class.

Labels

Perhaps the simplest control in the Visual Studio toolbox is the Label control, represented by the System.Windows.Forms.Label class. The Label control is often used to provide descriptive text for another control.

Most of the time, the text of a Label control is static; it doesn't change throughout the life cycle of the application. However, there are times when a Label control is used to display information that changes but which is not directly editable by the user. For example, in the Visual Studio .NET IDE, the text below the Properties window provides a brief summary of the currently selected property. This changes when selecting a different property but is obviously not editable. Therefore, you should use a Label control when you want text displayed on the screen, but you don't want that text to be editable.

Although there doesn't seem to be very much to the Label control, there are several interesting things you can do with it that are not immediately apparent. We'll look at those later, but first let's go ahead and put a label on our form.

Try It Out – Adding a Label Control

1. Select a Label control from the Toolbox, and place it on our form.

2. Change the Text property of the Label to PlayList, and change the Bold attribute of the Font property to True. Later, we'll add the control that this Label is describing.

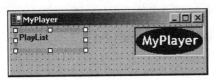

3. Finally, let's change the Name property of our Label to lblPlayList. This name is a bit more descriptive about what purpose the label serves, plus it will help us easily distinguish it from other labels we will add later in this chapter.

Textbox Controls

There are two textbox controls: TextBox control gives a user basic text entry and editing capability, whilst the RichTextBox supports Rich Text Format (.rtf) attributes on its contents. Both the TextBox class and RichTextBox class share the immediate base class of System.Windows.Forms.TextBoxBase. Most of the members belonging to the TextBox class are inherited from TextBoxBase while the RichTextBox adds support for formatted text font selection, URLs, and bulleted text. Therefore, we'll start by looking at the relevant members of TextBoxBase.

Property	Description
AcceptsTab	Determines whether pressing the tab key while in the TextBox will actually insert a tab into the text or if it will move the focus to the next control.
AutoSize	Will cause the control to size itself automatically whenever the size of the assigned font is changed.
HideSelection	When set to false, highlighted text will no longer appear so when the control loses focus.
MaxLength	Specifies the maximum number of characters the TextBox will allow.
Modified	This returns true when the contents of the TextBox have been changed by the user since the control was created or since the last time the contents were set.
Multiline	Determines whether the TextBox can accommodate multiple lines of text. Affects the behavior of the *Enter* key (as does the AcceptsReturn property of the TextBox control).
SelectedText	Returns whatever text is currently selected in the control.
SelectionLength	Returns the number of characters selected in the control.
SelectionStart	Allows you to get or set the starting point of text selected in the control.
WordWrap	Indicates whether a multiline TextBox control will automatically wrap words to the beginning of the next line when necessary.

In addition to these, TextBoxBase also provides built-in support for clipboard operations (Cut(), Copy(), and Paste() methods) and undo support by way of the Undo() method. TextBoxBase also includes automatic handling for the usual shortcut keys: *Ctrl-X* for cut, and so on. As for events, the one you'll usually be interested in for a TextBox is TextChanged that fires whenever the content of the TextBox is changed. This is the place to be when wishing to block the user from entering certain types of data into a TextBox (for instance when they attempt to enter alphabetic characters in a numeric only field).

Since we already looked at the properties that TextBoxBase provides, we should take a moment to take a look at the few properties that the actual TextBox control adds on.

Property	Description
AcceptsReturn	Determines whether pressing the *Enter* key in a multiline TextBox control will create a new line or activate the default button for the form.
CharacterCasing	Will cause all characters typed into the control to either be left alone, converted to uppercase, or converted to lowercase.

Table continued on following page

Property	Description
PasswordChar	Gets or sets the character used to mask input typed into a single line TextBox used for passwords.
ScrollBars	Gets or sets the scroll bars that should appear for a multiline TextBox control.
TextAlign	Gets or sets how text is aligned in the control.

Try It Out – Adding a TextBox Control

Let's look at an example of adding a regular TextBox to our application to allow a user to specify a directory containing playlists of audio tracks we wish to later select. We'll also explore the TextChanged event.

1. Select a TextBox control from the Toolbox and place it on our form to the right of the PlayList label.

2. Let's set the Text property of the TextBox to C:\MyPlayer\ to specify a default directory.

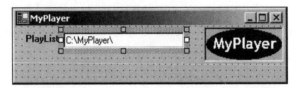

3. Set the Name property of our TextBox to txtDirectory to better identify its purpose.

4. Let's take advantage of some Visual Studio .NET Designer help by highlighting both the PlayList label and our new TextBox, then selecting Format | Align | Middles from the menu. This is a convenient way to make sure they are both aligned vertically.

5. Now, double-click on our new txtDirectory TextBox to create an event handler method in code. Enter the following highlighted lines (remember the Designer creates the others for us when we double-click on the TextBox):

```
private void txtDirectory_TextChanged(object sender, System.EventArgs e)
{
    if (txtDirectory.Text.StartsWith(@"C:\"))
    {
      txtDirectory.BackColor = SystemColors.Window;
    }
    else
    {
      txtDirectory.BackColor = Color.Tomato;
    }
}
```

6. Now, build the solution (Build | Build Solution) and then run it (Debug | Start), or press *F5*.
   Try entering different values in the TextBox.

How It Works

When we change the value of the text, the TextChanged event is fired and our handler method is
called. The Text property is a String, and the String class provides several methods of comparison
and manipulation. By using the boolean StartsWith() method, we can simulate some rudimentary
validation by making sure the value of Text always begins with "C:\". The @ symbol simply marks the
following string as a literal that doesn't process escape codes. The \ character denotes the beginning of
an escape sequence, so if we hadn't used the @ symbol, we would have had to test for "C:\\", which is
less intuitive. Finally, when the Text value meets the starting criteria the method will set the
BackColor property of the TextBox to the default color. When the value is incorrect, it will change
the BackColor property to a light red.

While this sample works well to demonstrate the TextChanged event, let's talk "real world" before
getting into the next pair of controls. Our next task will be to add a ListBox and a ComboBox to
further support our playlist selection theme. In most applications, you can make use of the
OpenFileDialog component to handle your file selection needs. In some situations you'll need to
piece together custom functionality, but we're only doing so in this sample application to make use of
three individual controls and demonstrate some of their properties and events.

List Controls

One common requirement of an interface is to present the user with a possibly dynamic list of multiple
items for selection. Both the ListBox and ComboBox accomplish this core task while adding unique
features of their own. Indeed, both controls inherit common elements from a base class named
System.Windows.Forms.ListControl.

ListBoxes

A ListBox can be sized to show a certain number of items at once, and it can be configured to allow
single or multiple selections. It can even display items in multiple columns. However, perhaps the most
useful aspect of a ListBox for a developer is its capacity for scrolling the item list, which means that it
takes up the same amount of space in the UI for two items or fifty. To get a better handle on the
ListBox class, let's take a look at a few of its properties:

Property	Description
ScrollAlwaysVisible	As the name implies, this determines whether the scroll bar for the ListBox is shown at all times or only when needed.
SelectedIndex	This is the index of the currently selected item starting with 0 for the first item. A value of -1 indicates no selection. If multiple items are selected, this will return the lowest index selected.
SelectedIndices	Returns a collection containing the index of each item selected. An empty collection is returned if no items are selected.

Table continued on following page

Property	Description
SelectedItem	Instead of an index, this returns the actual string value of the selected item and null if no item is selected.
SelectedItems	Returns a collection containing the value of all selected items.
SelectionMode	Determines how the user can select items in the list. The choices are None, One, MultiSimple, MultiExtended.
Sorted	Setting this to True will result in the ListBox always displaying its items in alphabetic order.
TopIndex	This property will return the index of the first item visible in the ListBox.

The SelectionMode property deserves a bit more explanation. Choosing the value One makes the ListBox enforce only one choice. When a user selects an item, it is highlighted, and any previously selected item is "un-selected" (denoted by the removal of its highlight). The second SelectionMode choice, MultiSimple, allows several items to be selected and highlighted. Click on any item to select it and click it again to unselect it. The user can click as many or as few as he or she likes. The last SelectionMode choice, MultiExtended, is something like what you experience in Windows Explorer. The user can click an item to select it and then extend their selection by *Shift*-clicking to select a range or *Ctrl*-click to select additional individual items.

ComboBoxes

One variation on the ListBox is the ComboBox control. In addition to its visual appearance, another thing that makes the ComboBox object unique is its ability to also act as a TextBox if we so desire. This allows users to manually enter a choice not presented in the list of items. The following list shows the properties that the ComboBox adds to those provided by the ListControl class.

Property	Description
DroppedDown	Indicates whether ComboBox is in fact dropped down.
MaxDropDownItems	This determines the maximum number of items to display in the drop-down portion of the ComboBox. This can range from 1-100 and a scroll bar will be provided when required.
MaxLength	This restricts the number of characters the user can type into the text portion of the ComboBox.
SelectedText	Returns the text currently selected in the text portion of the ComboBox.
SelectionLength	Returns the length, in characters, of the selection in the text portion of the ComboBox.

Property	Description
Style	This determines the type of ComboBox to display. The choices are DropDown (text editable and user must click to expand list), DropDownList (text is not editable), and Simple (text is editable and list is always displayed).
Text	Returns whatever text is currently in the editable portion of the ComboBox.

Now, let's try out these controls by adding them to our form and configuring them to operate together.

Try It Out – Adding Cooperative TextBox and ComboBox Controls

We'll use a simple DropDown-style ComboBox to present the user with a choice of music track playlists, and then display the individual tracks in a ListBox.

1. Stretch out our form to give us more room under our existing controls, then select a ComboBox control from the Toolbox and place it on our form just below the PlayList label. Next, select a ListBox control from the Toolbox and place it on our form just below the ComboBox.

2. We can take advantage of another Visual Studio .NET Designer formatting feature by selecting the PlayList label, our ComboBox, and our ListBox, then choosing Format | Align | Lefts to easily align the left edge of the three controls.

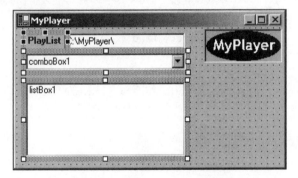

3. Now, let's change the Name property of our ComboBox and ListBox to cboPlayList and lstTracks, respectively, to better identify their purpose. Change the Text property for the ComboBox to an empty value.

4. Select the ComboBox and edit the Items property. You will be presented with a dialog box to enter multiple values. Enter Playlist 1, Playlist 2, and Playlist 3 for example:

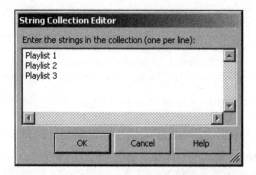

5. Double-click on the ComboBox control to create an event handler for the SelectedIndexChanged event. Enter the following highlighted lines (the designer creates the others for us when we double-click on the ComboBox):

```
private void cboPlayList_SelectedIndexChanged(object sender,
                                              System.EventArgs e)
{
    lstTracks.Items.Clear();
    switch (cboPlayList.Text)
    {
      case "Playlist 1":
          lstTracks.Items.Add("Garage Band Tune 1.mp3");
          lstTracks.Items.Add("Garage Band Tune 2.mp3");
          lstTracks.Items.Add("Garage Band Tune 3.mp3");
          lstTracks.Items.Add("Garage Band Tune 4.mp3");
          break;

      case "Playlist 2":
          lstTracks.Items.Add("My Violin Practice.mp3");
          lstTracks.Items.Add("My Dog Howling.mp3");
          lstTracks.Items.Add("My Cat Screaming.mp3");
          break;

      case "Playlist 3":
          lstTracks.Items.Add("Space Viking Symphony.mp3");
          lstTracks.Items.Add("Uller Concerto.mp3");
          lstTracks.Items.Add("Zarathustran Cycle.mp3");
          lstTracks.Items.Add("Tanith Sonata.mp3");
          break;
    }
}
```

6. Select the ListBox control. Instead of double-clicking on the control and creating the default event handler method, look in the Properties window for the lightning bolt icon. Select that icon to see a list of events for the control instead of a list of properties. Find the DoubleClick event line and double-click on it to create an event handler in the code:

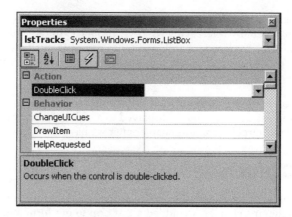

7. Enter the following highlighted line in the event handler method (the designer created the others for us when we double-clicked on the `DoubleClick` event line):

```
private void lstTracks_DoubleClick(object sender, System.EventArgs e)
{
    this.Text = "MyPlayer - " + this.lstTracks.SelectedItem.ToString();
}
```

8. Now, build the solution and then run it. Click on the `ComboBox` arrow to dropdown a list of playlists. If we select Playlist 2, we will see the following tracks appear in the `ListBox`:

9. In addition, when we double-click to select a track item in the `ListBox`, we will see the title bar of the form change to inform us of the currently-selected track.

10. Finally, don't forget that we changed the Properties window to an event view instead of a property view. Go back and click on the button on the left of the lightning bolt to return to property view.

How It Works

Merely clicking on an item in the `ComboBox` dropdown list selects that item and closes the dropdown. By monitoring the `SelectedIndexChanged` event, we can clear the `Items` collection in the tracks `ListBox` using the `Items.Clear()` method, and then load a new list of tracks there using the `Items.Add()` method for each track we want to display.

To keep our example simple, we determine which literal string track names to load based on the value of the selected ComboBox item by referencing its Text property. In the real world, we would read a playlist file that contained the track names and load those names in our ListBox. Of course, in a real application, we would be getting the available playlists in our ComboBox from a directory rather than entering them in the Items collection at design time.

Another interesting variation on the standard ListBox control is the CheckedListBox. This control is basically identical to a regular ListBox but is displayed as a series of items with check boxes. We'll look at the CheckedListBox control later in this chapter after we have added a second form to our project.

Button-Based Controls

The Button is a control that is relatively simple to use but which has some capabilities that are not completely obvious. In the first chapter, we added a Button to our form and changed the Text property. We also attached some code to the Click event that displayed a message box. Now, we'll look more closely at this mainstay of UI design.

The first thing that usually comes to mind when thinking of a Button is the rectangular push-button that we're so familiar with. However, in .NET, a single class – ButtonBase – is the foundation for not only the Button class but also the CheckBox and RadioButton classes. We'll be looking at CheckBoxes and RadioButtons in the next couple of sections. We won't go into exactly what properties and methods are members of ButtonBase and which reside in the subclasses but you may want to take a moment to look up System.Windows.Forms.ButtonBase in the .NET class library reference to get a basic feel for how the Microsoft engineers have put things together.

Buttons

Like all controls in .NET, when you click on a Button in the designer, you will see the Properties window fill with properties that affect the appearance and behavior of the component. Many are properties you will become very familiar with, as they are available for nearly all controls – like BackColor, Enabled, Visible, and so on. The table below shows some of the properties related to the appearance of a button component:

Property	Description
FlatStyle	This controls how the button will appear to the user, both when the mouse moves over the button, and when it's clicked.
Image	Allows you to display an image on a button rather than just text.
ImageAlign	Sets the alignment of the image on the button. Available values are provided by the ContentAlignment enumeration.
ImageIndex	This is used to specify exactly which image in the associated image list control to display on the button.
ImageList	Identifies an image list control to be used in conjunction with the ImageIndex property to specify the image to display on the button.
TextAlign	Determines the alignment of text displayed on the button. Uses the same values from the ContentAlignment enumeration as ImageAlign.

Let's now add some buttons to our sample application.

Try It Out – Adding Buttons and an Options Dialog

In later sections, we're going to place controls on a second form that will act as a popup dialog screen with various options for our player. We will continue to place the most important, frequently used controls on our main form, but this Options dialog will serve to reduce clutter on the main interface. Let's get the basic dialog form ready while working with some buttons.

1. Right-click on our project in Solution Explorer, then choose Add | Add Windows Form. Let's change the Name property of this new form to frmOptions to distinguish it from the main form. Set the Text property of the form to Options. Change the FormBorderStyle property to FixedDialog, and the StartPosition to CenterParent. Finally, change the MaximizeBox, MinimizeBox, and ControlBox properties all to False.

2. Now, let's add some buttons to our new options form. Place two buttons in the lower right corner of the form. Name one Button btnOK and set its Text property to OK. Name the other Button btnCancel and set its Text property to Cancel.

3. Select the whole Options form again and set the AcceptButton property to btnOK. Also set the CancelButton property to btnCancel.

4. Double-click on each of the buttons to create default Click event handler methods. Enter the following highlighted code in the methods for the respective buttons.

```
private void btnOK_Click(object sender, System.EventArgs e)
{
    this.DialogResult = DialogResult.OK;
}

private void btnCancel_Click(object sender, System.EventArgs e)
{
    this.DialogResult = DialogResult.Cancel;
}
```

5. Select the main form again, and stretch it out to give us more room under our existing controls. Now select a Button control from the Toolbox and place it on our form just below the track ListBox. With the Button still selected, choose Format | Center In Form | Horizontally and set the Anchor property of the Button to Bottom so it will maintain its position at the bottom-center of the form. Set the Text property to Options, and let's change the Name of the Button to btnOptions. Just for style, let's change this button's FlatStyle property to Flat.

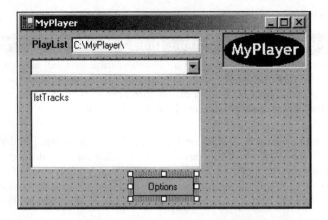

6. Double-click on the `Button` to create a default Click event handler method, and enter the following highlighted code.

```
private void btnOptions_Click(object sender, System.EventArgs e)
{
    frmOptions OptForm = new frmOptions();
    if (OptForm.ShowDialog(this) == DialogResult.OK)
    {
        // We would apply changes here since the user accepted them
    }
    OptForm.Dispose();
}
```

7. When we build and run the solution, clicking on the Options button will display our options form as a modal dialog box. We can close the options form by clicking on either the OK or Cancel button, and also by either pressing *Enter* or *Esc*.

How It Works

The `AcceptButton` property of a form allows us to specify a button to be "clicked" by hitting the *Enter* key while on that form. The `CancelButton` property of a form allows us to specify a button to be "clicked" by hitting the *Esc* key while on that form. That seems easy enough to understand, but what about the code behind our three buttons?

First, the button on our main form creates a new `frmOptions` object, and then calls its `ShowDialog()` method. This method displays the options form and halts execution of the `btnOptions_Click` method, waiting for the options form to be closed. The `this` parameter of the `ShowDialog()` method specifies that our main form is the owner of the options dialog box. When we are finished with a form we call as a modal dialog, we must explicitly dispose of it by calling its `Dispose()` method.

Our OK and Cancel buttons on the options form set the form's `DialogResult` property to the appropriate `DialogResult` enumeration value. Setting this property will cause the form to be hidden and control returned to the caller.

The `ShowDialog()` method is of type `DialogResult`, and it will return the value of the option form's `DialogResult` property. This is why the shorthand

```
if (OptForm.ShowDialog(this) == DialogResult.OK)
```

is possible instead of having to do the following two steps:

```
OptForm.ShowDialog(this);
if (OptForm.DialogResult == DialogResult.OK)
```

Now let's look at how we can add buttons that have images on top.

Try It Out – Adding Buttons With Images

Let's now create 5 more buttons that would control playing a track if this were a real world audio player application instead of a user interface example.

1. Create the buttons and place them somewhere below the logo.

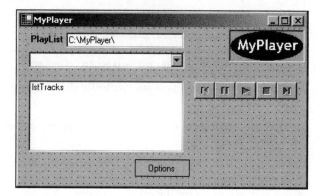

2. Set the `Name` and `Image` properties of the buttons according to the following table. The bitmap images are included in the chapter code download. Delete the `Text` property values or else the text will show through the image.

Button Name	Graphic
btnPrev	prev.bmp
btnPause	pause.bmp
btnPlay	play.bmp
btnStop	stop.bmp
btnNext	next.bmp

3. Make the buttons approximately 28 pixels wide and 23 pixels tall. If we planned on using text instead of the graphics, then we would need to make the buttons a bit larger to fit the words, of course.

It is worth mentioning that in a real world application, we would want to provide some other user clue about the button's function besides the graphic image. This is where the `ToolTip` component comes in handy. When the user's mouse hovers over a control for a period of time, then a small balloon of helpful text would pop up. Actually, we should provide a `ToolTip` for nearly every control on our forms. We'll look at ToolTips in Chapter 10.

CheckBoxes and GroupBoxes

The `CheckBox` class is another class derived from `ButtonBase` and its function is pretty self-explanatory. It allows you to select options from a choice of two. You should keep in mind that `CheckBoxes` are usually used to represent individual choices that are not mutually exclusive. On the other hand, `RadioButtons`, which we will look at next, are used when the user needs to pick one and only one of several options presented. Once again, we'll start by looking at those properties that are specific to the `CheckBox` class.

Property	Description
Appearance	Allows you to choose whether the control appears as a standard `CheckBox` or as a `Button` that will appear pressed when "checked".
AutoCheck	Determines if the `CheckBox` automatically changes its state when clicked. The default value is `true`.
CheckAlign	Specifies where the actual `CheckBox` itself appears in the control relative to the text.
Checked	Used to get or set the Boolean value indicating whether or not the `CheckBox` is checked. If using a three state `CheckBox`, this will return `false` for unchecked and `true` for the other two values.
CheckState	Similar to the `Checked` property but uses the `CheckState` enumeration instead of a Boolean value. Mostly used when dealing with three state `CheckBoxes`.
ThreeState	The actual property used to control whether or not a `CheckBox` will allow three states or two.

You will have noticed that in the table above we mentioned that a `CheckBox` can allow three states. A common use for a three state `CheckBox` is to have one `CheckBox` be the logical parent of several `CheckBoxes`. We'll see this in action later. The values for these states are defined by the `CheckState` enumeration as shown.

Value	Description
Checked	The CheckBox is checked. This will cause the Checked property to return true.
Indeterminate	The CheckBox appears checked but also has a shaded appearance. This will also result in the Checked property returning true.
Unchecked	The CheckBox is unchecked and the Checked property returns false.

A GroupBox control is a container control that can display a caption above and a border around a set of controls. As a container, the GroupBox will also apply certain of its properties (Enabled, for example) to the entire set of controls it contains.

Try It Out – Adding a GroupBox Full of CheckBoxes

We'll add a GroupBox that contains some CheckBoxes to our Options form and develop some code to demonstrate CheckState.

1. First, select our frmOptions dialog form and site a GroupBox control on the left side. Change its Text property to Effects and its Name property to grpEffects. Next, add four Checkboxes by dropping them inside the Effects GroupBox. Set the Text and Name properties of the checkboxes according to the following chart.

Name	Text
chkAllEffects	All
chkMegaBass	Mega Bass
chkEcho	Echo
chkReverse	Reverse

2. Position chkAllEffects as the top CheckBox and move it to the left side of the GroupBox interior. Align the lefts of the other three checkboxes with each other, and position them below, and to the right of chkAllEffects.

3. Select the `chkAllEffects` CheckBox. Instead of double-clicking on the control and creating the default event handler method, change the **Properties** window to display events instead of properties. Now find the `Click` event line and double-click on it to create an event handler in code. (We did this earlier for the `DoubleClick` event of a `ListBox` so you can refer back to there for detailed instructions.) Next, we type the following highlighted code in the handler that was created for us.

```
private void chkAllEffects_Click(object sender, System.EventArgs e)
{
    chkMegaBass.CheckState = chkAllEffects.CheckState;
    chkEcho.CheckState = chkAllEffects.CheckState;
    chkReverse.CheckState = chkAllEffects.CheckState;
}
```

4. Now, instead of letting the designer make more handlers for us, let's hook up one handler method to multiple control events. Go to the form's constructor method and add the following highlighted lines.

```
public frmOptions()
{
    //
    // Required for Windows Form Designer support
    //
    InitializeComponent();
    //
    // TODO: Add any constructor code after InitializeComponent call
    //
    this.chkMegaBass.Click += new System.EventHandler(this.ChildCheckBoxClicked);
    this.chkEcho.Click += new System.EventHandler(this.ChildCheckBoxClicked);
    this.chkReverse.Click += new System.EventHandler(this.ChildCheckBoxClicked);
}
```

5. Next, we must define the `ChildCheckBoxClicked` method we refer to above. Using the `chkAllEffects_Click` method from earlier as a template for parameters, we can add the following new method to our form. It may look intimidating as we type it all in, but we'll explain it in detail later.

```
private void ChildCheckBoxClicked(object sender, System.EventArgs e)
{
    long CheckedChildren = 0;
    // loop through each Control in the GroupBox's Controls
    // property collection
    foreach (Control tmpControl in grpEffects.Controls)
    {
        // make sure we're dealing with a CheckBox
        // and that it's not our "All" box
        if ((tmpControl.GetType() == typeof(CheckBox)) &&
                        (tmpControl.Name != chkAllEffects.Name))
        {
```

```
        // cast the Control object we are dealing
        // with into a CheckBox
        if (((CheckBox)tmpControl).Checked)
        {
            CheckedChildren++;
        }
    }
}
if (CheckedChildren == (grpEffects.Controls.Count - 1))
{
    chkAllEffects.CheckState = CheckState.Checked;
}
else if (CheckedChildren == 0)
{
    chkAllEffects.CheckState = CheckState.Unchecked;
}
else
{
    chkAllEffects.CheckState = CheckState.Indeterminate;
}
}
```

Now, build and run the project. Click on our **Options** button to bring up the `Options` dialog. Clicking on the **All** `CheckBox` should check or uncheck all the individual effect `CheckBoxes`. Clicking on the individual effect `CheckBoxes` so that only one or two of them are checked will give the **All** `CheckBox` the shaded `Indeterminate CheckState` we mentioned back in our discussion of `CheckBox` properties.

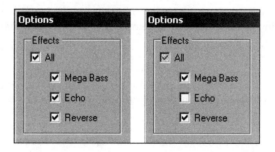

How It Works

Because we left each `CheckBox`'s `ThreeState` property set to `False` (its default setting), the user cannot select the grayed `Indeterminate` state even though we are free to select this state in our code. Clicking on the **All** `CheckBox` will merely toggle it between `Checked` and `UnChecked`. This will also execute our `chkAllEffects_Click` event handler method to set the `CheckState` property of each individual effects box to match the `CheckState` of our **All** box.

Now, what about that big `ChildCheckBoxClicked()` method? We want all of the individual effect boxes to exhibit the same behavior regarding the **All** box. Each time an individual effect box is clicked, we want to appropriately update the `CheckState` of the **All** box. To achieve this, we attached the same general handler method to all their `Click` events.

```
this.chkMegaBass.Click += new System.EventHandler(this.ChildCheckBoxClicked);
this.chkEcho.Click += new System.EventHandler(this.ChildCheckBoxClicked);
this.chkReverse.Click += new System.EventHandler(this.ChildCheckBoxClicked);
```

As far as the code in the handler method itself, we first declare a counter `CheckedChildren` to keep track of the total number of individual effect `CheckBoxes` that are actually checked at the moment.

We use the `foreach` loop to iterate through a `Controls` collection. Notice we create an object of type `Control` named `tmpControl` that is relevant inside the scope of the loop. Also of special interest is the fact that the loop is going to execute once for each `Control` in the `grpEffects.Controls` collection property, not for each `Control` in the `frmOptions.Controls` collection property. Since a `GroupBox` control is a container control, which in our case contains all our `CheckBox` controls, we can access them via the `GroupBox`'s `Controls` collection to avoid having to loop through every `Control` on the whole `Form`.

```
foreach (Control tmpControl in grpEffects.Controls)
{
    if ((tmpControl.GetType() == typeof(CheckBox)) &&
                        (tmpControl.Name != chkAllEffects.Name))
    {
        if (((CheckBox)tmpControl).Checked)
        {
            CheckedChildren++;
        }
    }
}
```

Inside the loop, we test each `tmpControl` and do further processing only if the control is actually a `CheckBox` and is not our All `CheckBox`. This leaves us with our individual effect `CheckBoxes`.

```
        if (((CheckBox)tmpControl).Checked)
```

With the above line of code, we cast each `tmpControl` (which remember is simply of type `Control`) into a `CheckBox` object so we can test its `Checked` property. If the `Checked` property is true, then we increment our `CheckedChildren` counter.

After looping through each `Control`, we finally make use of our `CheckedChildren` counter. If it is zero, then we know none of our individual effect `CheckBoxes` were checked, and we can set `CheckState` property of our All `CheckBox` to `CheckState.UnChecked`. Since we know that this `GroupBox` only contains our `CheckBoxes`, we can find the total number of `Controls` in the `GroupBox` by accessing the `Count` property of its `Controls` collection.

```
        if (CheckedChildren == (grpEffects.Controls.Count - 1))
```

Since we also know that one of those controls in the collection is going to be our All `CheckBox`, we can subtract one from that `Count` to determine the true number of individual effect `CheckBoxes`. If that number is the same as our `CheckedChildren` counter, then we set the `CheckState` property of our All `CheckBox` to `CheckState.Checked`. Finally, we are left with the situation that at least one, but not all of the effects have been selected. In that case we set the `CheckState` property of our All `CheckBox` to `CheckState.Indeterminate`.

While this method might be a bit of overkill for just 4 CheckBoxes, it would certainly be appropriate for lots of them. More importantly, it serves to illustrate some important properties and behaviors of the CheckBox and GroupBox controls.

RadioButtons

The RadioButton control is nearly identical to the CheckBox control. However, RadioButtons are usually utilized when the user must make a single choice from a number of options. Therefore, selecting an option in the group unselects all the other options in the group. RadioButtons are grouped together with containers. This means if you have 5 RadioButtons on a Form, they will all act as a group. If we need to have 10 of them on a form acting as 2 independent groups of 5, then we need to place each group of 5 in a container such as a GroupBox.

Try It Out – Adding RadioButtons to the Options Form

Let's add some RadioButtons in a GroupBox to our options dialog. In our discussion about ListBoxes earlier, we also talked about seeing a CheckedListBox. We'll add one of those now too, which will finish our work on the Options dialog form.

1. Stretch our options form a bit to make some room. Now add two GroupBox controls. Set the Text property of one to Optimize For and the Text property of the other to Associated File Types.

2. Add three RadioButtons to the GroupBox with the **Optimize For** caption. Set the Text properties of the RadioButtons to HeadPhones, Small Speakers, and Large Speakers.

3. Add a CheckedListBox control to the GroupBox with the **Associated File Types** caption. Add the following line items to the Items collection of the CheckedListBox. (see our ComboBox discussion earlier in the chapter if you need a refresher): Audio File (.wav), CD Audio Track (.cda), MP3 (.mp3), MIDI (.mid), and Windows Media Audio File (.wma).

Now we should be able to arrange our controls to make our options form look similar to the following screenshot.

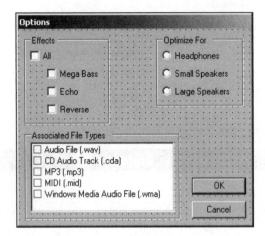

We can build and run the application to see how the RadioButtons only allow one selection. We can also see the default behavior of our CheckedListBox, a hybrid between the CheckBox and the ListBox.

Well, that's it for the Options form. The next chapter will cover the TabControl, which is often used in applications that need to present several sets of options as we have in our MyPlayer application. While our Options form isn't necessarily trendy, we have learned about some very frequently used controls in the process of building it.

Bar Controls

We'll end this chapter by talking about a couple of controls that are relatively simple but can come in very handy when the right situation arises for their use. These controls are the System.Windows.Forms.TrackBar, and the System.Windows.Forms.ProgressBar. The TrackBar is a scrollable bar control. The ProgressBar is a bar indicator control that fills from left to right.

Instead of going through a list of all the properties for these controls, we'll just go through an example using them. This will also give you a chance to repeat some of the skills we used earlier in the chapter and provides a good warm-up for when we start moving on to more complex controls in the next chapter.

Try It Out – Adding a TrackBar and a ProgressBar

Let's finish the user interface of our sample application by adding a TrackBar to represent a volume slider control, and a ProgressBar to represent a volume level indicator.

1. Let's go back to our main form and make it a little bigger. Add two GroupBox controls. Set the Text property of one to Balance and the Text property of the other to Volume.

2. Place one TrackBar control inside the GroupBox with the Volume caption. Set the Name property of this TrackBar to trkVolume. Set the Maximum property to 20, and then set the Value property to 6.

3. Just for comparison, add another `TrackBar` and two `Labels` in the `GroupBox` with the **Balance** caption. Set its `Value` property to 5. Set the `Text` properties of the `Labels` to `Left` and `Right` and position them accordingly on each side of the `TrackBar`.

4. Finally, add a `ProgressBar` control just below the **MyPlayer** logo. Set the `Maximum` property to 20, and then set the `Value` property to 6. Our main form should now look like the following screenshot:

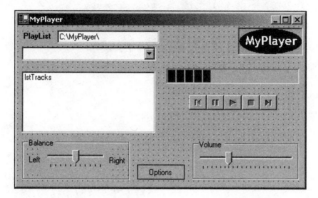

5. Double-click on our **Volume** `TrackBar` to create the `Scroll` event handler, and enter the following highlighted code.

```
private void trkVolume_Scroll(object sender, System.EventArgs e)
{
    this.progressBar1.Value = trkVolume.Value;
}
```

6. Build and run the project. Now we can move the **Volume** slider and see the setting mirrored in the `ProgressBar`.

While the `ProgressBar` is in a visual position better suited to represent the progress of playing an audio track instead of the selected volume from the `TrackBar`, our example serves to simply illustrate the use of both. Notice how the **Volume** `TrackBar` resized the increment marks when we changed its `Maximum` property in design mode.

Summary

In this chapter, we started out by looking at some general concerns to keep in mind when building a UI for a Windows desktop application. We then moved on to a survey of some of the more fundamental controls available in the Visual Studio .NET toolbox. The goal here was not to make you an expert in every one of these controls but to give you an introduction to each of them so that you're aware of what's available and start to get a feel for when each should be used in your own applications. The next chapter will continue along this path by introducing you to even more controls with increasing power and flexibility. As you progress through the remainder of this book and then into building your own "real-world" applications, all of the controls in this chapter will become like old familiar friends.

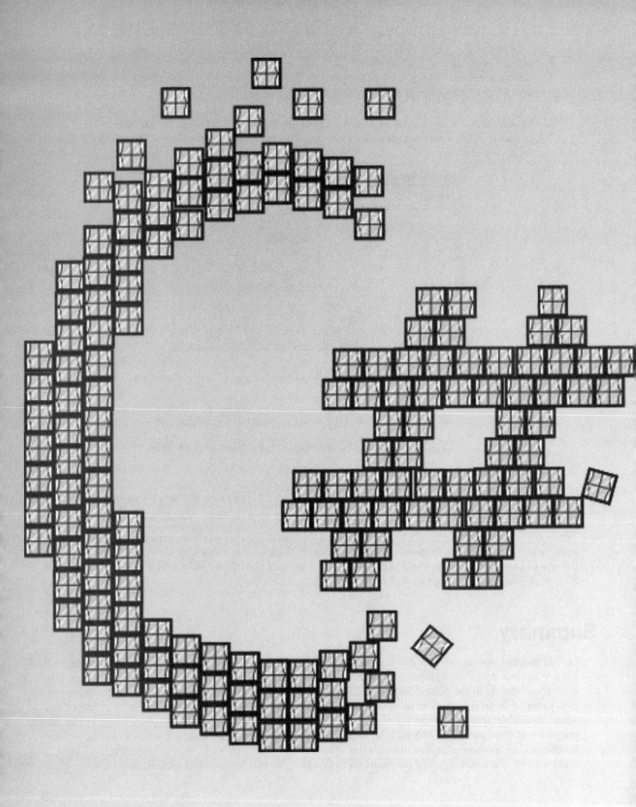

Advanced User Interface Controls

In the previous chapter we looked at different types of simple user interface controls and demonstrated how to use them to create Windows applications. In this chapter, we will expand our knowledge beyond these simple controls, by taking a look at some of the advanced user interface controls that allow us to create advanced, effective, and intuitive Windows Form-based GUIs.

As with the previous chapter, we will discuss the important properties and methods of the advanced controls, although we will not attempt to be completely comprehensive. We will also show you how to incorporate them into your Windows applications via examples.

Specifically we will cover the following topics:

❑ Introductions to the advanced user interface controls contained in the `System.Windows.Forms` namespace

❑ How to use the `TabControl` to create effective applications

❑ How to use `TreeView` and `ListView` to create Explorer-style applications

❑ How to incorporate dynamic resizing functionality using a `Splitter` control

❑ How to use `DateTimePicker` and `MonthCalendar` controls to add date selection features to an application

❑ How to change the cursor mouse pointer by making use of the properties and methods of the `Cursor` class

Along the way we will encounter a few other controls that are useful when used in conjunction with the controls and classes above.

Tour of Advanced Controls

In this section we'll take a tour of the most commonly encountered advanced controls. Let's begin with a general overview of the controls we will be looking at.

Overview

Before we dive into a discussion of each control in turn, let's briefly introduce you to the functionality of the controls we're going to be covering in this chapter:

❑   TabControl – You should be pretty familiar with dialog boxes that are subdivided into pages through the use of tabs. The TabControl is the control we can use to implement this feature.

❑   TreeView – A common way to present hierarchical information, like the hierarchy of folders on a hard disk, is to display it in a tree view format. You can see an example of this if you select View | Explorer Bar | Folders in Windows Explorer. A TreeView control allows us to create this same feature in our Windows applications.

❑   Splitter – Using the Splitter control, the users of an application can dynamically resize the width and height of the individual (or more commonly groups of) controls that make up the application form.

❑   DateTimePicker – The DateTimePicker does exactly what its name suggests, allowing the user to select a date.

❑   MonthCalendar – This is similar to the DateTimePicker but it allows the user to select a range of dates.

As you can see, we can use the TabControl and TreeView to present a lot of information to the user in an organized yet concise way. The Splitter lets the user personalize your application to some degree. The DateTimePicker and the MonthCalendar controls are obviously great for applications that require date input.

Let's start our tour of advanced controls now by discussing the TabControl in more depth.

TabControl

A TabControl is normally used when we have lots of information to present in one window, and we wish to subcategorize this information, presenting it one category at a time to make it more readable. By using a TabControl we can define multiple pages for the same window or dialog box, thereby saving the screen real estate. Each page is known as a **tab**, and is labeled at the top with a name. We can move between tabs by clicking on the tab name. This is illustrated below:

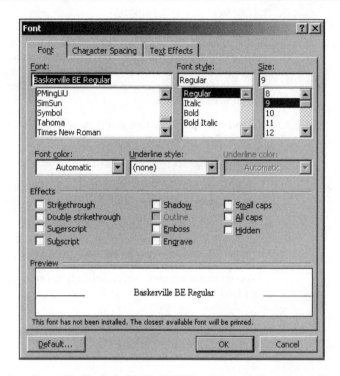

The above screenshot shows the **Font** dialog in MS Word that can be accessed by selecting **Format | Font**. Each tab in the dialog box is used to contain information related to a specific set of operations. For example, all the controls that allow us to change the font size and type are contained in the **Font** tab.

Using the tab control is very easy. Each tab in the `TabControl` is represented by a `TabPage` object. You simply add each `TabPage` you want to display to the `TabControl.TabPages` collection object. Once you have finished creating the tabs, you can drag and drop controls from the toolbox onto the individual tabs in the same way as you normally add controls to the form.

Most of the properties of the tab control class are used to control the way the tabs are displayed.

Property	Description
Alignment	Read-write property that determines where in the tab control the tabs are displayed. The default is at the top.
Appearance	Read-write property that allows us to control way the tabs appear in the tab control. It can have any one of the following values: `Buttons`, `FlatButtons`, and `Normal`.

Table continued on following page

53

Property	Description
Multiline	Using this read | write property, we can display several rows of tabs in the tab control. If this property is set to `false` and there are too many tab pages to show on a single line, it automatically adds scroll buttons.
RowCount	Read-only property that provides information about the number of rows of tabs that is displayed.
SelectedTab	Allows us to set or get the currently selected tab page.
SelectedIndex	Similar to the `SelectedTab` property except that it performs the selection of a tab page using an index (as opposed to a `TabPage` object).
TabPages	Using this property, we can get reference to the group of `TabPage` objects that are contained in the `TabControl`.
TabCount	As the name suggests, this read-only property provides the number of tabs contained in the `TabControl`.
ImageList	To display images in the tabs of the `TabControl`, we need to add the images to the `ImageList` object which can then be referenced in the `TabControl` to display the images.

Let's now create an example application that uses a tabbed dialog box.

Try It Out – Creating a Tabbed Dialog Box

In this example, we will use the `TabControl` to create a Windows application that allows us to specify font type and size.

1. Select File | New | Project and create a new Windows Application under C# Projects. Name the project AdvancedControls.

2. Rename the default `Form1.cs` to `TabControlExample.cs`. Change its `Name` property to `TabControlExample` and the `Text` property to `Advanced Controls - TabControl`.

3. Drag and drop a `TabControl` from the Toolbox onto the Designer. Name the control `tabFormattingControl`. In `tabFormattingControl`'s Properties window, click the ellipsis (. . .) button for the `TabPages` property to bring up the TabPage Collection Editor. From the TabPage Collection Editor, add a new tab to the `TabControl`. Name the tab `tabFont` and set its `Text` property to `Font`. Click OK.

4. Add a `RichTextBox` control to the form and name it as `rtfText`. Also clear its `Text` property. Now add a `Label` to the form. Change its `Name` property to `textLabel` and change its `Text` property to `Text`.

5. Navigate to the Font tab of the `TabControl` and add the following controls.

Control Type	Name	Text
Label	selectFontLabel	Select Font Type:
Label	selectFontSizeLabel	Select Font Size:
ComboBox	selectFontType	none
ComboBox	selectFontSize	none

After adding the above controls, the form should look like the following.

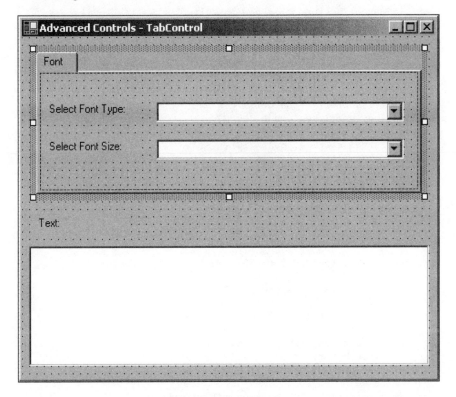

6. Set the `DropDownStyle` property for both the `selectFontType` and `selectFontSize` controls to `DropDownList`. This allows us to ensure that the user can only select only from the list of options shown in the `ComboBox`.

7. Select the `selectFontSize` `ComboBox` and for the `Items` property click the ellipsis (. . .) button. In the String Collection Editor dialog enter font sizes you want available in the application. Sizes within the regions of 6 to 72 are those normally found in most fonts.

8. Open up the Code Editor for the `TabControlExample` class, and add the following line of code to import the `System.Drawing.Text` namespace:

```
using System.Drawing.Text;
```

9. The above line is required since we directly want to reference the `InstalledFontCollection` class (contained in the `System.Drawing.Text` namespace) in our application. If you go back into the Designer and double-click the form, the load event will automatically be created. Modify the load event of the form to look like the following:

```
private void TabControlExample_Load(object sender, System.EventArgs e)
{
    InstalledFontCollection col = new InstalledFontCollection();
    //Enumerate all the FontFamily objects in the collection
    foreach (FontFamily fontFamily in col.Families)
    {
        selectFontType.Items.Add(fontFamily.Name);
    }

    //Set the first item as the default item
    if (selectFontType.Items.Count > 0)
        selectFontType.SelectedIndex = 0;
    if (selectFontSize.Items.Count > 0)
        selectFontSize.SelectedIndex = 0;
}
```

10. Add a method named `UpdateFont()` to the `TabControlExample` class.

```
private void UpdateFont()
{
    //Set the default font size to 10
    int fontSize = 10;
    if (selectFontSize.SelectedIndex > 0 )
        //Get the selected Font Size
        fontSize = Convert.ToInt32(selectFontSize.SelectedItem.ToString ());

    //Set the default font type as Arial
    string fontType = "Arial" ;
    if (selectFontType.SelectedIndex > 0 )
        //Get the selected Font type
        fontType = selectFontType.SelectedItem.ToString();

    //Create a new Font object with the specified font type and size
    Font newFont = new Font(fontType,fontSize);
    //Assign the newly created Font to the RichTextBox
    rtfText.Font = newFont;
}
```

11. Double-click on the `selectFontType` and `selectFontSize` ComboBoxes to add code for the `SelectedIndexChanged` event:

```
private void selectFontType_SelectedIndexChanged(object sender,
                                                 System.EventArgs e)
{
    //Update the RichTextBox based on the selection
    UpdateFont();
}


private void selectFontSize_SelectedIndexChanged(object sender,
                                                 System.EventArgs e)
{
    //Update the RichTextBox based on the selection
    UpdateFont();
}
```

12. Change the `Main()` method to run our form class, as shown below:

```
static void Main()
{
    Application.Run(new TabControlExample());
}
```

13. Build the application and then run it by pressing *F5*. In the form, whenever you change the font type or font size values in the ComboBox, it automatically reflects in the RichTextBox:

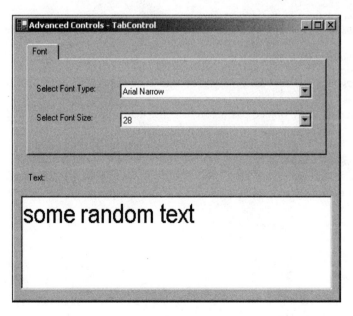

How It Works

Let us first consider the form load event. We start by instantiating the `InstalledFontCollection` object which allows us to retrieve the fonts installed on the system.

```
InstalledFontCollection col = new InstalledFontCollection();
```

Once we have an instance of the `InstalledFontCollection` object, we can then loop through the available fonts, adding the names of all the installed fonts to the `ComboBox` named `selectFontType`:

```
foreach (FontFamily fontFamily in col.Families)
{
    selectFontType.Items.Add(fontFamily.Name);
}
```

Finally, we set the first item as the default selection in both of the `ComboBoxes`.

```
if (selectFontType.Items.Count > 0)
    selectFontType.SelectedIndex = 0;
if (selectFontSize.Items.Count > 0)
    selectFontSize.SelectedIndex = 0;
```

Let us now consider the `UpdateFont()` method. In this method, we start by assigning default values for local variables that represent font type and font size. However, if an item is selected in the ComboBoxes, we assign that value to the local variables:

```
int fontSize = 10;
if (selectFontSize.SelectedIndex > 0 )
    fontSize = Convert.ToInt32(selectFontSize.SelectedItem.ToString());

string fontType = "Arial" ;
if (selectFontType.SelectedIndex > 0 )
    fontType = selectFontType.SelectedItem.ToString();
```

Then we create a new `Font` object, passing to its constructor the `fontType` and `fontSize` values as arguments.

```
Font newFont = new Font(fontType,fontSize);
```

Finally we assign the newly created `Font` object to the `Font` property of the `RichTextBox` control:

```
rtfText.Font = newFont;
```

Adding Tabs to a TabControl

In our previous example, we created a tab called Font in the `TabControl` and provided all the font-related functionality. As we already discussed, one of the important advantages of the `TabControl` is the ability to add a similar set of related functionality to the same form without taking any extra space in the form. In our case, let us say, for example, we want to provide the users of our application with the ability to change the style attributes (such as bold, italic, underline and so on) of the text displayed in the `RichTextBox`. Since this functionality has a lot in common with the font style and font size attributes, it should ideally be added as a separate tab to the same `TabControl`.

Let's see how to incorporate this functionality into our application.

Try It Out – Adding More Tabs to the Tabbed Dialog Box

In this Try It Out we are going to add another tab to our example that will allow the user to select the font style they require.

1. Open the Designer for `TabControlExample`.

2. Right click on `tabFormattingControl` and select **Properties** from the menu to bring up the Properties window. In the Properties window, click the ellipsis (. . .) button next to the `TabPages` property to bring up the TabPage Collection Editor.

3. From the TabPage Collection Editor, add one more tab to the `TabControl` as shown below. Name the tab as `tabStyle` and set its `Text` property to `Style`.

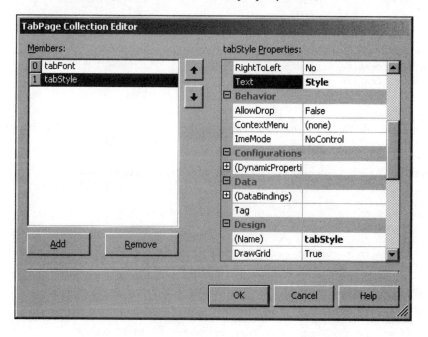

4. Navigate to the **Style** tab of the `TabControl` and add the following controls. Set their properties as shown below:

Control Type	Name	Text
CheckBox	checkBoldStyle	Bold
CheckBox	checkUnderlineStyle	Underline
CheckBox	checkItalicStyle	Italic

5. That concludes the visual part of the example. Now we'll move straight to the code. Double-click on the `checkBoldStyle` CheckBox to create the `CheckedChanged` event handler:

```
private void checkBoldStyle_CheckedChanged(object sender,
                                           System.EventArgs e)
{
    Font newFont;
    Font oldFont;

    //Get the font that is being used in the selected text
    oldFont = this.rtfText.SelectionFont;

    //If the font is using Bold style now, remove the formatting
    if (checkBoldStyle.Checked)
        newFont = new Font(oldFont,oldFont.Style | FontStyle.Bold);
    else
        newFont = new Font(oldFont,oldFont.Style & ~FontStyle.Bold); .

    //Insert the new font and return focus to the Richtextbox
    this.rtfText.SelectionFont = newFont;
    this.rtfText.Focus();
}
```

6. Similarly, add the following lines of code to the `CheckedChanged` events handlers of the `checkUnderlineStyle` and `checkItalicStyle` CheckBoxes:

```
private void checkUnderlineStyle_CheckedChanged(object sender,
                                                System.EventArgs e)
{
    Font newFont;
    Font oldFont;
    //Get the font that is being used in the selected text
    oldFont = this.rtfText.SelectionFont;
    //If the font is using Underline style now, remove the formatting
    if (checkUnderlineStyle.Checked)
        newFont = new Font(oldFont,oldFont.Style | FontStyle.Underline);
    else
        newFont = new Font(oldFont,oldFont.Style & ~FontStyle.Underline);
    //Insert the new font and return focus to the Richtextbox
    this.rtfText.SelectionFont = newFont;
```

```
        this.rtfText.Focus();
    }

    private void checkItalicStyle_CheckedChanged(object sender,
                                            System.EventArgs e)
    {
        Font newFont;
        Font oldFont;
        //Get the font that is being used in the selected text
        oldFont = this.rtfText.SelectionFont;
        //If the font is using Italic style now, remove the formatting
        if (checkItalicStyle.Checked)
            newFont = new Font(oldFont,oldFont.Style | FontStyle.Italic);
        else
            newFont = new Font(oldFont,oldFont.Style & ~FontStyle.Italic);
        //Insert the new font and return focus to the Richtextbox
        this.rtfText.SelectionFont = newFont;
        this.rtfText.Focus();
    }
```

7. Run the application by pressing *F5*. It should look like this:

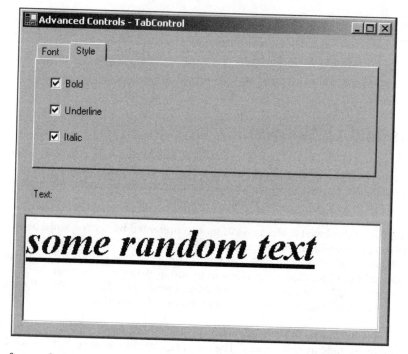

In the above form, whenever you select the text and check or uncheck an item in the checkbox, it automatically reflects in the RichTextBox.

How It Works

Let's look at the CheckedChanged event handler for the checkBoldStyle CheckBox. We start by getting the font being used in the current selection and assigning it to a local variable. Then we check if this selection is already bold. If it is, we remove the bold setting; otherwise we add the bold setting. We achieve this by creating a new font using the oldFont as the prototype, but add or remove the bold style as needed.

```
private void checkBoldStyle_CheckedChanged(object sender,
                                           System.EventArgs e)
{
    Font newFont;
    Font oldFont;

    oldFont = this.rtfText.SelectionFont;
    if (checkBoldStyle.Checked)
        newFont = new Font(oldFont,oldFont.Style | FontStyle.Bold);
    else
        newFont = new Font(oldFont,oldFont.Style & ~FontStyle.Bold);
```

Finally, we assign the new font to the selection and return focus to the RichTextBox:

```
    this.rtfText.SelectionFont = newFont;
    this.rtfText.Focus();
}
```

The code for the other event handlers is very similar except that we check for underline style or italic style.

TreeViews and ListViews

As you might have seen in many places, a TreeView control allows us to display a set of related information using a hierarchical structure. Using TreeView, we can organize related information into easy-to-manage blocks. For example, the TreeView control is most commonly used to display a the directory structure of disk drives, as in Windows Explorer.

Each individual item displayed in the TreeView is represented by a TreeNode object. To get references to the list of child nodes under a specified node, we use the Nodes collection property of the TreeNode object, which returns an object of type TreeNodeCollection. The important methods of the TreeNodeCollection object that allow us to add or delete a node from the TreeView are Add() and Remove(). We can also empty the Nodes property collection using the Clear() method, and the Count property returns the number of nodes in the collection.

At run time, any particular node in the hierarchical structure of the TreeView can be expanded or contracted to show or hide its child nodes. The user can expand the node by clicking the + sign that is displayed next to the node (if the node has any child nodes). It is also possible to programmatically expand a TreeNode by invoking its Expand() method.

When we are displaying nodes in the `TreeView`, it is also possible to display images right next to the nodes. To display images, you need to perform the following steps:

1. Add a set of images that you want to display in the `TreeView` to an `ImageList` control. An `ImageList` control simply contains a collection of images that can be used by other controls. We add images (represented by the `Image` class) to the `ImageList` using its `AddImage()` method.

2. Associate the `ImageList` with the `TreeView` by setting the `ImageList` property of the `TreeView` to refer to the `ImageList` object.

3. Once the initial association is done, we can then easily reference the images contained in the `ImageList` object from the `TreeView` by making use of the `ImageIndex` property.

The following table discusses some of the important properties of the `TreeView` control:

Property	Description
CheckBoxes	Allows us to specify if we want to display checkboxes next to the nodes in the `TreeView`
HotTracking	Allows us to specify if the tree node label looks like a hyperlink when the mouse pointer is moved on top of it
ImageList	Allows us to associate an `ImageList` object that is used as the repository for all of the images used by the `TreeView`
ImageIndex	Allows us to refer to the images stored in the `ImageList` by using the index number
Indent	Allows us to specify the indent that is used for each of the child tree node levels
Nodes	Allows us to get the collection of tree nodes that are part of the `TreeView` control
PathSeparator	Allows us to get or set the delimiter string used by the tree nodes
SelectedImageIndex	Allows us to get or set the index of the image (that is stored in the `ImageList`)
SelectedNode	Allows us to get or set the tree node that is currently selected in the `TreeView` control
ShowLines	Allows us to get or set the value that determines if lines are drawn between the nodes in the `TreeView` control
ShowPlusMinus	Determines if we want to set or get a value indicating if we want to display plus-sign (+) and minus-sign (-) next to the nodes in the `TreeView`
ShowRootLines	Determines if we want to draw lines between the root nodes in the `TreeView`

A `ListView` control allows you to display a list of items. Each item is represented by a `ListViewItem` object, and the `ListViewItem` objects associated with the `ListView` are stored in a property collection called `Items`. To add `ListViewItem` objects to `ListView.Items`, we use the `Add()` method.

Similarly, the `ListViewItem` class has a property collection called `SubItems` which is used to store `ListViewSubItem` objects. These `ListViewSubItems` are displayed when the `View` property of the `ListView` control is set to `View.Details`. In other words, the `ListViewSubItem` objects represent details about a particular list item.

In the following example, we will demonstrate how to use `TreeView` and a `ListView` together to create a Windows Explorer-style application.

Try It Out – Adding TreeView Functionality to the Tabbed Dialog Box

In this example, we will enhance our `TabControl` application by adding the functionality needed for the user to be able to select a file from a hard disk, and display the contents of the file in a `RichTextBox`. To be able to perform that, we need to provide the users with the ability to navigate through the file system and pick a file from it; we will use a `TreeView` control for this.

You may not have encountered many of the objects we use to read text from a file, and to get information about directories and files before. However, we are not too concerned with these file and directory handling aspects of the application at this stage; we are much more interested in how to incorporate a `TreeView` in a "real world" style application. If you feel you need to know more, then you should refer to the later chapter on file, directory, and Registry handling (Chapter 8).

1. Open the Designer for `TabControlExample`, and right click on `tabFormattingControl`. Select **Properties** from the menu to bring up the Properties window.

2. Next to the `TabPages` property, click the ellipsis (. . .) button to bring up the TabPage Collection Editor, and using this add another tab to the `TabControl`. Name the tab `tabSelectFile` and set its `Text` property to `Select File`.

3. Open the **Select File** tab, and drag and drop a `TreeView` control from the Toolbox onto the left of the tab and name it `treeExplorer`. Also add a `ListView` control to the right of the tab and name it as `listExplorer`.

4. In the Properties window for the `treeExplorer` change the `Sorted` property to `True`; this will then sort alphabetically the displayed directories.

5. In the Properties window for `listExplorer`, set the `MultiSelect` property to `false` to prevent multiple items from being selected. Then, click the ellipsis button next to the `Columns` property to bring up the ColumnHeader Collection Editor. In this editor add a couple of `ColumnHeader` items named `colName` and `colModified`. Also set their `Text` properties to `Name` and `Modified` respectively:

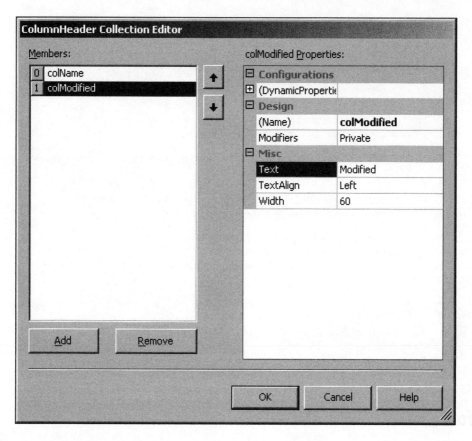

6. Now change the `View` property for `listExplorer` to `Details`. You should now see your two columns in the `ListView`.

7. Add the following line of code at the top of the file for `TabControlExample`, to import the `System.IO` namespace into our application:

```
using System.IO;
```

8. Declare an instance variable named `folder` directly inside the `TabControlExample` class:

```
private DirectoryInfo folder;
```

9. Add the `LoadTree()` private method as part of the class:

```
private void LoadTree()
{
    DirectoryInfo directory;

    // Clear the TreeView
```

```
        treeExplorer.Nodes.Clear();

        // Loop through the drive letters and find the available drives
        foreach(string drive in Environment.GetLogicalDrives())
        {
            try
            {
                // get the directory information for this path.
                directory = new DirectoryInfo(drive);

                // If the retrieved directory is valid, add it to the TreeView
                if (directory.Exists == true )
                {
                    TreeNode newNode = new TreeNode(directory.FullName);
                    treeExplorer.Nodes.Add(newNode);

                    // Add the new node to the root level
                    GetSubDirectories(newNode);
                    // scan for any sub folders on this drive
                }
            }
            catch
            {
                //Ignore Exceptions
                return;
            }
        }
}
```

10. Add the `GetSubDirectories()` private method:

```
private void GetSubDirectories(TreeNode parent)
{
    DirectoryInfo directory;
    try
    {
        // Check if we have already scanned this folder
        if ( parent.Nodes.Count == 0 )
        {
            directory = new DirectoryInfo(parent.FullPath);
            foreach( DirectoryInfo dir in directory.GetDirectories())
            {
                TreeNode newNode = new TreeNode(dir.Name);
                parent.Nodes.Add(newNode);
            }
        }
        // Scan the first level of sub folders to create + or - sign
        foreach(TreeNode node in parent.Nodes)
        {
            // If we have not scanned this node before.
            if (node.Nodes.Count == 0)
            {
```

```
            // Get the folder information for the specified path.
            directory = new DirectoryInfo(node.FullPath);
            // Check this folder for any possible subdirectories
            foreach( DirectoryInfo dir in directory.GetDirectories())
            {
                //Create a new TreeNode and add it to the TreeView.
                TreeNode newNode = new TreeNode(dir.Name);
                node.Nodes.Add(newNode);
            }
        }
    }
}
catch
{
    //Ignore Exceptions
    return;
}
}
```

11. Add the `ReadFile()` private method too:

```
private void ReadFile(string path)
{
    try
    {
        Stream stream = new FileStream(path, FileMode.Open);
        FileInfo fileInfo = new FileInfo(path);

        string fileExtension = fileInfo.Extension.ToUpper();

        if (fileExtension.Equals(".RTF"))
            rtfText.LoadFile(stream, RichTextBoxStreamType.RichText);
        else
            rtfText.LoadFile(stream, RichTextBoxStreamType.PlainText);

        stream.Close();
    }
    catch
    {
        //Ignore the Exceptions
        return;
    }
}
```

12. Add the following event handlers to the `treeExplorer` control:

```
private void treeExplorer_BeforeSelect(object sender,
    System.Windows.Forms.TreeViewCancelEventArgs e)
{
    //Get all the subdirectories for the selected node
    GetSubDirectories(e.Node);
```

```
        //Get the DirectoryInfo object and assign it to the module level variable
        folder = new DirectoryInfo(e.Node.FullPath);
}

private void treeExplorer_BeforeExpand(object sender,
    System.Windows.Forms.TreeViewCancelEventArgs e)
{
        //Get all the subdirectories for the selected node
        GetSubDirectories(e.Node);

        //Get the DirectoryInfo object and assign it to the module level variable
        folder = new DirectoryInfo(e.Node.FullPath);
}

private void treeExplorer_AfterSelect(object sender,
    System.Windows.Forms.TreeViewEventArgs e)
{
        //Get reference to the selected node
        DirectoryInfo dirInfo = new DirectoryInfo(e.Node.FullPath);

        //Clear all the items in the ListView
        listExplorer.Items.Clear();

        //Check if the Directory exists or not
        if (dirInfo.Exists)
        {
            //Get reference to all the files
            FileInfo[] fileInfos = dirInfo.GetFiles();

            //Add all the files to the ListView
            foreach(FileInfo info in fileInfos)
            {
                ListViewItem item = new ListViewItem();
                item = listExplorer.Items.Add(info.Name);
                item.SubItems.Add(info.LastAccessTime.ToString());
            }
        }
}
```

Then go to the Properties window for the TreeView control, and click on the Events button (the one with the lightning flash). Find the BeforeSelect, BeforeExpand, and AfterSelect events and set them to treeExplorer_BeforeSelect, treeExplorer_BeforeExpand, and treeExplorer_AfterSelect respectively.

13. Add the SelectedIndexChanged event handler as shown below, and then set the SelectedIndexChanged event in the Properties windows for the ListView control to listExplorer_SelectedIndexChanged. In this method we make use of the SubItems property of the ListViewItem object to retrieve the selected file name from the ListView control.

```
private void listExplorer_SelectedIndexChanged(object sender,
                                              System.EventArgs e)
{
   //Check if an item is selected in the Listview
   if (listExplorer.SelectedItems.Count > 0)
   {
      string fileName = listExplorer.SelectedItems[0].SubItems[0].Text;

      //Create proper path by passing the selected path
      // to the GetFullPath method of Path class
      string folderName =
         Path.GetFullPath(treeExplorer.SelectedNode.FullPath) + @"\";

      //Invoke the ReadFile method to display the contents
      // of the file in the RichTextBox
      ReadFile(folderName + fileName);
   }
}
```

14. Add the following lines of code to the end of the `TabControlExample_Load()` event handler:

```
//Load the TreeView
LoadTree();
```

15. Start the application by pressing *F5*. Navigate to the **Select File** tab from the `TabControl` and select a file (that has an extension of either `.txt` or `.rtf`) from the `ListView` and you should see the contents of the file in the `RichTextBox` control.

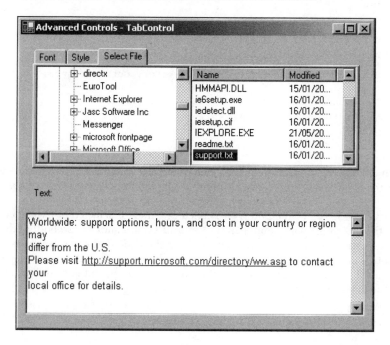

How It Works

When we first start up the application, the form load event handler is called, which in turn invokes the LoadTree() method. This method populates not only the root elements in the TreeView but also their child nodes. We're interested in several lines of code from this method. The first empties the Nodes collection of the TreeView:

```
treeExplorer.Nodes.Clear();
```

After this we use a DirectoryInfo object get directory information for each drive. Provided a particular directory exists, we create a new TreeNode object with for this directory, and add this TreeNode to the Nodes collection using the Add() method:

```
TreeNode newNode = new TreeNode(directory.FullName);
treeExplorer.Nodes.Add(newNode);
```

Then we call our GetSubDirectories() method, passing it the node we've just added to the Nodes collection:

```
GetSubDirectories(newNode);
```

In this method, we first check the Nodes collection of this node in order to see if we've already processed this node. If not, we use a DirectoryInfo object to obtain directory information about the Node, and then for each subdirectory of this "parent" node we add a "child" node to the parent node's Nodes collection:

```
if ( parent.Nodes.Count == 0 )
{
    directory = new DirectoryInfo(parent.FullPath);
    foreach( DirectoryInfo dir in directory.GetDirectories())
    {
        TreeNode newNode = new TreeNode(dir.Name);
        parent.Nodes.Add(newNode);
    }
}
```

Next, for each child node we go through the same procedure as for the parent node – we fill the Nodes collection for the child node. In this way we build up the full directory tree in Nodes.

The GetSubDirectories() method is also called as a node is selected or expanded by the user (as we can see in the BeforeSelect and BeforeExpand event handlers), so both of these user actions result in the generation of a directory tree starting from the node that was selected or expanded. However, if a tree node is selected rather than expanded, the AfterSelect event handler clears the ListView control, gets a reference to all the files in the directory, and adds the name and last access time of each file to a ListViewItem:

```
FileInfo[] fileInfos = dirInfo.GetFiles();

foreach(FileInfo info in fileInfos)
```

```
    {
        ListViewItem item = new ListViewItem();
        item = listExplorer.Items.Add(info.Name);
        item.SubItems.Add(info.LastAccessTime.ToString());
    }
```

Notice how we add the last access time to the `SubItems` collection of the `ListViewItem`, and we also add the `ListViewItem` to the `Items` collection of the `ListView` control.

Now that the `ListView` is loaded with items, let's consider what happens when the user selects a particular file in the list. In this case the `SelectedIndexChanged` event is fired. In the event handler, we see that (provided there is at least one file in the list) we retrieve the full path name to the file selected, and then call our `ReadFile()` method, passing it this full path:

```
    string fileName = listExplorer.SelectedItems[0].SubItems[0].Text;

    string folderName =
        Path.GetFullPath(tvwExplorer.SelectedNode.FullPath) + @"\";

    ReadFile(folderName + fileName);
```

Finally, in the `ReadFile()` method, we get some information about the file using a `FileInfo()` object, work out whether or not the file is a rich text file, and then load the contents of the file into the `RichTextBox` using its `LoadFile()` method:

```
    FileInfo fileInfo = new FileInfo(path);

    string fileExtension = fileInfo.Extension.ToUpper();

    if (fileExtension.Equals(".RTF"))
        rtfText.LoadFile(stream, RichTextBoxStreamType.RichText);
    else
        rtfText.LoadFile(stream, RichTextBoxStreamType.PlainText);
```

Obviously, as we mentioned earlier we've glossed over many of the objects associated with file and directory handling. But we'll look at these in more detail in Chapter 8.

Splitter

Using the `Splitter` control, the users of an application can dynamically resize the width and height of the individual controls that make up the form. To enable this to happen, we need to dock controls to the edge of the `Splitter` control. After that, when the user moves the mouse over the `Splitter` control, the mouse cursor changes its shape to indicate that the controls docked to the `Splitter` can be resized.

There are two important properties of the `Splitter` control that allow us to ensure that the controls that are docked to the `Splitter` are not resized too small to be of any use. These properties are `MinExtra` and `MinSize`.

As you may have guessed, the core functionality of the `Splitter` control is provided by the `Dock` property. This property allows us to specify the edge of the parent container a control is docked to. It is specified using the `DockStyle` enumeration, which can take any one of the following values:

Member Name	Description
Bottom	The bottom edge of the control is docked to the bottom of its container control
Fill	All the edges of the control are docked to the edges of the container control
Left	The left edge of the control is docked to the left edge of its container control
None	No docking takes place
Right	The right edge of the control is docked to the right edge of its container control
Top	The top edge of the control is docked to the top of edge of its container control

It is important to note that the resizing of controls using a `Splitter` control can only be done by means of mouse.

Try It Out – Adding Splitter Functionality to the Tabbed Dialog Box

You might have noticed in our previous example, we did not provide the capability to resize the `TreeView` and `ListView` controls at run time. In this example, we will see how to add the resizing feature to our `TreeView` explorer that makes this possible.

1. Open the Designer for the `TabControlExample`, and navigate to the **Select File** tab.

2. Drag and drop a `Splitter` control from the Toolbox onto the form and name it as `explorerSplitter`.

3. Make sure the following properties for the controls present in the **Select File** tab have the following values:

Control Name	Property	Value
treeExplorer	Dock	DockStyle.Left
explorerSplitter	Dock	DockStyle.Left
listExplorer	Dock	DockStyle.Fill
explorerSplitter	MinSize	50
explorerSplitter	MinExtra	50

In the above list, since we want to allow the user to resize the TreeView control, we set the Dock property for the TreeView and the splitter to DockStyle.Left. We also set the Dock property for the ListView control to DockStyle.Fill to allow the ListView to occupy the remaining space on the form. After that, to ensure that the Splitter control does not resize the TreeView and ListView controls to a very small size, we also set MinSize and MinExtra properties to appropriate values.

4. Run the application by pressing *F5*. You will see that both the TreeView and ListView controls can be dynamically resized at run time.

DateTimePicker

The DateTimePicker control allows us to display a placeholder that allows easy date selection. It is also possible to display the date according to our desired format. In addition, the DateTimePicker can also be customized to select the date from a drop-down calendar interface.

The following table summarizes the important properties of the DateTimePicker control:

Property	Description
CustomFormat	Using this property, we can specify the custom date-time format string that can be used to control the way in which the date and time are displayed in the DateTimePicker
MaxDate	Allows us to set or get the maximum date that can be selected in the control
MinDate	Allows us to set or get the minimum date that can be selected in the control
ShowCheckBox	Allows us to determine if we want to show a CheckBox to the left of the selected date
ShowUpDown	Allows us to determine whether an up-down control is displayed to adjust the date – time value

As you might have already guessed, by using the combination of MinDate and MaxDate properties, we can perform validations without even writing a single line of code.

Apart from the above properties, we can also change attributes such as the font, foreground color, and background color using the following properties:

- ❑ CalendarFont
- ❑ CalendarForeColor
- ❑ CalendarMonthBackground
- ❑ CalendarTitleBackColor
- ❑ CalendarTitleForeColor
- ❑ CalendarTrailingForeColor

Let's now make use of a `DateTimePicker` in our example application.

Try It Out – Selecting Dates in a Control

In this example, we will see how to use the `DateTimePicker` control to allow the user to select dates.

1. Add a new Windows Form by right-clicking on the project **AdvancedControls** from the Solution Explorer, select **Add | Add New Item** and select **Windows Form** from the list of available items. Name the form as `DateTimePickerSample.cs`, and set its `Text` property to `Advanced Controls - DateTimePicker`.

2. Add the following controls and set their properties according to the table shown below:

Control Name	Property	Value	Property	Value
Label	Name	selectFormLabel	Text	Select Format
Label	Name	startDateLabel	Text	Start Date
Label	Name	endDateLabel	Text	End Date
ComboBox	Name	formatSelection	Text	None (Empty)
DateTimePicker	Name	startDatePicker		
DateTimePicker	Name	endDatePicker		
Button	Name	calculateNoOfDays	Text	Calculate the number of days

The form should now look like the following:

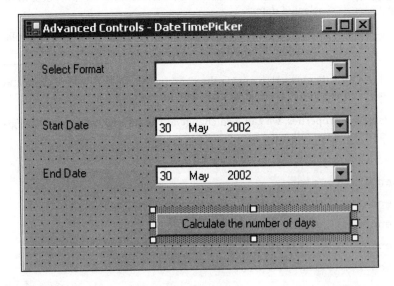

3. Select the ComboBox control, and in the Items property click on the ellipsis button. Add Long to the String Collection Editor.

4. Double click on the form to bring up the Code Editor. Modify the form load event handler to look like the following:

```
private void DateTimePickerSample_Load(object sender, System.EventArgs e)
{
    //Select the Long as the Default selection in the ComboBox
    formatSelection.SelectedIndex = 0;

    //Set the Default date style for both the controls to Long style
    startDatePicker.Format = DateTimePickerFormat.Long;
    endDatePicker.Format = DateTimePickerFormat.Long;

    //Get the current Date and Time
    DateTime now = DateTime.Now;

    //Set the MaxDate and MinDate to values which
    //only allow the user to select the start date
    //that falls within the last month
    startDatePicker.MaxDate = now;
    startDatePicker.MinDate = now.AddDays(-30);

    //Allow the user to select the maximum date that falls in the next month
    endDatePicker.MaxDate = now.AddDays(30);
}
```

5. Add the following lines of code for the click event handler for the button:

```
private void calculateNoOfDays_Click(object sender, System.EventArgs e)
{
    //Get the difference in number of days
    int noOfDays =
        (endDatePicker.Value.Subtract(startDatePicker.Value).Days + 1;
    MessageBox.Show(noOfDays.ToString());
}
```

6. Add the following Main() method to the DateTimePickerSample class just after the **Windows Form Designer generated code** section:

```
static void Main()
{
    Application.Run(new DateTimePickerSample());
}
```

Save and build the code, and change the startup object to `DateTimePickerSample` by right-clicking the **AdvancedControls** project in **Solution Explorer** and selecting **Properties**. In the Property Pages dialog change the `Startup Object` to `AdvancedControls.DateTimePickerSample`.

7. Run the application by pressing *F5*. Based on the selected date format in the **Select Format** `ComboBox`, the `startDatePicker` and `endDatePicker` controls display the date. When you click on the button, you will see a message box that displays the number of days between the start date and end date.

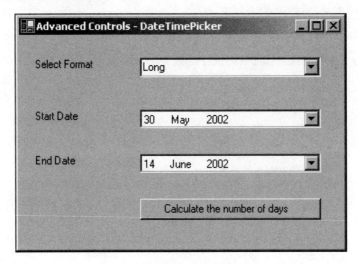

How It Works

Let us consider the code of the form load event.

```
private void DateTimePickerSample_Load(object sender, System.EventArgs e)
{
    formatSelection.SelectedIndex = 0;
```

Here, we set the default format for the `DateTimePicker` controls as `Long`:

```
    startDatePicker.Format = DateTimePickerFormat.Long;
    endDatePicker.Format = DateTimePickerFormat.Long;
```

We also restrict the user to only start dates that fall within the last month, by setting the `MinDate` and `MaxDate` properties to appropriate values:

```
    DateTime now = DateTime.Now;
    startDatePicker.MaxDate = now;
    startDatePicker.MinDate = now.AddDays(-30);
    endDatePicker.MaxDate = now.AddDays(30);
}
```

MonthCalendar

This control is similar to the `DateTimePicker` control except that it provides a user interface in which we can select a range of dates. As it is similar to the `DateTimePicker`, this control also allows users to set the minimum and the maximum dates by means of `MaxDate` and `MinDate` properties. However, the `MonthCalendar` control does not allow the user to provide a custom formatting string for the selected date(s). If your application needs custom formatting, it is recommended that you use the `DateTimePicker` control and take advantage of the built-in custom formatting capabilities.

The following table summarizes the important properties of the `MonthCalendar` control:

Property	Description
MaxSelectionCount	Using this property, we can set or get the maximum number of days that can be selected in the `MonthCalendar` control (by default this is seven).
SelectionStart	If we want to select a group of dates, this property can be used to provide the starting date for that range of dates.
SelectionEnd	It is similar to the `SelectionStart` except that it allows us to provide the end date for the range of dates.
SelectionRange	This property can be used to set or get the range of dates in the `MonthCalendar` control. It is normally used as an alternative to the combination of `SelectionStart` and `SelectionEnd` properties to select a date range.
ShowToday	Allows us to specify whether we want to display today's date in the bottom of the control.
ShowTodayCircle	Allows us to specify whether we want to circle today's date in the bottom of the control.
TodayDate	Allows us to get or set today's date in the `MonthCalendar` control.

Let's dive into an example that uses the `MonthCalendar` control.

Try It Out – Allowing Multiple Selection of Dates

In this example, we will see how to use the `MonthCalendar` control to allow the user to select a range of dates.

1. Add a new Windows Form as we did at the start of the previous example. Name it `MonthCalendarSample.cs`, with a form `Text` property of `Advanced Controls – MonthCalendar`.

2. Add the following controls to the form and set their properties as shown below:

Control Name	Property	Value	Property	Value
MonthCalendar	Name	timeCalendar		
Button	Name	calculate NoOfDays	Text	Calculate the number of days

3. Double-click on the form to bring up the Code Editor. Modify the form load event handler to look like the following:

```
private void MonthCalendarSample_Load(object sender, System.EventArgs e)
{
    // Get the current Date and Time
    DateTime now = DateTime.Now;

    //Set the default properties
    timeCalendar.ShowToday = true;
    timeCalendar.ShowTodayCircle = true;
    timeCalendar.TodayDate = now;
    timeCalendar.MaxSelectionCount = 61;

    //Set the MinDate and MaxDate properties
    timeCalendar.MinDate = now.AddDays(-30);
    timeCalendar.MaxDate = now.AddDays(30);

    //Select the last 7 days as the default range
    timeCalendar.SelectionStart = now.AddDays(-6);
    timeCalendar.SelectionEnd = now;
}
```

4. Add the following lines of code to the button click event handler:

```
private void calculateNoOfDays_Click(object sender, System.EventArgs e)
{
    //Get the Start and End Dates
    DateTime startDate = timeCalendar.SelectionRange.Start;
    DateTime endDate = timeCalendar.SelectionRange.End;

    //Get the difference in number of days
    int noOfDays  = (endDate.Subtract(startDate).Days + 1);
    MessageBox.Show(noOfDays.ToString());
}
```

5. Add the following code to the `MonthCalendarSample` class just after the Windows Form Designer generated code section:

```
static void Main()
{
    Application.Run(new MonthCalendarSample());
}
```

Save and build the project. Change the startup object to `MonthCalendarSample` as we did in the previous example.

6. Run the application by pressing *F5*. You will see a calendar display, and you will be able to select a range of days (by default this will be the last seven days). When you click on the button, you will see a message box that displays the number of days between the start date and end date of the range. You will also not be allowed to select a start date more than a month ago, and an end date more than a month ahead.

How It Works

In the load event of the form we find today's date:

```
DateTime now = DateTime.Now;
```

Then we set the various properties of the `MonthCalendar` control:

```
timeCalendar.ShowToday = true;
timeCalendar.ShowTodayCircle = true;
timeCalendar.TodayDate = now;
timeCalendar.MaxSelectionCount = 61;
```

We also set the `MinDate` and `MaxDate` properties to appropriate values to restrict the user from selecting an invalid date range:

```
timeCalendar.MinDate = now.AddDays(-30);
timeCalendar.MaxDate = now.AddDays(30);
```

Finally we set the last week as the default selected dates in the `MonthCalendar` control:

```
timeCalendar.SelectionStart = now.AddDays(-6);
timeCalendar.SelectionEnd = now;
```

Controlling the Appearance of the Cursor

As you've played around with Windows in the past, you will have noticed that the shape of the mouse cursor changes depending upon the operation being performed by the application (shapes include the usual arrow, an hourglass, and a hand, among many others). This is very useful, because it provides the user with a visual indicator of the state of an application. The `System.Windows.Forms.Cursor` class gives you the ability to control the cursor shape for your application.

> *You should note that since the `Cursor` class is not derived from the `System.Windows.Forms.Control` class it is not technically a control (and therefore you won't find a `Cursor` control in the Toolbox). However, we have included a section about it in this chapter because you should consider the behavior of the cursor when you create advanced GUIs using Windows Forms.*

The `Cursor` property exposed by the `Control` class is the one that allows us to perform operations related to the cursor. Since all of the controls in the `System.Windows.Form` namespace derive from `Control` class, the `Cursor` property is available to all the controls.

The `Cursor` object can be created from any one of the following sources.

- ❑ From the handle of an existing cursor object. To perform this, we need to use the `CopyHandle()` method that returns the handle of the cursor

- ❑ From an external cursor file (a file that is saved with extension `.cur`)

- ❑ From an external resource

- ❑ From a data stream (for more about streams, see Chapter 8)

The `DrawStretched()` method of the `Cursor` class allows us to stretch the size of the cursor. This is very useful in situations where you are using an external resource as a cursor image and the image is too small for the cursor. Other useful methods exposed by the cursor class are `Show()` and `Hide()`. As the name suggests, these methods are used to control the cursor display behavior.

The following table summarizes the important properties of the Cursor class:

Property	Description
Current	Allows us to get or set the mouse cursor that determines the mouse cursor shown on the screen. This is a read | write property.
Handle	This read-only property allows us to retrieve the handle of the cursor. This will be useful in situations if you are creating a new cursor object from an existing cursor object.
Size	Using this read-only property, we can get the size of the cursor object in the form of a Size object (see Chapter 5 for more about the Size object).
Clip	Allows us to clip the cursor within the specified clipping rectangle (for more about clipping rectangles see Chapter 5).

In the above list, the most frequently used property that we will be requiring in our applications is the Current property. The collection of cursor shapes that can be set though the Current property is contained in the Cursors class. Some of the important shapes contained by the Cursors class include:

- ❑   AppStarting
- ❑   Arrow
- ❑   Cross
- ❑   Default
- ❑   Hand
- ❑   Help
- ❑   IBeam
- ❑   WaitCursor

There are lots more. Please refer to the MSDN documentation for the Cursors class at http://msdn.microsoft.com/library/ for the list of cursor shapes available.

Try It Out – Using the Cursor Class to Change the Cursor Appearance

In this example, we will see how to use the Cursor class and change the mouse pointer object to different values.

1.   Add a new Windows Form to our project, and name it CursorSample.cs.

2.   Add a Button named startProcessButton and set its Text property to Do Processing. Double-click on the button to generate a click event handler, and add the following lines of code to it:

```
private void startProcessButton_Click(object sender, System.EventArgs e)
{
    //Set the cursor to WaitCursor to indicate that the used needs to wait
    Cursor.Current = Cursors.WaitCursor;

    //Dummy variable used to simulate the real processing behavior
    Int64 i = 100000000;

    //Replace these set of statements with your
    //time consuming process invocation
    for(i=0; i<100000000; i++)
    {
        // Do nothing inside the loop
    }

    //Set the cursor back to the default shape
    Cursor.Current = Cursors.Default;
}
```

3. Add the following code to the `CursorSample` class just after the **Windows Form Designer generated code** section:

```
static void Main()
{
    Application.Run(new CursorSample());
}
```

Save and build the project. Change the startup object to `CursorSample` as we described in previous examples.

4. Run the application by pressing *F5*. If you click on the **Do Processing** button, you will see the mouse pointer changing to the `WaitCursor` shape to indicate that it is executing a long process. Once the process is done, the mouse pointer changes back to the default shape.

How It Works

As usual we'll look at the click event of the button. Before starting the process, we change the cursor shape to `WaitCursor`:

```
Cursor.Current = Cursors.WaitCursor;
```

Then we simulate a long performing process by executing a huge `for` loop:

```
Int64 i = 100000000;

//Replace these set of statements with your
// time consuming process invocation
for(i=0; i<100000000; i++)
{
    // Do nothing inside the loop
}
```

Finally we change the cursor back to the default shape:

```
Cursor.Current = Cursors.Default;
```

Summary

In this chapter we looked at some of the more advanced user interface controls present in the
`System.Windows.Forms` namespace, including:

- ❏ `TabControl`
- ❏ `TreeView`
- ❏ `Splitter`
- ❏ `DateTimePicker`
- ❏ `MonthCalendar`

We noted that the `TabControl` and `TreeView` controls are very useful for organizing large amounts
of information in a readable and concise way. The `DateTimePicker` and `MonthCalendar` controls
are great for working with dates. The `Splitter` can be used to give our applications a more user-
friendly feel, as can the intelligent use of the `Cursor` class. We discussed the important properties and
methods of each of the above-mentioned controls and classes, and demonstrated their use
through examples.

In the next chapter we will be discussing the use of menus and toolbars in Windows applications.

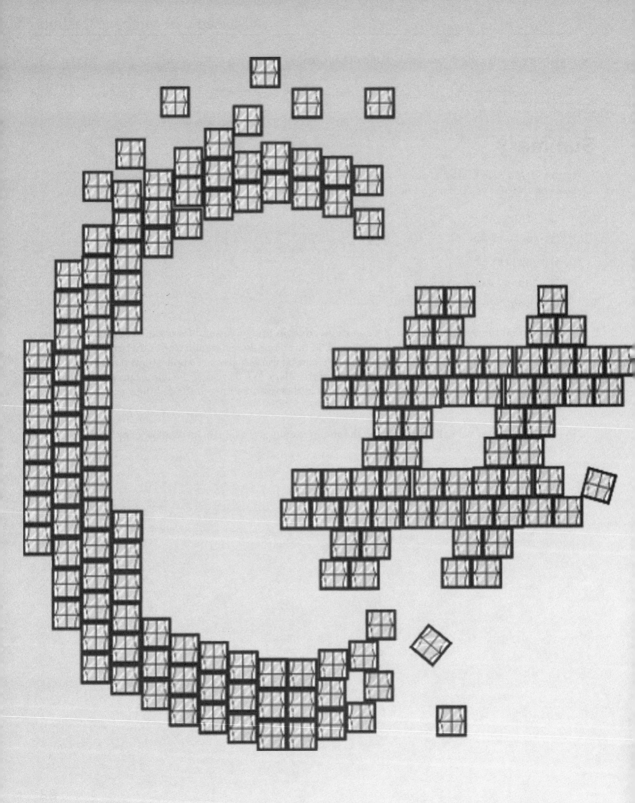

Menus and Toolbars

In the previous chapters we covered most of the controls that you will need to create a reasonably complex and robust Windows application. However, there are a couple of controls that you will be very familiar with that we have yet to discuss:

- ❏ Menu – a drop-down list of options

- ❏ Toolbar – a bar (usually anchored at the top or the side of the window) that contains buttons

Of these two, menus crop up so commonly in Windows applications that it easy to overlook them since we take them for granted. Toolbars are also pretty common, especially in applications of reasonable complexity, for instance Microsoft Word. Often toolbars and menus provide different ways to present the user with the same options (you will probably have noticed that many of the buttons on Microsoft Word's toolbars perform the same actions as menu items at the top of the window).

Visual Studio .NET allows us to add menus and toolbars to our Windows applications quickly and easily; we can just drag them onto a form from the toolbox and configure them like any other control.

In this chapter we are going to show you how to add menus and toolbars to a Windows form. We will show you how to:

- ❏ Create a main menu for the form, and discuss menu design standards

- ❏ Navigate around menus using the keyboard, and add keyboard shortcuts to menu items

- ❏ Create a context menu

- ❏ Create a toolbar and add buttons to it

- ❏ Add icons to toolbar buttons

- ❏ Wire up the menu and toolbar items to event handlers in code

Let's start by looking at menus.

Menu Controls and Classes

Everyone that has used a Windows application in the past will have used menus before, because they are used in almost every Windows application. One of the main reasons for this is that a drop-down menu provides a great way to present a selection of options to the user in a non-invasive manner – as soon as we select an item from the menu, or cancel the menu by clicking somewhere else, the drop-down menu list disappears.

As you will probably already know, there are two types of menus associated with most Windows applications:

- ❑ **Main menus** – these exist at the top of a window, and typically have top-level menu items that include File, Window, and Help.
- ❑ **Context menus** – these pop-up when we right-click the mouse somewhere in a window. The options available in the context menu usually vary according to the application and the application feature (the control for example) that we right-click on.

Working with menus in Visual Studio .NET is very easy. The built-in Form Designer provides support for design-time editing of menus (of both types) and menu options in much the same way that we can manipulate controls on forms – by using the mouse to drag the menu onto the form from the ToolBox, by using the Properties window to set properties on the menu options, and by adding event handlers.

As with any other control, any menus you see in the Form Designer correspond to objects of a class. Both types of menus are represented by classes derived from the abstract System.Windows.Forms.Menu class. Main menus are represented by the MainMenu class, while context menus correspond to the ContextMenu class. All menu classes contain a collection of MenuItem objects, which you won't be surprised to learn correspond to the options available in the menu.

Let's now take a closer look at how to create your own main and context menus on a Windows form.

Creating Main Menus

Adding a main menu to a form in Visual Studio .NET is a piece of cake; we just drag a MainMenu control from the ToolBox onto our form. If you do this on a blank form you will see the following:

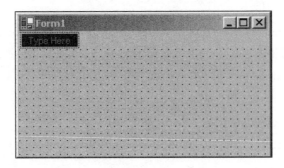

To add options to this blank menu we just type where it says **Type Here**. As you add options you will see that Visual Studio .NET provides you with the opportunity to add new menu options below the menu option you just added, and to the right of the last top-level menu option you entered. As with any other control, we can configure the name of the menu (among many other properties) using the Properties window.

Given that this is pretty straightforward, let's dive quickly into a Try It Out example where we create a simple main menu and add some options to it.

Try It Out – Creating Menus

In this Try It Out we will add a main menu to a blank form. The menu will have one top-level menu item, and when this is selected a submenu with three more menu items in it pops up.

1. Create a new **Visual C# | Windows Application** project. Call it **MenuAndToolbarDemo**. Change the Text property for the form to Menu and Toolbar Demo. Change the Size of the form to 400 by 200.

2. Drag a new MainMenu control from the ToolBox onto the form. The control will appear at the bottom of the Designer window (mainMenu1). Click in the left-hand **Type Here** box, and enter **MyMenu**:

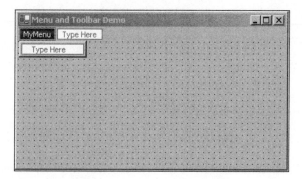

3. You'll notice that two new boxes appear to the right-of and underneath the menu option. Click the **Type Here** box *underneath* MyMenu, and enter **Option 1**. Press *Return*. Now, enter **Option 2** and **Option 3**:

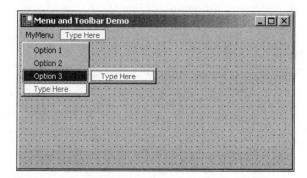

4. At this point, we have four menu items: a top-level menu item **MyMenu**, which appears in the menu bar, and three child menu items of **MyMenu**. If you select these options, you'll notice that the Properties window changes. One important property is the `Name` property. Change the name of **MyMenu** to `menuMyMenu`. Change the name of the **Option 1** to `menuMyMenuOption1`, **Option 2** to `menuMyMenuOption2` and **Option 3** to `menuMyMenuOption3`. Finally, make sure that the `Menu` form property (which governs which menu control is used for the main menu of the form) is set to `mainMenu1`.

5. Double-click on **Option 1** and add this code to the method below:

```
private void menuMyMenuOption1_Click(object sender, System.EventArgs e)
{
    MessageBox.Show("You selected Option 1!");
}
```

6. Build and run the application. If you select **MyMenu**, the three child options will appear. Select **Option 1** and you'll see the message box appear:

Selecting the other options will have no effect.

How It Works

This example is pretty straightforward until we double-click on **Option 1** and start adding code to the `menuMyMenuOption1_Click()` method. When we run the example, a message box pops up only if we select **Option 1**, so it's not difficult to see that the code that we added must be responsible for this.

So what's going on? When the user selects a menu item, a `Click` event is fired. We can respond to this event using a `Click` event handler method. When we double-clicked on the **Option 1** menu item, Visual Studio .NET automatically generated the empty `menuMyMenuOption1_Click()` event handler method for us. We added the following line of code to it:

```
MessageBox.Show("You selected Option 1!");
```

We've seen before that `MessageBox.Show()` simply pops up a message box that displays the contents of the string that we pass to the method. Of course we are free to add just about any code we wish to the handler, so we can respond to the `Click` event in just about any way we like.

You may have noticed that the naming scheme for the menu items that we've chosen here is quite verbose, but it does make it easy to understand what each menu item does. For example, just by looking at the name `menuMyMenuOption1`, we know that:

❑ The control is a `MenuItem` control, because it's prefixed with `menu`

❑ The control is a child of the **MyMenu** menu option

❑ The control refers to the menu item **Option 1**

Of course, we're forced to remove invalid characters like whitespace from the name. Although I personally don't tend to replace invalid characters with underscores, if I did the name would be `menuMyMenuOption_1`.

Navigating a Menu Using the Keyboard

As you have played with Windows before, you will have noticed that there are many keyboard combinations and shortcuts that allow you to perform all kinds of useful actions, like closing a window (*Alt+F4*), accessing the system menu (*Alt+Space*), and maximizing a window (*Alt+Space*, then *X*).

Menus can also be navigated using the keyboard, but in modern versions of Windows, Microsoft decided to turn off by default the "keyboard hints" that show you how to do this for some applications. For example, here's the menu for the Notepad text editor on Windows 2000:

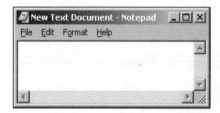

Technically, you can directly shortcut to the **File, Edit, Format,** and **Help** menu options using the *Alt* key plus a letter key. To get at the **File** menu, press *Alt+F*. To get at the **Help** menu, press *Alt+H*.

Although we can guess what most of the shortcuts to the top-level menu items are, we don't need to. If you press and release the *Alt* key, you'll notice the focus goes to the menu bar, plus underscores will appear under a single letter of each menu item. This is the keyboard shortcut key for the menu.

If you press the down arrow key or *F*, the **File** menu will pop up. If you access the menu using the mouse, the shortcut keys do not appear.

This gives you one quick way of accessing menu items through the keyboard. For example, if we want the File | Save option, we can press *Alt+F*, then *S*.

To obtain this effect in our own applications, you just have to modify the `Text` property of the menu item you want to add a shortcut for, by prefixing the shortcut character with the & symbol.

Try It Out – Adding Keyboard Shortcuts for Menu Navigation

Let's add some shortcuts that will allow us to navigate around our example menu using a keyboard.

1. Open the Designer for `Form1` of our Demo app, and select the MyMenu option.

2. Change the `Text` property to &MyMenu. Look at the MyMenu option in the Designer: the first letter is underlined and the & symbol is not displayed.

3. Change the Text property of the other three options to Option &1, Option &2 and Option &3.

4. Now run the application and access the menu using the mouse. The navigation shortcut keys will not appear.

5. Press *Alt*. The shortcuts appear. At this point, we can shortcut MyMenu | Option 1 with the keys *Alt+M* followed by *1*:

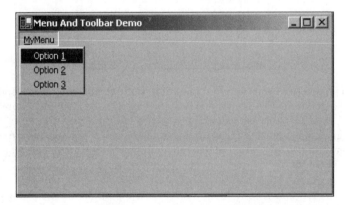

Adding Accelerator Shortcuts

Of course, since selecting one menu option often gives rise to another menu, and so on, navigating through several layers of menus using *Alt*-based shortcuts can become tiresome. One way around this is to assign **accelerator** shortcuts to menu items that are often used. For example, in the screenshot of Notepad we saw earlier, we can see that the *Ctrl+N* combination will activate the File | New option directly, without us having to navigate through the menu.

To add an accelerator shortcut, we simply set the `Shortcut` property of the menu item to the key combination we want.

Try It Out – Adding Accelerator Shortcuts

Let's add an accelerator shortcut to our example.

1. Open the Designer for Form1 and select **Option 1**.

2. Set the Shortcut property to CtrlL.

3. Run the project. The shortcut will appear next to the option no matter which way we access the menu. You will now be able to shortcut to the **MyMenu | Option 1** menu option by pressing Ctrl+L:

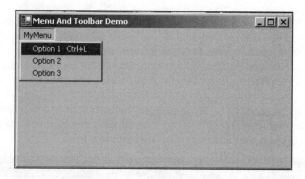

Shortcut Conventions

One thing before we go on. Some shortcuts should be avoided as they have some common meanings in applications. Here are some of them:

❏ *Ctrl+N* – create new document (or in IE, new window)

❏ *Ctrl+O* – open an existing document

❏ *Ctrl+S* – save current document

❏ *Ctrl+Z* – undo

❏ C*trl+X* – cut

❏ *Ctrl+C* – copy

❏ *Ctrl+V* – paste

❏ *F10* – shortcut menu (like a single press of *Alt*)

❏ *F2* – save current document

❏ *Alt+F4* – close window

To be consistent with other applications, you should avoid using those shortcut combinations for your own menu items, unless they perform the functionality usually associated with them.

Main Menu Conventions

You should have noticed that there are some conventions on how to present menu items to the user. Traditionally, the top-level menu items should include File, Edit, and View options from left to right. The top-level menu should also end with a Window option, followed by a Help option. Your own application-specific top-level menu items should go between these, assuming that they don't belong in the submenus of File, Edit, View, Window, or Help.

There are also some submenu conventions; for example, the last option on the File menu should be Exit. The last option on the Help menu should be About. The Edit menu should contain Undo, Cut, Copy, and Paste options, in that order. The File menu should contain New..., Open..., Save and Save As... options in that order. You'll probably have noticed that any menu item that displays a dialog box when selected should be suffixed with an ellipsis (...) too. So, because the File | Open option brings up the common Open File dialog box, the menu option should actually be presented as Open.... Finally, in many submenus you will see that related actions (such as File | New..., Open..., Close and File | Save, Save As..., Save as Web Page..., Versions... in Microsoft Word) are grouped together, with the groups separated by lines. We can create a line separator in a menu by entering a single dash as the Name of a menu item.

The best technique for this is not to try to remember the rules, but to try to follow the rules that Microsoft Office applications follow. However, you will probably find that these applications contain more options than you would implement in your own applications.

Try It Out – Creating the Main Menu for a Text Editor

In this Try It Out, we're going to make our Demo app a little more "real world". We'll pretend that we're creating a text editor application, so we'll add top-level, File, Edit, and Help menu options to the menu of our Demo app. To the File submenu, we'll add:

- ❑ New
- ❑ Open
- ❑ Save
- ❑ Save As
- ❑ Exit

To the Edit submenu we'll add:

- ❑ Undo
- ❑ Cut
- ❑ Copy
- ❑ Paste

To the Help menu we'll add an About... menu option. Although we're going to be adding a lot of menu options, we'll actually only implement the Edit menu options.

1. To the Designer for `Form1`, add a new top-level menu item with the text `&File`. Change its `Name` property to `menuFile`.

2. You'll notice that the **File** menu appears to the right of the **MyMenu** menu. As **File** should be the first level menu option, use the mouse to drag it to the appropriate position.

3. To the **File** menu, add **&New**, **&Open...**, **&Save**, and **Save &As...** options. Set their `Name` properties to `menuFileNew`, `menuFileOpen`, `menuFileSave`, and `menuFileSaveAs`.

4. To create a separator, enter a single dash ("`-`") as the name of the menu item. Then, create the **E&xit** menu item with a `Name` property of `menuFileExit`.

5. Next, create a new **E&dit** top level menu item (`menuEdit`), with the options **&Undo** (`menuEditUndo`), then a separator, then **Cu&t** (`menuEditCut`), **&Copy** (`menuEditCopy`) and **&Paste** (`menuEditPaste`). Set `Shortcut` properties against these four as `CtrlZ`, `CtrlX`, `CtrlC` and `CtrlV`. The shortcuts will not appear against the menu items at design time, but they will appear at run time.

6. For completeness, add a new **Help** menu (`menuHelp`) with an **&About...** option (`menuHelpAbout`).

The menu should look like this now:

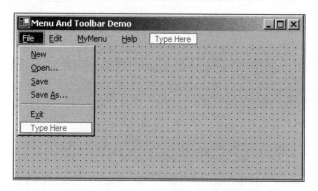

If you build run the application now, you'll be able to see the menus and navigate through them, but nothing will happen because we haven't wired in the code yet. So let's do that.

7. The first thing to do is add a new `TextBox` control to the form (this will contain the text that the user modifies in the editor). Do this, and set its `Name` property to `textEditor`. Clear the `Text` property, set the `MultiLine` property to `True`, and the `Dock` property to `Fill`. The control will fill the entire space of the form and will automatically stretch to fill the form if the form is resized.

8. Using the Designer, we can now add the functionality to both the menus and buttons. Double-click on the **Edit | Undo** menu option in the Designer and add the code:

```
private void menuEditUndo_Click(object sender, System.EventArgs e)
{
    Undo();
}
```

9. Then, add this method to `Form1`:

```
public void Undo()
{
    textEditor.Undo();
}
```

10. Now, do the same with Edit | Cut:

```
private void menuEditCut_Click(object sender, System.EventArgs e)
{
    Cut();
}
```

```
public void Cut()
{
    textEditor.Cut();
}
```

11. Edit | Copy:

```
private void menuEditCopy_Click(object sender, System.EventArgs e)
{
    Copy();
}
```

```
public void Copy()
{
    textEditor.Copy();
}
```

12. Edit | Paste:

```
private void menuEditPaste_Click(object sender, System.EventArgs e)
{
    Paste();
}
```

```
public void Paste()
{
    textEditor.Paste();
}
```

Build and run the application, and try typing some text into the TextBox. You should be able to perform the undo, cut, copy, and paste actions on the text, by selecting the appropriate menu item or by using a keyboard shortcut:

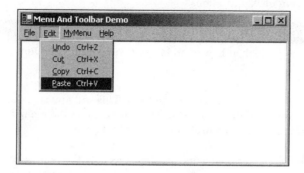

How It Works

We haven't really done anything in this Try It Out that we haven't done in several others. However, the thing to look at here is the coding methodology we used to wire up the menu items.

We usually recommend that the actual code that provides the functionality to the menu item should be broken out into a new method. That's precisely what we've done here, for example:

```
private void menuEditUndo_Click(object sender, System.EventArgs e)
{
    Undo();
}

public void Undo()
{
    textEditor.Undo();
}
```

This is great from a reusability perspective, because now we've exposed the functionality to perform an undo action through a method. Here we've made the method public so that anyone can call it. We might have made it protected instead so that only people extending the class can call it, or even private, meaning that only this class can access the method. We will see the advantage of moving the functionality into a new method outside the click handler when we add toolbars to our example later.

Also note that we cheated a little here because all of the functionality to undo, cut, copy, and paste is actually implemented in the TextBox control itself (although this technique is to be encouraged, because it is a great example of code encapsulation and reuse!)

Creating Context Menus

A context menu is a pop-up menu that is assigned to a control or group of controls on a form. It is usually activated by right-clicking the mouse. In most Windows applications, almost everything on the screen that you can position the mouse cursor over will respond to a right-click in some way.

If you look in the Visual Studio .NET ToolBox, you will see a `ContextMenu` control, which as we mentioned earlier is associated with the `ContextMenu` class derived from the base `System.Windows.Forms.Menu` class. This `ContextMenu` class gives us everything we need to build our own context menus in our applications.

Try It Out – Adding a Context Menu to the Text Editor

In this example, we'll take a look at how to add a context menu to our **Demo** form and associate it with the `TextBox` control.

1. Add a new `ContextMenu` control to the form. This will appear in the region at the bottom of the Designer. Note as well the **ContextMenu** edit area on the menu bar. Set the `Name` property of the new `ContextMenu` control to `contextEditor`.

2. The editor for a context menu works in almost exactly the same way as the `MainMenu` control editor. In this case, however, we don't get top-level menu items, as we don't get a menu bar with a context menu. If you click the **ContextMenu** edit area on the menu bar, you'll get the familiar **Type Here** box. Add two new options. The first, **Show Me**, should have a property `Name` of `contextEditorShowMe`. The second, **Clear**, should have a `Name` of `contextEditorClear`. If you need to get back to the editor for the `MainMenu` control, just select the `mainMenu1` control and the editor will re-appear.

3. To bind the `ContextMenu` control to the `TextBox` control, select the `TextBox` control and set the `ContextMenu` property to `contextEditor`.

4. Double-click the **Show Me** menu option. Add this code:

```
private void contextEditorShowMe_Click(object sender, System.EventArgs e)
{
    MessageBox.Show(textEditor.Text);
}
```

5. Then, do the same with **Clear**:

```
private void contextEditorClear_Click(object sender, System.EventArgs e)
{
    textEditor.Clear();
}
```

6. Now build and run the project. You'll be able to right-click on the `TextBox` control and see the context menu:

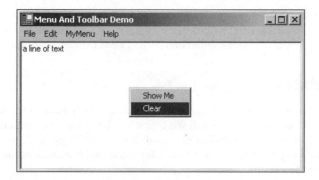

If you now select Show Me, a message box pops up containing any text you've entered into the TextBox. If you select Clear, the TextBox is cleared.

How It Works

Again, this example is pretty straightforward. We set the Name and Text properties of the context menu using the Properties window, and also used the Properties window to bind the context menu to the TextBox. Finally we added click event handlers for the menu items.

All of the controls in the Framework have a ContextMenu property. However, it doesn't make sense to put context menus on every control. For example, what's the point of putting a context menu on a Button control or a Label control? Although the Framework allows us to do this, most users won't be expecting to see this functionality, so it's usually best to avoid it.

Then we created event handlers for the menu items and added some code to them so that something would happen when the items are selected.

Toolbar Controls and Classes

Toolbars provide another way to present the Windows user with quick shortcuts to common operations. A toolbar contains buttons that usually have images on the top; the images graphically represent the action performed by the toolbar button. For instance, the default toolbar button that brings up the Open dialog in Microsoft Word has an image that shows a folder opening. It is also common to find that running the mouse over the top of a toolbar button causes a tooltip to pop up, which describes the action of the button in a few words.

Although toolbars are usually "docked" at the top, bottom, or sides of a window, many can be dragged away from their default positions, to float in a position that is more convenient to the user. In more complex applications, the user can often also configure which buttons are shown in the toolbar.

In a normal application, toolbars represent a subset of the functionality shortcuts through the menu. The principle behind creating a toolbar is to have the right balance of options present in the toolbar. Too few and the user will become frustrated at having to hunt around in the menus (you should assume that the average user will *not* try and learn the key combinations to navigate via keyboard shortcuts through the menus). Too many options and the user may become overwhelmed.

In .NET, a `ToolBar` control is the visual representation of the `System.Windows.Forms.ToolBar` class. Toolbar buttons are associated with the `System.Windows.Forms.ToolBarButton` class. The `ToolBar.Buttons` property gets the collection of `ToolBarButtons` assigned to the toolbar.

Creating Toolbars

We can add a `ToolBar` control to a Windows form by dragging the control from the ToolBox onto the form in the Designer. If you do this you will see that a blank toolbar (one with no buttons) is added to the top of the form. To add buttons, and to configure the toolbar in general, we use the Property Inspector, as we would expect from any control. Given that this is a fairly intuitive process, let's throw ourselves into another Try It Out.

Try It Out – Adding a Toolbar and Toolbar Buttons with ToolTips

What we're going to do in the next few Try It Outs is to build a basic toolbar that has seven buttons that mimic functionality provided in the **File** and **Edit** submenus:

- ❏   New (file)
- ❏   Open (file)
- ❏   Save
- ❏   Undo
- ❏   Cut
- ❏   Copy
- ❏   Paste

In this example, we'll just add the buttons and name them. In the next section we'll look at adding images to the top of the buttons and in the section after that we'll wire up the buttons so that they actually do something.

1.   Add a new `ToolBar` control to the form. This will automatically dock at the top of the form, underneath the menu. Set its `Name` property to `toolbarStandard`.

2.   You will notice that the `ToolBar` is covering the top of the `TextBox`. This is a slight problem, because when we actually come to use the editor, we won't be able to see the first few lines of what we write! The reason that the `ToolBar` overlaps the `TextBox` is that any control that you use to fill the form should be added last to the form. However, it's pretty easy to get around the problem with a quick cut and paste. Right-click on the `TextBox` control. Select **Cut**, and then right-click in the same area again and select **Paste**. This will add the control back, but it will not be created until *after* the `ToolBar` control. Therefore, the docking and automatic resizing functionality should work properly.

3.   Now we want to add some buttons to the `ToolBar`. Find the `Buttons` property of the `ToolBar`, and click the ellipsis button ("...") to open the Collection Editor.

4. Click the Add button to create a new button. Set its `Name` property to `toolbarStandardNew` and set its `ToolTipText` property to `New Document`. Add buttons for Open (`toolbarStandardOpen`) and Save (`toolbarStandardSave`) too.

5. Next we need a separator, so add a new button and change its `Style` property to `Separator`. Don't worry about the `Name` property – leave it as it as.

6. Next, add an Undo button (`toolbarStandardUndo`), then a separator, then a Cut (`toolbarStandardCut`), a Copy (`toolbarStandardCopy`), and finally a Paste button (`toolbarStandardPaste`).

7. If you build and run the project now, you'll be able to press the buttons, but they won't do anything. You'll also be able to see the ToolTips against the buttons by hovering the mouse over them.

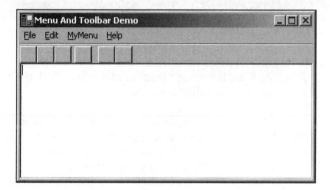

Adding Toolbar Button Images

Next we'll add the toolbar's images. To do this, we need to:

1. Find or draw the images

2. Add a new `ImageList` to the form and import the images into the `ImageList` control

3. Bind the `ImageList` control to the toolbar

4. Assign an image to each button

Where you get the button images from is completely up to you. Some buttons are commonly available – we'll show you where to get the ones we need – other buttons you'll need to design yourself. Some software developers try to get a very "groovy" feel out of their applications and so hire professional graphic designers to come up with images for them. Whatever you decide to do, it's just a matter of getting `.bmp` files (or `.gif` or `.png` files) together for the images.

When you add the images to the `ImageList` control, you will need to consider transparency. Imagine that we have an image for a toolbar button. That image will have a background color – in the ones you've found, this background color is probably light gray or "silver" in .NET parlance. If you put this image onto a button that is the same color (that is, gray background against a gray control), everything will look fine. However, if you put that image onto a button that is not the same color, for example a gray background against a blue button, things are going to look odd.

However, even if you do match colors there are problems. In Windows, the user has the ability to change the appearance of GUI objects on the screen, such as buttons. In addition (and nowadays this is particularly true of Windows XP), some operating systems may use a different color by default.

To get around these problems, we nominate a color on the image as the "transparent" color on the `ImageList`. When .NET draws the image, any pixels of the nominated color are skipped, allowing the color of the pixel below to show through. As we mentioned before, this color is most likely "silver".

Try It Out – Adding Images to Toolbar Buttons

Now that we understand how to add images to buttons in theory, let's see how easy it is in practice.

1. Using Windows Explorer, find the installation folder for Visual Studio .NET. In most cases, this will be C:\Program Files\Microsoft Visual Studio .NET. Click the Search button on the Explorer toolbar. Look for a file called `new.bmp`.

2. You'll get a number of hits back. To open the folder, right-click on the file and select Open Containing Folder. Avoid any folder that contains the word Large, as we want "normal" button size images (16x16 pixels). We also need an Undo button image, and you may find that some of the folders don't contain that. We're going to use the \Common7\Graphics\bitmaps\Tlbr_W95 subfolder for this demonstration. Copy the folder name into the clipboard.

3. Add a new `ImageList` control to the Designer for `Form1`. Set the `Name` property to `imagesToolbarStandard`. Set the `TransparentColor` property to `Silver`.

4. Open the Collection Editor for the `Images` property. Add images for New, Open, Save, Undo, Cut, Copy, and Paste. The images on the left appear a bit distorted, but the bitmaps are not affected, this is purely an artifact of this list display. Click OK to close the Collection Editor.

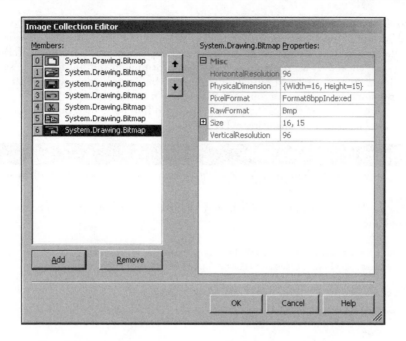

5. Select the toolbar and set its `ImageList` property to `imagesToolbarStandard`.

6. Open the `Buttons` Collection Editor and assign images to each of the buttons by using the `ImageIndex` property on each button. Click **OK** and you'll find that the images have been added:

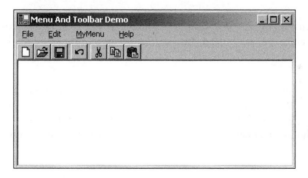

Now we can look at how to wire code up to the buttons.

Handling Toolbar Click Events

Luckily for us, the `TextBox` control already includes functionality to power the undo, cut, copy, and paste actions. All we have to do is write code that calls the provided methods when we click on the appropriate menu item or toolbar button.

We're not going to worry about the file handling through File menu options and associated toolbar buttons. We cover file handling in more detail in Chapter 8.

Before we start, we need to warn you about some odd behavior in the design of the `ToolBar` control! We're already aware of how most controls in the Framework raise their own events when the user manipulates them. In particular for this chapter, we've seen how `MenuItem` objects raise `Click` events whenever they are clicked. It would seem to make sense for toolbar buttons to do the same, but they do not. The `ToolBar` control itself will raise a `Click` event, but to determine which button was actually pressed requires some extra effort on our part; we have to make use of the `ToolBarButtonClickEventArgs.Button` property to find out which button was clicked by the user. Let's see how we might do this using a Try It Out.

Try It Out – Wiring-Up Toolbar Buttons

In this Try It Out we'll add a button click event handler for the buttons of the toolbar in our Demo app.

1. Using the Designer again, double-click on the toolbar control. Add this code to the resulting event handler:

```
private void toolbarStandard_ButtonClick(object sender,
    System.Windows.Forms.ToolBarButtonClickEventArgs e)
{
    if(e.Button == this.toolbarStandardUndo)
        Undo();
    if(e.Button == this.toolbarStandardCut)
        Cut();
    if(e.Button == this.toolbarStandardCopy)
        Copy();
    if(e.Button == this.toolbarStandardPaste)
        Paste();
}
```

2. Build and run the project now, and you'll find that you're able to manipulate the text in the textbox using the toolbar buttons (as well as the menu items and keyboard shortcuts).

How It Works

In this example we see the advantage of the approach we took in an earlier Try It Out, where we moved the code that performs the undo, cut, copy, and paste actions into separate methods (`Undo()`, `Cut()`, `Copy()` and `Paste()`), instead of placing it in the click event handlers for menu items. The advantage of this technique is that we can call these methods from the toolbar button click event handler too:

```
private void toolbarStandard_ButtonClick(object sender,
    System.Windows.Forms.ToolBarButtonClickEventArgs e)
{
    if(e.Button == toolbarStandardUndo)
        Undo();
    if(e.Button == toolbarStandardCut)
        Cut();
    if(e.Button == toolbarStandardCopy)
        Copy();
    if(e.Button == toolbarStandardPaste)
        Paste();
}
```

By being able to reuse a method in this way, we don't have to duplicate code, making it easier to maintain.

You will also note that we determine which toolbar button has been pressed by comparing the value of the `Button` property of `ToolBarButtonClickEventArgs` (this object contains state information for the control when it was pressed, and is made available to us by the `ToolBarButtonClickEvent` object) to the names of the toolbar buttons.

Showing and Hiding Toolbars

In many complex applications, there are several toolbars available to the user, and it is often possible for the user to show or hide toolbars according to their personal preference. This is usually achieved in the main menu through a **View** submenu that contains a list of the toolbars available. Selecting a toolbar in the submenu makes it visible if it is currently hidden, or hides it if it is currently visible. The toolbars that are visible are indicated by a check next to the name of the toolbar in the submenu.

In this final section of the chapter, we'll take a look at how we can incorporate this toolbar show/hide feature into our Windows applications. This is actually much easier than it may seem at first sight. Controlling the visibility of a `ToolBar` control is achieved by controlling the value of its `Visible` property (either `true` or `false`). To add/remove a check to/from a menu item, we set the value of the `MenuItem.Checked` property (again to either `true` or `false`).

Let's take a look at how we can use these properties to give our **Demo** application a toolbar show/hide option.

Try It Out – Showing and Hiding Toolbars

In order to be able to demonstrate the toolbar show/hide feature more fully, we'll start by adding another toolbar to our application. We won't wire up the buttons, though, since that is unnecessary extra work for this example. We'll then add a **View** top-level menu item to our main menu, which brings up a submenu that allows the user to select the toolbars they require.

For the actual buttons, we're going to add three buttons for **MyMenu | Option 1**, **MyMenu | Option 2** and **MyMenu | Option 3**. It doesn't really matter what images you use for these, since we are not worried about their functionality.

1. Add a new `ToolBar` control to the **Demo** form. Set its `Name` property to `toolbarOptions`.

2. As with a previous example, we have a problem that the new toolbar is obscuring the top of the `TextBox`. Right-click the `TextBox` and select **Cut**, then right-click in the same place and select **Paste**.

3. Add a new `ImageList` control to the form. Set its `Name` property to `imagesToolbarOptions`. Set its `TransparentColor` property to `Silver`.

4. Use the `Images` Collection Editor to add three new images. As we mentioned before, it doesn't really matter what these images are.

5. Select the `toolbarOptions` toolbar. Set its `ImageList` property to `imagesToolbarOptions`.

6. Use the `Buttons` Collection Editor to add three new buttons to the toolbar: `toolbarOptionsOption1`, `toolbarOptionsOption2`, and `toolbarOptionsOption3`. Assign images to each of the buttons using the `ImageIndex` property.

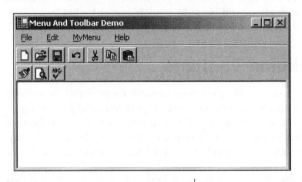

Now we have two toolbars. Next we're going to add a new top-level View menu, and under this create a Toolbars option. Against this option we're going to add a submenu containing items that let us toggle on and off either of the toolbars.

7. Create a new top level **&View** menu item. Set its `Name` property to `menuView`. To be in line with standard Windows application design, the View menu should appear immediately to the right of the Edit menu. Use the mouse to drag it to its proper position.

8. Create a new option under the **View** menu called **&Toolbars**. Set its `Name` property to `menuViewToolbars`.

9. To the *right* of this option, add a new option called **&Standard**. Set its `Name` property to `menuViewToolbarsStandard`. In addition, set its `Checked` property to `True`.

10. Underneath this new option, add a new option called **&Options**. Sets its `Name` property to `menuViewToolbarsOptions`. In addition, set its `Checked` property to `True`.

11. Double-click on the **Standard** option and add this code:

```
private void menuViewToolbarsStandard_Click(object sender, System.EventArgs e)
{
    ToggleStandardToolbar();
}
```

```
public void ToggleStandardToolbar()
{
    StandardToolbarVisibility = !(StandardToolbarVisibility);
}

public bool StandardToolbarVisibility
{
    get
    {
```

```
            // Is the toolbar visible?
            return toolbarStandard.Visible;
        }
        set
        {
            // Make the toolbar visible or invisible...
            toolbarStandard.Visible = value;

            // Check the menu option...
            menuViewToolbarsStandard.Checked = value;
        }
    }
```

12. Now we need to do the same with the Options toolbar. Add the following code:

```
    private void menuViewToolbarsOptions_Click(object sender, System.EventArgs e)
    {
        ToggleOptionsToolbar();
    }
```

```
    public void ToggleOptionsToolbar()
    {
        OptionsToolbarVisibility = !(OptionsToolbarVisibility);
    }
public bool OptionsToolbarVisibility
    {
        get
        {
            // Is the toolbar visible?
            return toolbarOptions.Visible;
        }
        set
        {
            // Make the toolbar visible or invisible...
            toolbarOptions.Visible = value;

            // Check the menu option...
            menuViewToolbarsOptions.Checked = value;
        }
    }
```

13. If you build and run the application now, you'll find that you're able to turn on and off the toolbars using the menu.

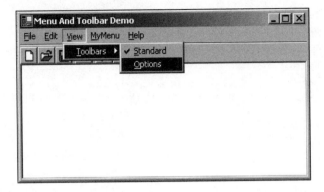

How It Works

The trick here is to use Windows forms' automatic resizing functionality to make the `TextBox` control fill the available space on the form when the `ToolBar` controls are hidden or shown, using the `Visible` property.

What we've done is we've abstracted the **Visible** properties of the `ToolBar` controls into their own properties (`StandardToolbarVisibility` and `OptionsToolbarVisibility`). We did this because not only do we want to affect the **Visible** property of the `ToolBar` control, but we also want to affect the `Checked` property of the associated menu item whenever the visibility of the toolbar is changed:

```
public bool StandardToolbarVisibility
{
    get
    {
        // is the toolbar visible?
        return toolbarStandard.Visible;
    }
    set
    {
        // make the toolbar visible or invisible...
        toolbarStandard.Visible = value;

        // check the menu option...
        menuViewToolbarsStandard.Checked = value;
    }
}
```

This is an important step in making sure that user interface widgets like the menus keep in step with what the user is trying to achieve.

The `ToggleStandardToolbar()` and `ToggleOptionsToolbar()` methods are important in this scenario. We use the `!` (not) operator to take whatever Boolean value is being returned by `StandardToolbarVisibility` or `OptionsToolbarVisibility` and flip it around so that `True` becomes `False` and `False` becomes `True`. By passing that flipped value back into whichever of the two properties it was retrieved from, it has the effect of acting like an on/off toggle switch.

```
public void ToggleStandardToolbar()
{
    StandardToolbarVisibility = !(StandardToolbarVisibility);
}
```

Summary

In this chapter, we took a detailed look at how to add menu and toolbar controls to our Windows applications – these are two essential UI controls that your users will expect to find in their applications.

We started off by looking at menus. We noted that there are two types of menu:

❑   Main Menus

❑   Context Menus

We can find a main menu at the top of most Windows applications, often with top-level menu items that include **File**, **Edit**, and **Help**. Context menus are also common, and are usually invoked by right-clicking the mouse. We saw that the functionality of menu controls is provided in .NET the `MainMenu`, `ContextMenu`, and `MenuItem` classes, and through examples we showed how to add these controls to a form, and connect them up to click event handlers. We also demonstrated how to configure keyboard shortcuts to navigate around a main menu, or activate a particular menu item directly.

After this, we moved on to look at toolbar controls. We noted that toolbars are represented by the `ToolBar` class in .NET, and we showed how to add buttons to a `ToolBar` using the `Button` property. We also discussed how to add images to the top of the buttons, and how to give the buttons ToolTips that flash up as the user runs their mouse over the button. We finished by demonstrating how we can add code to the form that will allow the user to show or hide toolbars.

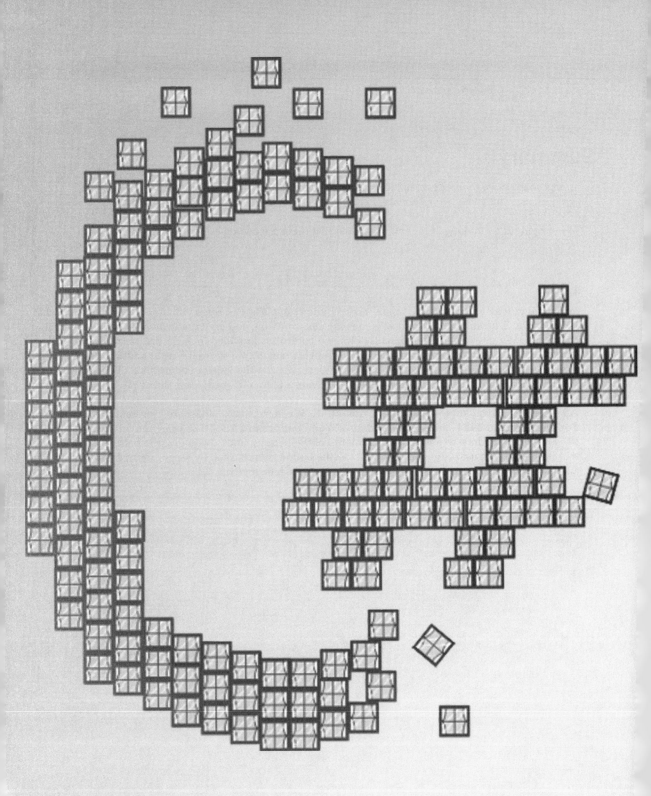

Using Graphics

Someone once said that "a picture is worth a thousand words". Chances are, sooner or later you will want to add some graphics to your Windows application. You may want to display pictures or draw graphs, change the visual appearance of existing Windows controls, or create new controls. You may even get involved in creating picture editors or CAD programs.

At the lowest level, graphics programming is supported through a set of Windows 32 APIs collectively known as the Graphical Device Interface, or GDI for short. GDI is quite complicated, quite primitive, and offers ample opportunity for locking up your machine if you are not careful. To remedy this situation, Microsoft has now introduced GDI+.

GDI+ is an excellent encapsulation of GDI. It offers a number of helper classes that let you do most common graphical tasks quickly. Combine this with the help you get from IntelliSense, and graphics development has never been easier. However, GDI+ is huge; it spans 6 namespaces and a total of some 300 classes and enumerations. Fortunately you don't have to know them all to get started or to write a meaningful application.

The purpose of this chapter is to give you an overview of using graphics and GDI+ in Windows applications. We will cover the following topics:

❑ Drawing – The classes and methods used to draw lines and shapes, including curves, ellipses, rectangles, and piecharts, and tools such as pens and brushes

❑ Specifying position, size and color – We need to specify where on the form we want shapes and lines to be drawn, what color(s) they should be, and how large they should be

❑ Drawing on demand – How Windows calls your drawing code, and what you must do to make it work optimally

❑ Drawing text and images – How to display text of various font styles and sizes, and how to manipulate and display images on forms

As we move through the chapter, we will gradually build up a user control that graphically plots share prices, so that you can see how we might use graphics in a real-world application. But let's start by briefly reviewing GDI and GDI+.

The Device Context

The **G**raphical **D**evice **I**nterface (GDI) is exactly what its name says: an interface to graphical devices, such as a screen or a printer. At the lowest level all graphics operations are routed through a GDI element called the **Device Context (DC)**.

The Device Context is responsible for implementing device independence. Through the use of device drivers the DC is able to translate high-level method calls into very low level instruction needed to draw a line on a particular device. Thanks to the DC, you can write your graphics program without having to worry about which device – screen or printer – will ultimately render your artistic expression.

The Device Context is also responsible for managing the relationship between the different visual entities on the Windows desktop, and keeping these isolated. If, for example, you get hold of a DC associated with a particular window, GDI makes sure that you will only be able to draw within that window. Further, all graphics operations are relative to the top left corner of the window. You can therefore write your graphics code without worrying if the user moves the window around on the desktop.

The Graphics Class

Although GDI is a relatively high-level API, it is still one that is based upon the old Windows API, with C-style functions. In the move to .NET, GDI+ was introduced, which is basically an object-based wrapper around GDI. In GDI+, the DC is encapsulated by a class called `Graphics`; it's much easier to use the `Graphics` class to create graphics than to work directly with a Device Context.

Using the Graphics Class

Almost everything in GDI+ is done by invoking methods on an instance of the `Graphics` class from the `System.Drawing` namespace. The general procedure is as follows:

1. **Obtain a Graphics object.**
There are several ways of doing this. In some situations you will ask another object to create a `Graphics` object for you, using the `CreateGraphics()` method. In other situations a `Graphics` object will be provided for you. Either way, the `Graphics` object will be associated with the graphical entity on which you want to paint. Therefore operations made on the `Graphics` object will ultimately be rendered on a target (like a bitmap, a window on the screen, or an area on a printout).

2. **Obtain a tool to use on the Graphics object**.
GDI+ provides a host of standard tools. An example of a tool could be a **pen**; the action of a pen object mimics the action of a real world pen. It has many properties, including color and width. Other tools include **brushes** and **fonts**. You can also create your own tools.

3. **Call methods on the Graphics object to draw your picture.**
The `Graphics` object has many methods that mimic what you would do if you stood in front of a canvas with a painting tool in your hand. One example of such a method is `Graphics.DrawLine()`, which (as the name suggests) draws a straight line between two points (using the pen we described in the previous step).

4. Dispose of the Graphics object and painting tools.

If your code allocated any `Graphics` object or painting tool, you should dispose of them as soon as they are not needed. Graphical objects require a lot of resources, and you should not rely on the .NET runtime to free them up eventually. Instead you should do it explicitly at the end of your drawing routine.

> GDI+ object disposal is very important. The DC is allocated from the underlying GDI sub-system, and it consumes lot of resources. However, the .NET runtime only monitors the resources directly used by GDI+ objects. It is not aware that a few GDI+ objects may hold up resources in GDI, and it will not expedite garbage collection even if GDI resources start to run low. This is almost equivalent to opening a database connection and locking a record on a database server. If you do not explicitly close the database connection, it would only be freed up when the .NET runtime eventually decided to collect it.

Methods of the Graphics Class

At first sight the number of methods available in the `Graphics` class is quite overwhelming. Luckily they can be broken down into six main categories.

❑ **Draw methods**

The `Graphics` class offers no less than 19 methods with a name starting with `Draw`. These include `DrawLine()`, `DrawArc()`, `DrawPie()`, `DrawImage()`, `DrawString()`, and so on. As the names imply, the draw methods allow you to draw different shapes onto the drawing surface. Most of these methods are intended to draw empty shapes. For example, if you call `DrawEllipse()`, you will draw the boundaries of the ellipse, but the ellipse will be not be filled.

❑ **Fill methods**

Likewise the `Graphics` class offers 8 methods starting with `Fill`. These include `FillEllipse()`, `FillPie()`, `FillPolygon()`, and so on. All fill methods are intended to draw filled shapes. For example, if you call `FillEllipse()` it will draw a filled ellipse.

❑ **Measure methods**

There are two measure methods: `MeasureString()` and `MeasureCharacterRanges()`. These two methods are used to find out how much space a given text string will take up on the graphics surface.

❑ **From methods**

Methods starting with `From` are responsible for creating a `Graphics` object from some other object. One example is `FromImage()`, which can generate a `Graphics` object from an `Image` (a class representing a bitmap).

❑ **Clip methods**

A number of methods are available to deal with something called the **clipping region** of our `Graphics` object. When you operate on the `Graphics` object, any operation which would be rendered outside the clipping region will not be visible. You can adjust the size and shape of the clipping region to geographically limit the output of any graphical operation.

❑ **Transform methods**

Graphical transformations are a powerful, but somewhat complicated subject. It is possible to specify a 3-dimensional transformation matrix to a `Graphics` object. Transformations are used to change the scale, orientation, and position of drawing operations. For example, by applying a transformation we could shift the position of the center of a circle in a window. A typical application of graphical transformations is a 3-D drawing program, where you can use the transformation to change the perceived viewpoint of the observer. Due to the complexity of the subject, we will not be dealing with transformations in this chapter.

We will be using many of the methods from the `Graphics` class throughout the chapter.

Specifying Position, Size, and Color

When working with the `Graphics` object we are constantly required to specify size and position of the objects we want drawn. We usually do this through the use of `Size`, `Rectangle`, `Point`, and `Color` structures in the `System.Drawing` namespace. In this section we are going to take a look at these structures.

Position and Size

Each of the `Size`, `Rectangle`, and `Point` structures come in an integer and a floating-point version. The floating-point version has an `F` at the end of the structure name. The floating-point versions are mostly used when dealing with graphics applications such as 2D or 3D image rendering, involving complex transformations. For our purposes we will stay with the integer versions, since integer-based computations are much faster than their floating-point counter-parts.

Here's a summary of these structures:

Classes	Description
`Point, PointF`	These structures are used to specify a position, and each has two member variables `X` and `Y` which specify the coordinates of the point (in pixels) from the upper left corner of the drawing surface.
`Size, SizeF`	These structures are used (you've guessed it) to specify the size of an object. They each have two member variables, `Height` and `Width` (in pixels).
`Rectangle, RectangleF`	You can think of each of these structures as a combination of their associated Point and Size structures. Each specifies a rectangle with the location of its upper left corner specified by a point object, and with a size specified by a size object.
	These Rectangle structures have four member variables, but since they are used in different contexts most of these variables have more than one name.

All of these structures have a number of conversion methods and overloaded operators that make them very easy to work with. You can, for example, add an object of type `Point` to an object of type `Size`, to get a new object of type `Point`.

```
Point P1=new Point(10,10);
Size S=new Size(10,10);
Point P2=P1+S; //P2 is now (20,20)
```

The Rectangle Structure

As mentioned, the `Rectangle` structure boasts quite a number of public properties, some of which are equivalent to each other.

Property	Description
int Left	x-coordinate of left-hand edge
int Right	x-coordinate of right-hand edge
int Top	y-coordinate of the top of the rectangle
int Bottom	y-coordinate of the bottom of the rectangle
int X	x-coordinate of left-hand edge. Same as `Left`.
int Y	y-coordinate of the top of the rectangle. Same as `Top`.
int Width	The width of the rectangle (in other words `Right-Left`).
int Height	The height of the rectangle (in other words `Bottom-Top`).
Point Location	The location of the rectangle. This is equivalent to (`Left`, `Top`) or (`X`, `Y`).
Size Size	Size of the rectangle, equivalent to (`Width`, `Height`).

Rectangle Methods

The `Rectangle` structure has a number of handy methods. These include:

Method	Description
Inflate()	This method can be used to inflate (or decrease) the width and height of a `Rectangle`. When the `Rectangle` changes size its location properties are changed so that the center of the `Rectangle` remains the same. The method takes three arguments: a `Rectangle` to inflate, and two integers (x,y) as the inflation parameters. For instance, for a 50 by 50 `Rectangle` object `rect`, `Inflate(rect,50,100)` will inflate `rect` by 50 pixels in the x-direction and minus x-direction, and by 100 pixels in the y-direction and minus y-direction, making `rect` 150 by 250 pixels.

Table continued on following page

Method	Description
Offset()	Adjusts the location of a Rectangle by a specified amount. The offset is defined by a Point or by two integer values (x,y).
Intersect()	Replaces this Rectangle with the Rectangle created by the intersection of this Rectangle and another Rectangle supplied as a parameter to this Intersect() method.
Union()	Replaces this Rectangle with a Rectangle created by the union of the Rectangle itself and a Rectangle supplied as a parameter to the Union() method.

ClientRectangle and the Client Area

If you obtain a Graphics object for a Windows form, you will be able to draw within the form's **client area**. The client area is the area inside a form that is not occupied by the any captions, menus, toolbars, sliders or status bars. A Form has a ClientRectangle property, which is a Rectangle that specifies the size of the client area.

You can think of the client area as an x-y coordinate system, where each (x,y) point represents a dot on the screen. In Windows these dots are called **pixels**. The pixel at the upper left corner of the client area will have the coordinates (0,0). Moving to the right increases the x-coordinate and moving down increases the y-coordinate. You should note that since coordinates are relative to the client area, you will not have to change your code if the user moves the whole window on the screen.

It is rare that you will actually change the colors of individual pixels directly. Most of the time you will use one of the methods available in the Graphics object to change the colors of a group of pixels at the same time, by drawing a line or shape, or filling the shape with color.

Colors

We use a variable of the Color structure (in the System.Drawing namespace) to specify the color of the pens, brushes, fonts and other tools that are painted onto a Graphics drawing surface.

Internal Color Representation

The Color structure is internally represented by four member variables:

❑ We can create any color by mixing together different amounts of the primary colors red, blue and green. Therefore Color contains member variables R, B, and G that specify the amount of red, blue, and green in the color respectively. In GDI+ each of these are represented by a byte with values ranging from 0 to 255. This gives us the ability to specify a maximum of 255 x 255 x 255, or 16,777,216 different colors.

❑ The other member variable of Color, A (also called Alpha), is used to specify the **transparency**. A is also a number between 0 and 255. A Color with A=0 is completely transparent, whereas a Color with A=255 is completely opaque. We can use transparency to create the effect of dimming an image or to partially overlay one image on another. However, most of the time we will work with colors that are completely opaque (A=255).

Creating Color Objects

Although the underlying color representation is RGB+A as described above, there are a number of different ways of specifying which color we want.

Native Representation

We can specify the color by directly setting the value of those four components using the `FromArgb()` method. Below are a couple of examples.

```
Color CRed = Color.FromArgb(255, 0, 0);
```

This would give an opaque intense red (R=255). Note that if A is undefined, it defaults to A=255 (opaque). The following line would give an opaque blue color that is only half as intense as the red above:

```
Color CBlue = Color.FromArgb(0, 0, 128);
```

Finally, the next line would give an intense pink (R=255, G=128, B=255), although it would be semi-transparent since we have defined A=128 (the first parameter in the list):

```
Color CSemiPink = Color.FromArgb(128, 255, 128, 255);
```

While the ability to precisely specify a particular color from its component values is powerful, it is also a little cumbersome. Luckily the `Color` structure comes with predefined colors, and there are also predefined colors available in the `SystemColors` class too.

Web Colors

The `Color` structure has 141 predefined colors ready to go. These include the simple colors, like `Red`, `Yellow`, `Blue`, and so on. You will also find color mixes like `Khaki`, `LemonChiffon`, `MediumSpringGreen`, and `Aquamarine`. But why exactly 141 colors? Well, 140 colors are taken from an HTML specification for web browsers. If you designed your web site using only one of these 140 colors, you were pretty sure that the pages would be rendered in the same way by all browsers. Today, Internet Explorer is by far the dominant browser, and most systems are capable of displaying millions of colors, so this is less of a concern. Nevertheless, Microsoft adopted the colors and the naming convention. The 141st color is the color `Transparent`. You can find a full list of the colors available from the `Color` structure in the MSDN library at http://msdn.microsoft.com/library.

System Colors

Another place to look for predefined colors is the `SystemColors` class in the `System.Drawing` namespace. These represent the colors used for different UI elements according to the color scheme selected by the user. A selection of these colors is shown below:

Color Name	Color Applies To...
ActiveBorder	Border of the active windows
ActiveCaption	Caption bar of active window

Table continued on following page

Color Name	Color Applies To...
ActiveCaptionText	Caption bar text of active window
Control	Background color of controls
Desktop	Color of the Windows desktop
WindowText	Color of window text

If you are creating user controls you should seriously consider using these colors to make your application's appearance consistent with other applications, and with Windows itself.

Drawing Lines and Shapes

Now that we know how to set the position, size, and color of a line or shape, let's start looking at the tools and methods we can use to draw the lines or shapes with. We'll start by looking more closely at the tool used to draw lines, the **pen**.

The Pen Class

The Pen class is used to draw lines. The simplest type of pen will draw a solid line with a specified width (the default is one pixel) and color. The code below specifies a green solid pen with a width of 3 pixels:

```
Pen GreenPen = new Pen(Color.Green, 3);
```

If you just want to use a pen with a width of one pixel in one of the 141 standard colors, you can grab it directly from the Pens (not Pen) class. Below is an example of using the Aquamarine pen:

```
Pen AquamarinePen = Pens.Aquamarine;
```

Properties of the Pen Class

The Pen class has a number of properties. A partial list is shown below:

Property	Description
StartCap, EndCap	Defines the style of cap used at the start and end of a line.
DashPattern, DashStyle, DashOffset, DashCap	Defines if and how a line should be dashed instead of solid.
Alignment	Defines where the lines of a shape should be drawn in relation to the outline of the shape (we can draw lines centered on the outline, or lines that are just inside the outline).
LineJoin, MiterLimit	This defines how two lines should be joined. You can, for example, specify if you want a corner to be sharp or rounded.

To use some of these properties (`DashStyle`, `DashCap`, and `LineJoin`) you will need to import the `System.Drawing.Drawing2D` namespace.

It should finally be mentioned that it is also possible to create a `Pen` from other tools, such as the brushes or images we will meet a little later.

Draw Methods

As we mentioned earlier, the `Graphics` class comes equipped with a host of different draw methods, which can be used to draw many different types of curves and shapes. Let's discuss a couple of these in a little more detail now.

Lines and Curves

These methods are quite straightforward. The simplest is `DrawLine()`, which draws a line between two points. You need to pass the method a `Pen` and two `Point` objects.

If you have an array of points, there are two methods you can use to connect up the points. Whereas `DrawLines()` will draw straight lines between the points, `DrawCurve()` will draw a nice smooth curve. This kind or curve is called a cardinal **spline**. When using `DrawCurve()`, you can even specify how tense you want the curve to be. A couple of examples are shown below.

This was generated by this code:

```
Point[] pointList = {new Point(10,250), new Point(60,200),
                     new Point(160,300),new Point(210,250)};
aGraphics.DrawLines(curvePen,pointList);
curvePen.Color=Color.Red;
aGraphics.DrawCurve(curvePen,pointList);
curvePen.Color=Color.Green;
aGraphics.DrawCurve(curvePen,pointList,1.5F);
```

Notice how a tension of 1.5 makes the curve pretty sluggish. The higher the number, the less tense. The default setting (used by the red curve) is `tension=0.5`.

Rectangles

Rectangles can be drawn using the `DrawRectangle()` method, which takes a `Pen` (or a standard pen from `Pens`) and a `Rectangle` as arguments, like this:

```
aGraphics.DrawRectangle(Pens.Black, paintRectangle);
```

Obviously here the `paintRectangle` is an instance of a `Rectangle` object.

Bezier Curves

Another type of smooth curve is a Bezier curve. If you have ever worked with a drawing program, I'm sure you have come across these creations.

A single Bezier curve element is defined by 4 points. Two of the points define the end points of the curve element. The two other points are control points that define how the line is drawn between the two end points. The control points function like magnets that pull the line towards themselves. The further away the control point, the stronger the pull.

The curve element shown above was generated using this code:

```
Point startPoint=new Point(10,350);
Point endPoint=new Point(210,400);
Point controlP1=new Point(50,200);
Point controlP2=new Point(150,500);
aGraphics.DrawBezier(curvePen,startPoint,controlP1,controlP2,endPoint);
```

Notice how `controlP1` pulls the curve upwards because it's located at y=200, which is above the `startPoint` (y=350) while `controlP2` pulls the curve downwards because its y value is 500, which is below the `endPoint` (y=400).

If you connect several Bezier curve elements using the `DrawBeziers()` method, the endpoint of one curve element is the start point for the next element. To draw a curve with *n* elements, you must therefore supply an array of exactly *3n+1* points, otherwise an exception will be thrown.

Ellipses and Arcs

An ellipse is a circular shape defined by its bounding rectangle. `DrawEllipse()` will draw an "empty" ellipse within the rectangle.

Whereas `DrawEllipse()` will draw a closed curve around the whole boundary of the ellipse, `DrawArc()` will only draw part of the ellipse. Which part should be drawn is defined by a `StartAngle` and a `SweepAngle`.

The graphics above is created by the following code:

```
aGraphics.DrawEllipse(Pens.Blue,new Rectangle(10,50,200,40));

//Create wide pen with Arrow
Pen arcPen = new Pen(Color.Black,5);
arcPen.EndCap=LineCap.ArrowAnchor;
//Create Arc
aGraphics.DrawArc(arcPen,new Rectangle(10,50,200,40),0,180);
arcPen.Dispose();
```

As you can see from the picture a `StartAngle` of 0 will cause the arc to start to the far right. The arc will then move clockwise, the number of degrees specified by the `SweepAngle` (in this case 180 degrees).

Piecharts

The method `DrawPie()` is also closely related to the ellipse. You specify an ellipse by supplying the enclosing rectangle. In addition you specify a `StartAngle` and a `SweepAngle`, to define where the pie starts, and how large of a section of the ellipse it spans.

Other Draw and Fill Methods

Although we have not discussed all of the drawing and filling methods available to us, the ones above should keep you going for quite a while. For further information please refer to the online help supplied with Visual Studio .NET, or examine the methods of the `Graphics` class at http://msdn.microsoft.com/library/.

We've covered quite a lot so far in this chapter, so it's about time we used what we've learned in a Try It Out.

Try It Out – Wrox PortFolio Monitor

Living in Silicon Valley, there really is only one thing that springs to mind: stocks. So over the next few pages we will build the skeleton for a miniature graph control that can show the performance of several stocks in a portfolio (an array of stocks). We will create a user control that plots the stock price when we feed it our stock data. Later in the chapter we will add some text and an image (a Wrox logo) to the graph.

Each stock will contain the following fields:

- **Ticker** – text with the ticker symbol (MSFT, INTL)
- **Color** – the color we want applied to the stock on the graph
- **Price** – an array of price values

To test out the control, we will create a portfolio containing Microsoft (MSFT) and Intel (INTL). For each stock we will register the stock price on January 1 in each of the years from 1996 to 2002.

Please remember that this data representation is overly simplified for the purpose of this example. In real life our test application would read the data from a file, take it from a web site, or obtain it through a web service (in the *File and Registry Operations* chapter we will see how to create an application that serializes and deserializes portfolio data to file).

1. Create a new C# Windows Application project, calling it StockChart. Give the default form a size of about 500 by 400 pixels, and change its Text property to StockChart.

2. Add a Button to the top left of the form, and change its Text property to Plot Stocks.

3. Double click on the Button to open the code editor for the form. Add the following namespace import to the top of the file:

```
using System.Drawing.Drawing2D;
```

4. Just after the start of the StockChart namespace, before the definition of the Form1 class, enter the following definition of our Stock class:

```
public class Stock
{
  public Color m_Color;
  public String m_Ticker;
  public float[] m_Price;
}
```

5. At the start of the definition of the Form1 class, make the following entries:

```
public class Form1 : System.Windows.Forms.Form
{
  private System.Windows.Forms.Button button1;
  /// <summary>
```

```
/// Required designer variable.
/// </summary>
private System.ComponentModel.Container components = null;

private float m_MaxY = 100F;
private float m_MinY = 0F;
private float m_MaxX = 1;
private float m_MinX = 10;
private float m_TickX = 1;
private float m_TickY = 10;

private ArrayList m_StockList;
private Rectangle m_PaintRectangle;

public float MaxY
{
  set {m_MaxY=value;}
}
public float MinY
{
  set {m_MinY=value;}
}
public float MaxX
{
  set {m_MaxX=value;}
}
public float MinX
{
  set {m_MinX=value;}
}

public void AddStock(Stock aStock)
{
  m_StockList.Add(aStock);
}
public float TickX
{
  set {m_TickX=value;}
}

public float TickY
{
  set {m_TickY=value;}
}

public Form1()
...
```

6. Insert code to construct m_StockList into the Form1 constructor:

```
public Form1()
{
    ...
    InitializeComponent();

    m_StockList = new ArrayList();
}
```

7. Add the following code, which adds stock data to the m_StockList array, to the start of the button handler:

```
private void button1_Click (object sender, System.EventArgs e)
{
    this.MaxX = 2000;
    this.MinX = 1996;
    this.MaxY = 140;
    this.MinY = 0;

    // Add Stocks for Microsoft and Intel
    StockChart.Stock aStock = new StockChart.Stock();
    aStock.m_Ticker = "MSFT";
    aStock.m_Color = Color.Red;
    aStock.m_Price = new float[5]{36.1F, 71.3F, 119.35F, 45.2F, 64.9F};

    this.AddStock(aStock);

    aStock = new StockChart.Stock();
    aStock.m_Ticker = "INTL";
    aStock.m_Color = Color.Blue;
    aStock.m_Price = new float[5]{10.3F, 23.34F, 22.2F, 8.78F, 20.19F};

    this.AddStock(aStock);
```

8. Add the following code, which creates the gridlines for the plot and plots the data, to the end of the button click handler:

```
    Graphics aGraphics = this.CreateGraphics();

    // calculate the location and size of the rectangle
    // within which we want to draw the graph...
    m_PaintRectangle = new Rectangle(this.ClientRectangle.Location,
                                     this.ClientRectangle.Size);
    Size s = new Size(12, 14);
    m_PaintRectangle.Inflate(-(6*s.Width), -(6*s.Height));
    aGraphics.DrawRectangle(Pens.Black, m_PaintRectangle);

    // create horizontal gridlines...
    float y;
    Pen aGridPen = new Pen(Color.Black);
```

```
    aGridPen.DashStyle = DashStyle.Dot;
    for (y=m_MinY+m_TickY;y<m_MaxY;y+=m_TickY)
    {
      aGraphics.DrawLine(aGridPen,
                         PixelPoint(new PointF(m_MinX,y)),
                         PixelPoint(new PointF(m_MaxX,y)));
    }
    aGridPen.Dispose();

    // create the y axis tick marks...
    for (y=m_MinY;y<=m_MaxY;y+=m_TickY)
    {
      PointF xaxisPoint = PixelPoint(new PointF(m_MinX, y));

      aGraphics.DrawLine(Pens.Black,
                         xaxisPoint,
                         new PointF(xaxisPoint.X-s.Width/2, xaxisPoint.Y));
    }

    // create the x-axis tick marks...
    float x;
    for (x=m_MinX;x<=m_MaxX;x+=m_TickX)
    {
      PointF yaxisPoint = PixelPoint(new PointF(x, m_MinY));

      aGraphics.DrawLine(Pens.Black,
                         yaxisPoint,
                         new PointF(yaxisPoint.X,
                         yaxisPoint.Y+s.Height/2));
    }

    // plot the stock data...
    foreach (Stock newStock in m_StockList)
    {
      Pen aPen = new Pen(newStock.m_Color, 2);
      float startX = m_MinX;

      PointF startPoint = new PointF(m_MinX, newStock.m_Price[0]);
      PointF endPoint = new PointF(m_MinX, newStock.m_Price[0]);

      foreach(float price in newStock.m_Price)
      {
        endPoint.Y = price;
        aGraphics.DrawLine(aPen,
                           PixelPoint(startPoint),
                           PixelPoint(endPoint));
        startPoint = endPoint;
        endPoint.X += 1;
      }
      aPen.Dispose();
    }
}   // end of button click handler
```

9. Finally, add the following utility method to the `Form1` class:

```
PointF PixelPoint(PointF valuePoint)
{
  PointF newPoint = new PointF();
  newPoint.X = m_PaintRectangle.X + (valuePoint.X - m_MinX) *
               m_PaintRectangle.Width / (m_MaxX - m_MinX);
  newPoint.Y = m_PaintRectangle.Bottom - (valuePoint.Y - m_MinY) *
               m_PaintRectangle.Height / (m_MaxY - m_MinY);
  return newPoint;
}
```

10. Build and run the project, and press the button. You should see the bare bones of the stock chart displayed: the gridlines and the colored lines representing stock prices. Obviously we don't know how to draw text on a form yet, so we can't label the plot or the axes yet – we'll leave that until a little later in the chapter.

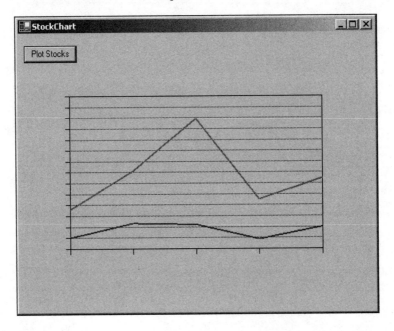

How It Works

Although this Try It Out looks quite involved, we will see that it is actually reasonably easy to follow what is happening.

We start off by importing the following namespace, which is needed to be able to manipulate the `DashStyle` pen property later:

```
using System.Drawing.Drawing2D;
```

Next, we add another class to the `StockChart` namespace, `Stock`. This is the class that will hold the ticker text, the stock prices and the color we will use to represent the stock on the graph:

```
public class Stock
{
  public Color m_Color;
  public String m_Ticker;
  public float[] m_Price;
}
```

Then we turn our attention to the `Form1` class. We start by creating member fields to hold the values for the maximum and minimum values of the graph axes, and the number of units between tick marks, and we also create some properties to get and set these fields:

```
private float m_MaxY = 100F;
private float m_MinY = 0F;
private float m_MaxX = 1;
private float m_MinX = 10;
private float m_TickX = 1;
private float m_TickY = 10;

public float MaxY
{
  set {m_MaxY=value;}
}
...

public float TickX
{
  set {m_TickX=value;}
}
...
```

We also declare an `ArrayList` member to hold the stock data values, and a `Rectangle` member that represents the size of the graph:

```
private ArrayList m_StockList;
private Rectangle m_PaintRectangle;
```

We can add stocks to this using the `AddStock()` method:

```
public void AddStock(Stock aStock)
{
  m_StockList.Add(aStock);
}
```

Inside the constructor we instantiate the `ArrayList`:

```
m_StockList = new ArrayList();
```

The real action happens inside the button click handler. We start by setting the maximum and minimum values of the graph axes:

```
this.MaxX = 2000;
this.MinX = 1996;
this.MaxY = 140;
this.MinY = 0;
```

Then we add values to some Stock objects and add these objects to m_StockList using AddStock():

```
StockChart.Stock aStock = new StockChart.Stock();
aStock.m_Ticker = "MSFT";
aStock.m_Color = Color.Red;
aStock.m_Price = new float[5]{36.1F, 71.3F, 119.35F, 45.2F, 64.9F};

this.AddStock(aStock);
```

Next we initially define the m_PaintRectangle to be the same size as the client area, but because we don't want the graph grid to take up the whole form, we use the Inflate() method to shrink this plot area a little. Notice how we have just guessed at the values to supply as parameters to the Inflate() method. We'll see a more efficient way of deriving these parameters later when we learn how to draw text.

```
m_PaintRectangle = new Rectangle(this.ClientRectangle.Location,
                                 this.ClientRectangle.Size);
Size s = new Size(12, 14);
m_PaintRectangle.Inflate(-(6*s.Width), -(6*s.Height));
```

Then we draw the outline of the graph, using DrawRectangle() and a black pen:

```
aGraphics.DrawRectangle(Pens.Black, m_PaintRectangle);
```

Our next step is to create the horizontal gridlines for the plot. We create a black pen that gives a dotted line (using DashStyle.Dot), and then use DrawLine() to draw the gridlines:

```
float y;
Pen aGridPen = new Pen(Color.Black);
aGridPen.DashStyle = DashStyle.Dot;
for (y=m_MinY+m_TickY;y<m_MaxY;y+=m_TickY)
{
  aGraphics.DrawLine(aGridPen,
                     PixelPoint(new PointF(m_MinX,y)),
                     PixelPoint(new PointF(m_MaxX,y)));
}
aGridPen.Dispose();
```

The `PixelPoint()` method is a method we create that is responsible for translating from (x,y) values on the graph to (x,y) values representing pixels. Also note how we dispose of the `Pen` after we have used it.

Next we draw the tick marks for the y-axis of the graph. For each tick mark, we find the pixel coordinates for the point where the tick mark joins the y-axis, and then draw a black line from this point, 6 pixels long (6 is the value of `s.Width/2`):

```
for (y=m_MinY;y<=m_MaxY;y+=m_TickY)
{
    PointF xaxisPoint = PixelPoint(new PointF(m_MinX, y));

    aGraphics.DrawLine(Pens.Black,
                       xaxisPoint,
                       new PointF(xaxisPoint.X-s.Width/2, xaxisPoint.Y));
}
```

We use the same principle for the x-axis tick marks too.

Finally we plot the stock data. For each `Stock` object, we create a `Pen` 2 pixels wide that has a color defined by the `Stock` object's `m_Color` member:

```
foreach (Stock newStock in m_StockList)
{
    Pen aPen = new Pen(newStock.m_Color, 2);
```

Then we move sequentially through the array of stock values in `m_Price`, drawing a line (using the `Pen` we just created) from one data point to the next:

```
    float startX = m_MinX;

    PointF startPoint = new PointF(m_MinX, newStock.m_Price[0]);
    PointF endPoint = new PointF(m_MinX, newStock.m_Price[0]);

    foreach(float price in newStock.m_Price)
    {
        endPoint.Y = price;
        aGraphics.DrawLine(aPen,
                           PixelPoint(startPoint),
                           PixelPoint(endPoint));
        startPoint = endPoint;
        endPoint.X += 1;
    }
    aPen.Dispose();
```

Note how we finish by disposing of the `Pen` as usual.

Drawing on Demand

While few will dispute the artistic qualities of our portfolio plotter, you will quickly find out that our claim to fame is only ephemeral. If you move another window in front of any part of our masterpiece, and then move it away again, you will see that the area of the drawing that was covered has been erased. Also, if you minimize and restore the form, the drawing will disappear completely. The graph is only repainted if we click Plot Stocks again.

This problem occurs because Windows doesn't usually store information about what is drawn in each window. Doing so would require much too much memory. Depending on the color resolution of the screen, the information to store the color for one pixel can require up to 3 bytes. So storing information for our little 600 by 500 form could require as much as 900KB. While this may not seem much for a modern laptop which may have up to 1 GB of RAM, remember that this is only one window, and you may have many windows open at the same time.

Storing the state of all windows would a very wasteful representation of what is actually visible on the screen. After all, we were able to completely define the drawing with about 50 lines of code! Windows therefore requires that every control (and therefore every form) must be able to redraw itself at any point in time. While the user is moving different forms around on the desktop, Windows keeps track of which areas are being obscured. When an obscured area is no longer hidden, Windows will ask the application that owns the form to redraw all or part of its contents (whatever the application decides it needs to redraw).

Raising and Responding to Paint Events

When a form or control needs to redraw itself, Windows will raise a Paint event. The form already has an event handler for Paint. It simply fills the whole client area with the specified background color. It then forwards Paint events to all of its child controls, so that they can also repaint themselves. This is why you will see that our drawing disappears, while the Plot button is not erased. This button already has code built in to repaint itself, including its borders and text.

It is very easy to modify our form so that it will get repainted. As part of the event processing the form's event handler will call its own virtual method OnPaint(). The signature for OnPaint() is shown below:

```
protected virtual void OnPaint(PaintEventArgs e);
```

The PaintEventArgs argument (e) has two properties.

Property	Description
ClipRectangle	The area (a Rectangle) that needs to be repainted
Graphics	The Graphics object used to paint

While OnPaint() is called with every repaint, you often don't have to repaint the whole area. You only want to repaint the part which was previously obscured, but which is now visible. By inspecting the value of ClipRectangle your code can make intelligent decisions on how much should be redrawn, and this can speed up the application tremendously.

When drawing in the OnPaint() method you can immediately use the Graphics object argument. Since the object has been passed into your method, you shouldn't dispose of it at the end of the method either.

Try It Out – Repainting the Portfolio Monitor on Demand

In this Try It Out we are going to do two things. First, we are going to move all of the functionality used to plot the Stock Graph into a user control, to give the application better separation of logic and make it more reusable. Second, we will move the painting code inside the OnPaint() method, so that the form gets repainted when it needs to be.

1. Open up the **StockGraph** project again. Create a User Control called **StockGraph**. To do this, right-click on the project in the Solution Explorer, and select **Add | Add User Control**. A dialog box will appear, with the user control selected. Set the name to StockGraph and press **Open**.

2. The form designer will now switch to show the user control. Use the Properties window to set the control's BackColor property to Window.

3. Open the control's code editor by pressing *F7*, and move the code that we added to the Form1 class in Steps 4 to 6 of the previous Try It Out into the corresponding positions in the StockGraph class. In other words: move the definition of the Stock class to between the StockChart namespace definition and the StockGraph class definition. Move the code added in Step 5 to the start of the Form1 class to the start of the StockGraph class instead, and move the line of code added in Step 6 from the Form1 constructor to the StockGraph constructor.

4. Add the namespace import statement below to the top of the file:

```
using System.Drawing.Drawing2D;
```

5. Create the GraphPaint() method in the StockGraph class. Move the code to plot the graph (which we added in Step 8 of the previous Try It Out) into this method, and modify the initialization of the Graphics object as shown:

```
protected void GraphPaint(PaintEventArgs e)
{
    Graphics aGraphics = e.Graphics;

    // calculate the location and size of the rectangle
    // within which we want to draw the graph...
    m_PaintRectangle = new Rectangle(this.ClientRectangle.Location,
                                     this.ClientRectangle.Size);

    // etc... (rest of plotting code goes here)
```

```
      aPen.Dispose();
   }
}
```

6. Add an override for the `OnPaint()` method to the `StockGraph` class, which calls the `GraphPaint()` method when the form needs repainting:

```
protected override void OnPaint(System.Windows.Forms.PaintEventArgs e)
{
  base.OnPaint(e);
  GraphPaint(e);
  return;
}
```

7. Move the `PixelPoint()` utility method to the `StockGraph` class.

8. Remove the button from the main form (`Form1.cs`), and the button click handler from the `Form1` class. Then build the project (you need to do this to get the project to build properly so that the user control is created).

9. Next switch to the design view for `Form1`. Change the size of the form to 625 by 450. Drag the newly created **StockGraph** user control onto the right hand side of the form. You should be able to find the user control in the ToolBox. Use the Properties window to set the size to 450 by 350.

10. Reintroduce the **Plot Stocks** button to the top left of the form, and double-click on it to recreate the button click handler. Change the code in the button click handler to the following (note the minor differences from the code we added in Step 7 of the previous Try It Out):

```
private void button1_Click (object sender, System.EventArgs e)
{
    stockGraph1.MaxX = 2000;
    stockGraph1.MinX = 1996;
    stockGraph1.MaxY = 140;
    stockGraph1.MinY = 0;

    // add Stocks for Microsoft and Intel
    StockChart.Stock aStock = new StockChart.Stock();
    aStock.m_Ticker = "MSFT";
    aStock.m_Color = Color.Red;
    aStock.m_Price = new float[5]{36.1F, 71.3F, 119.35F, 45.2F, 64.9F};

    stockGraph1.AddStock(aStock);

    aStock = new StockChart.Stock();
    aStock.m_Ticker = "INTL";
    aStock.m_Color = Color.Blue;
    aStock.m_Price = new float[5]{10.3F, 23.34F, 22.2F, 8.78F, 20.19F};
```

```
    stockGraph1.AddStock(aStock);

    // invalidate control to show data
    stockGraph1.Invalidate();
}
```

11. Build and run the application. Try moving other windows over the top of the form, and notice how the form is immediately redrawn.

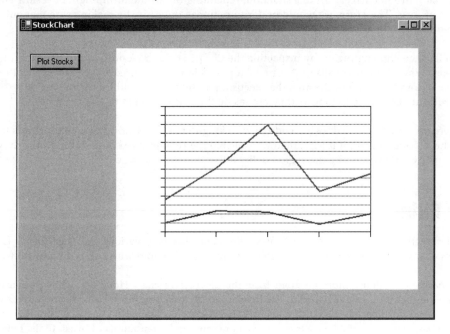

How It Works

There is not a lot to explain here. The code that we moved from `Form1` to the `StockGraph` user control is largely unchanged. We left the initialization of `Stock` objects in the button click handler of `Form1`, but moved the graph plotting code into the `StockGraph` user control to make it more reusable. We placed the plotting code into a method called `GraphPaint()`, and introduced an override of the `OnPaint()` method that called `GraphPaint()`:

```
protected override void OnPaint(System.Windows.Forms.PaintEventArgs e)
{
    base.OnPaint(e);
    GraphPaint(e);
    return;
}
```

By introducing the OnPaint() override, we are ensuring that the graph gets redrawn every time the form is partially or totally covered by another window.

Using the ClipRectangle During Repaint

You will probably have noticed that each time OnPaint() is called, the whole client area of the form is repainted, even when only a small portion of the form needs to be repainted. Now, although our drawing application doesn't do much painting, we can imagine a situation with an application that uses graphics far more intensively. In this situation, repainting the whole form might be a slow and resource-intensive process. Therefore, we would prefer to optimize the code, by making sure that only the portion of the form that has been covered (the clipping region) is repainted, not all of it.

We can find the clipping region by inspecting the ClipRectangle property of the PaintEventArgs parameter. When Windows calls OnPaint() it passes in a Graphics object and a ClipRectangle set to the size and location of the area that needs repainting. Draw and fill operations on a Graphics object will only be visible as long as they are inside the clipping region.

Therefore, we can optimize drawing code by checking to see if any drawing actually needs to be done inside the clipping region; if it isn't, then we can skip the repaint. We could optimize the drawing code still further by only repainting the region defined by ClipRectangle.

Color Fills

In the last section we considered how to draw lines and shapes of various colors on forms. However, for graphics of any real complexity, we are going to want to fill shapes with color. So how do we do this?

To fill shapes, we will use more methods from the Graphics class. However, while pens are used to draw lines and curves, we will need to use **brushes** to fill areas enclosed by lines and curves with color (and to draw text). There is a Brush class (in the System.Drawing namespace), but it is actually an abstract class, serving as the base class for five concrete implementations of brush tools. Let's take a closer look at these now.

Brush Tools

In this section we will give a brief introduction to each of the classes derived from Brush. We will then extend our framework with some examples of how to use them. The SolidBrush and TextureBrush classes are from the System.Drawing namespace; the others are from System.Drawing.Drawing2D.

SolidBrush

A SolidBrush is very simple; it represents a brush of a single color. It only takes one parameter: the color of the brush. However, if you just want a solid brush in one of the standard colors, you will probably want to take advantage of the Brushes (not Brush) class which has 141 brushes available in the standard colors. For example:

```
Brush aBrush = Brushes.Blue;
```

HatchBrush

A HatchBrush is used to fill the area with some small repeating pattern (a hatch). When creating an instance of a HatchBrush you can specify the type of pattern used for the hatch, as well as a foreground and background color. For example:

```
HatchBrush aHatchBrush =
    new HatchBrush(HatchStyle.DashedVertical, Color.Blue, Color.White);
```

There are over 50 different hatch styles defined in the HatchStyle enumeration, so feel free to experiment! We will be using some of them in our next Try It Out example, although a full list of all hatch styles is available in the MSDN library at http://msdn.microsoft.com/library.

TextureBrush

A TextureBrush is a brush where the fill pattern is not specified by a simple predefined hatch style and a couple of colors; instead the fill pattern is based on an image (a bitmap). For example:

```
TextureBrush aTextureBrush =
    new TextureBrush(aImage, WrapMode.Tile, aRectangle);
```

Here aImage is the image we want to use as the pattern. We will look at images a little later in this section. The aRectangle parameter can be used to specify which area of the image we want to use, if we are only interested in a part of it. Finally the WrapMode specifies how the brush should repeat the image, if the image is smaller than the area to be drawn. Options include Tile (default), TileFlipX, TileFlipY, TileFlipXY or Clamp.

LinearGradientBrush

A LinearGradientBrush is made up of two solid colors that blend along a line defined by two end-points. The default behavior is for the colors to blend linearly, but it is actually possible to customize the blending pattern by setting the brush's Blend property.

The simplest way to construct a LinearGradientBrush is to specify two end points and the two colors:

```
LinearGradientBrush aLGBrush = new LinearGradientBrush(new Point(0, 0),
                                                       new Point(200, 0),
                                                       Color.Blue,
                                                       Color.Orange);
```

This specifies a brush that blends from blue to orange along the horizontal axis. It is completely blue to the far left of the screen (x=0) and completely orange 200 pixels to right from the edge of the screen (x=200). In case you use the brush outside the area specified when the brush was created – the line from (0,0) to (200,0) – the gradient will be repeated according to the brush's WrapMode, which by default is Tile.

When you specify the two end points, it is important to remember that they are relative to the client area of the form, *not* to the shape that is being drawn. Say for example that you use the brush above to fill a 200 pixel wide rectangle, left side at x=100. The color of that rectangle will blend from blue/orange (at x=100) to pure orange (at x=200). From x=200 to x=300 we get a blend of pure blue to blue/orange in the rectangle, because the WrapMode is Tile, causing the brush to "repeat itself".

Take a look at the following image:

The output above was produced by the following two lines:

```
aGraphics.FillRectangle(aLGBrush, new Rectangle(10, 300, 200, 30));
aGraphics.FillRectangle(aLGBrush, new Rectangle(110, 335, 200, 30));
```

PathGradientBrush

The "mother of all gradient brushes" is the PathGradientBrush. This brush allows you to specify an enclosed complex area within which one color (the center color) will blend with one or more other colors (the surround colors).

We specify the enclosed area to fill using by passing a GraphicsPath object to the PathGradientBrush constructor. A GraphicsPath object stores a sequence of lines, curves, and/or shapes. We add a line, curve, or shapes to the object using an "add" method; for instance we can add an ellipse to the GraphicsPath using AddEllipse().

We will not discuss the PathGradientBrush further here, but just include an example in the next Try It Out.

Fill Methods

Once we have obtained a brush, we then use a fill method to fill a shape with color. The most common fill methods include:

- ❑ FillRectangle()
- ❑ FillEllipse()
- ❑ FillPie()

Each of these methods takes a brush as an argument, as well as a `Rectangle` that encloses the shape to be filled. The `FillPie()` method is slightly different, in that it can take several brushes (one for each slice of the pie), and it needs you to specify the starting angle and the sweep angle for each slice too, as this example illustrates:

```
int[] valueList = {35,45,20,15};
int valueTotal = 115;
Brush[] brushList= {Brushes.LightGreen,
                    Brushes.LightBlue,
                    Brushes.RosyBrown,
                    Brushes.Teal};
int I;
float Angle = 0F;
for (I=0;I<valueList.Length;I++)
{
   float sweepAngle = (360F*valueList[I])/valueTotal;
   aGraphics.FillPie(brushList[I],250,60,150,150,Angle,sweepAngle);
   aGraphics.DrawPie(Pens.Black,250,60,150,150,Angle,sweepAngle);
   Angle += sweepAngle;
}
```

Let's now dive into a Try It Out that uses many of these brushes and fill methods.

Try It Out – Using Shapes and Color Fills

In this example, we are going to draw a picture: specifically we are going to draw a tennis ball about to land on a grass court. To do this, we will use many of the brushes that we covered above, as well as some draw and fill methods.

1. Create a new C# Windows Application project called **SketchViewer**. Give the default form a size of about 600 by 400 pixels, and change its `Text` property to `SketchViewer`. Double-click on the form to open the code editor.

2. Add the namespace import statement below to the top of the file:

```
using System.Drawing.Drawing2D;
```

3. Add the following method that actually performs the painting:

```
private void PaintTennisCourt(PaintEventArgs e)
{
   Graphics aGraphics = e.Graphics;

   // fill the clientrectangle with "grass"
   Rectangle rect = new Rectangle(this.ClientRectangle.Location,
                                  this.ClientRectangle.Size);
   rect.Inflate(-1, -1);
   HatchBrush grassBrush = new HatchBrush(HatchStyle.LargeConfetti,
                                          Color.Yellow, Color.LawnGreen);
   aGraphics.FillRectangle(grassBrush, rect);
```

```
      grassBrush.Dispose();

      // add a chalk line
      Pen chalkPen = new Pen(Color.White, 50);
      aGraphics.DrawLine(chalkPen,
        new PointF(ClientRectangle.Left+150, ClientRectangle.Bottom+20),
        new PointF(ClientRectangle.Right-180, ClientRectangle.Top-20));
      chalkPen.Dispose();

      // add the ball's shadow on the grass
      Rectangle shadowRect = new Rectangle(400, 200, 70, 50);
      HatchBrush shadowBrush = new HatchBrush(HatchStyle.LargeConfetti,
                                              Color.LightGray,
                                              Color.LawnGreen);
      aGraphics.FillEllipse(shadowBrush, shadowRect);
      shadowBrush.Dispose();

      // add the tennis ball
      Rectangle ballRect = new Rectangle(300, 50, 150, 150);
      GraphicsPath aGraphicsPath = new GraphicsPath();
      aGraphicsPath.AddEllipse(ballRect);

      PathGradientBrush ballBrush = new PathGradientBrush(aGraphicsPath);
      ballBrush.CenterPoint = new Point(ballRect.Left + ballRect.Width/3,
                                        ballRect.Top + ballRect.Height/4);
      ballBrush.CenterColor = Color.White;
      ballBrush.SurroundColors = new Color[]{Color.Yellow};

      aGraphics.FillRectangle(ballBrush, ballRect);
      ballBrush.Dispose();

      // draw the seam in the tennis ball
      Pen curvePen = new Pen(Color.GhostWhite,6);
      Point startPoint = new Point(300,125);
      Point controlP1 = new Point(370,205);
      Point controlP2 = new Point(410,45);
      Point endPoint = new Point(450,125);
      aGraphics.DrawBezier(curvePen,startPoint,controlP1, controlP2,endPoint);

      // draw the outline for the ball
      aGraphics.DrawEllipse(Pens.LightGray, ballRect);
    }
```

4. Add the override for the OnPaint() method:

```
protected override void OnPaint(PaintEventArgs e)
{
  base.OnPaint(e);
  PaintTennisCourt(e);
}
```

5. Build and run the application. You should see the following (except in color!):

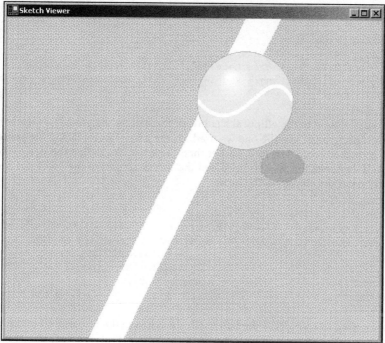

How It Works

As you should be able to spot, all of the actual painting in this example is performed inside the `PaintTennisCourt()` method. Let's take a closer look at this method.

After we have retrieved the `Graphics` object from the `PaintEventArgs` object passed to the `PaintTennisCourt()` method, our first step is to paint the background of the form: in other words, to paint the "grass" of the tennis court.

To do this, we create a `Rectangle` object that represents the client area inset by one pixel. Then we instantiate a `HatchBrush`. This `HatchBrush` has a `HatchStyle` of `LargeConfetti`; when we use this style with the colors yellow and lawn green, it looks a little like short grass:

```
Rectangle rect = new Rectangle(this.ClientRectangle.Location,
                               this.ClientRectangle.Size);
rect.Inflate(-1, -1);
HatchBrush grassBrush = new HatchBrush(HatchStyle.LargeConfetti,
                                       Color.Yellow, Color.LawnGreen);
aGraphics.FillRectangle(grassBrush, rect);
grassBrush.Dispose();
```

As you can see, we then fill the `Rectangle` using the `HatchBrush`, and then dispose of the brush.

Next we add a chalk line in the grass. We simply use a white `Pen` to do this, setting its width to 50 pixels:

```
Pen chalkPen = new Pen(Color.White, 50);
aGraphics.DrawLine(chalkPen,
    new PointF(ClientRectangle.Left+150, ClientRectangle.Bottom+20),
    new PointF(ClientRectangle.Right-180, ClientRectangle.Top-20));
chalkPen.Dispose();
```

Then we turn our attention to the elliptical shadow of the ball on the grass. To create this, we instantiate another `HatchBrush`, much like the one we used for the grass, but replacing the yellow component with light gray to make the shadow look darker than the grass. We define the size of the ellipse using a `Rectangle`, and then feed this `Rectangle` and the `HatchBrush` to the `FillEllipse()` method in order to actually paint the ellipse on the form:

```
// add the ball's shadow on the grass
Rectangle shadowRect = new Rectangle(400, 200, 70, 50);
HatchBrush shadowBrush = new HatchBrush(HatchStyle.LargeConfetti,
                                        Color.LightGray,
                                        Color.LawnGreen);
aGraphics.FillEllipse(shadowBrush, shadowRect);
shadowBrush.Dispose();
```

The last thing we need to consider is the ball itself, since it is in the foreground of the picture. We will give the ball a spherical look by using a `PathGradientBrush` fill. We begin by creating a `GraphicsPath` object, and adding an ellipse to it using the `AddEllipse()` method. The size and position of the ellipse is defined in a `Rectangle` object; note that it is 150 by 150 pixels in size, giving us a circle:

```
Rectangle ballRect = new Rectangle(300, 50, 150, 150);
GraphicsPath aGraphicsPath = new GraphicsPath();
aGraphicsPath.AddEllipse(ballRect);
```

Then we feed the `GraphicsPath` object to the `PathGradientBrush` constructor in order to create the brush:

```
PathGradientBrush ballBrush = new PathGradientBrush(aGraphicsPath);
```

Next we define the center point for the gradient fill, the color at this center point, and the color that should gradually become more intense as we move away from the center point:

```
ballBrush.CenterPoint = new Point(ballRect.Left + ballRect.Width/3,
                                  ballRect.Top + ballRect.Height/4);
ballBrush.CenterColor = Color.White;
ballBrush.SurroundColors = new Color[]{Color.Yellow};
```

To actually paint the ball we call the `FillRectangle()` method on the `Graphics` object, passing it the `PathGradientBrush`, and the `Rectangle` that defines the size and position of the ball:

```
aGraphics.FillRectangle(ballBrush, ballRect);
ballBrush.Dispose();
```

Our next step is to add a seam to the tennis ball in order to give it a more realistic look. We can give the seam the right kind of curve by using a Bezier curve. Therefore we define four points that define the shape of the curve, and then pass these to the `DrawBezier()` method which actually draws the curve. We also pass the method a `Pen` that we have defined to be 6 pixels wide and "ghost white" in color:

```
Pen curvePen = new Pen(Color.GhostWhite,6);
Point startPoint = new Point(300,125);
Point controlP1 = new Point(370,205);
Point controlP2 = new Point(410,45);
Point endPoint = new Point(450,125);
aGraphics.DrawBezier(curvePen,startPoint,controlP1, controlP2,endPoint);
```

Finally we make the ball stand out from the grass a little more by giving the ball a thin light gray outline:

```
aGraphics.DrawEllipse(Pens.LightGray, ballRect);
```

Using Text

Lines and shapes are great, but we often need to add text to our graphical creations too. The tool for drawing text is a `Font` object, from the `System.Drawing` namespace.

Fonts

If you are using a modern text editor, you are probably already familiar with some of the important characteristics of a font:

❑ **Font Names and Font Families**
If you look in the Font drop-down listbox on the Word toolbar, you will probably see the names of around 50 fonts, each with a unique character set. The fonts are generally grouped in families that have a similar "look". Examples of these families include "Times and Times New Roman", "Arial, **Arial Black**, and Arial Narrow" and "Lucinda Console and Lucinda Sans".

❑ **Font Size**
The size of a font is normally given in **points** (as opposed to pixels). A point is approximately 1/72nd of an inch.

❑ **Font Style**
These include whether a font is written in **bold**, *italics* or underlined.

Properties of the Font Class

The characteristics of a font described above are captured in the properties of the `Font` class. Below is a table with a selection of these properties:

Property	Description
FontFamily	Gets the font family name
Name	Gets the name of the font
SizeInPoints	Gets the size of the font, in points
Style	Gets a `FontStyle` enumeration value that contains font style information

The `FontStyle` enumeration can take the following values:

❑   Bold

❑   Italic

❑   Regular

❑   Strikeout

❑   Underline

This enumeration also has an attribute that allows bitwise combination of these values, so that we can have combinations of font styles.

> **All of the properties of the `Font` object are read-only. You cannot just change a `Font` from, say, regular to italic or bold by setting a property or calling a method on the Font. Instead you have to create a new `Font` (and destroy the old one if you are done with it).**

Creating a Font Object

There is no readily available collection of `Font` objects. You can either use the default font of the control or form, or you will have to create a `Font` yourself. The `Font` class has no less than 13 different constructors. Let's look at some examples of simple `Font` creation.

```
Font aFont = new Font("Times New Roman", 12);
```

Here we pass in the name of the font and the desired size in points. If you specify a font name that does not exist on the machine, the constructor will just return the default font, which is Microsoft Sans Serif. The following constructor will create the font `anItalicsFont` using `aFont` as a prototype, but with the `Italic` style:

```
Font anItalicsFont = new Font(aFont, FontStyle.Italic);
```

Finally, the constructor below specifies a font (aVerticalFont) that is Comic Sans MS, and has a height of one inch:

```
Font aVerticalFont = new Font("Comic Sans MS", 1, GraphicsUnit.Inch);
```

The GraphicsUnit enumeration specifies the unit of measure for the font; values include Point (the default), Inch, Millimeter, and Pixel, among others.

Drawing Text

Displaying text on a form is pretty easy. You call the Graphics.DrawString() method, passing the text string to display, a Font object, a brush, and a starting position as arguments. The following line displays text starting from (x,y) = (100, 100):

```
aGraphics.DrawString("Line of text", aFont, aBrush, new Point(100,100));
```

It becomes a bit more tricky when we want to write another text string next to the first one, or at an appropriate location on the following line. To do this properly you need to use a couple of methods. First, we can use the Font.GetHeight() method to return the height of a font, including the space needed to separate two lines. Second, we can use Graphics.MeasureString(), which will return the length and height of the text (in pixels), if we pass it the text string and the font.

You can also pass a Rectangle to DrawString(), in which case the DrawString() method will wrap and or clip the text so it fits inside the Rectangle.

Finally you can supply a StringFormat to DrawString(). The StringFormat object affects how the text is displayed. You create a StringFormat object by passing a StringFormatFlags enumeration value to the constructor, including:

- ❑ DirectionRightToLeft – Display text from right to left
- ❑ DirectionVertical – Display text vertically
- ❑ NoClip – Don't clip text if it does not fit within a supplied rectangle
- ❑ NoWrap – Don't wrap text if it does not fit within a supplied rectangle

The value passed can also be a bitwise combination of several of these attributes, along with an optional language specifier. You can also use the StringFormat.Alignment property to specify whether the text should be aligned Far, Near, or Center.

Now that we are equipped with these text-handling methods we are ready to experiment.

Try It Out – Adding Labels to the Portfolio Monitor

1. Open up the **StockChart** project. Open the code editor for the `StockGraph` class, and add the following method that adds labels to the graph:

```
void AddLabels(Graphics aGraphics)
{
  // add vertical axis label
  Font aVerticalFont=new Font("Arial Narrow",14,FontStyle.Bold);
  StringFormat aStringFormat =
    new StringFormat(StringFormatFlags.DirectionVertical);
  aGraphics.DrawString("Share Price (US$)", aVerticalFont,Brushes.Black,
    new Point((m_PaintRectangle.Left-60), (m_PaintRectangle.Top+40)),
    aStringFormat);
  aVerticalFont.Dispose();

  // add horizontal axis label
  Font aHorizFont=new Font("Arial Narrow", 14, FontStyle.Bold);
  aGraphics.DrawString("Year", aHorizFont, Brushes.Black,
                    new Point((m_PaintRectangle.Left+130),
                    (m_PaintRectangle.Bottom+30)));
  aHorizFont.Dispose();

  // add title of plot
  Font aTitleFont=new Font("Impact",28);
  aGraphics.DrawString("Portfolio Monitor", aTitleFont, Brushes.Crimson,
    new Point((m_PaintRectangle.Left+30),(m_PaintRectangle.Top-60)));
  aTitleFont.Dispose();
}
```

2. We want to call this method from `GraphPaint()`, but we also want to label the stock data, and add numbers to the axes. To do this, add/modify the highlighted code below to the `GraphPaint()` method:

```
protected void GraphPaint(PaintEventArgs e)
{
  Graphics aGraphics = e.Graphics;

  // Calculate the location and size of the rectangle
  // within which we want to draw the graph...
  m_PaintRectangle = new Rectangle(this.ClientRectangle.Location,
                              this.ClientRectangle.Size);

  // Size s = new Size(12, 14);
  SizeF s = aGraphics.MeasureString("H", this.Font);

  // Alter this line from the original version
  m_PaintRectangle.Inflate(-(int)s.Width*6, -(int)s.Height*6);
  aGraphics.DrawRectangle(Pens.Black, m_PaintRectangle);

  // Create horizontal gridlines...
```

```
...

// Create the y axis tick marks...
for (y=m_MinY;y<=m_MaxY;y+=m_TickY)
{
  PointF xaxisPoint = PixelPoint(new PointF(m_MinX, y));

  aGraphics.DrawLine(Pens.Black, xaxisPoint,
      new PointF(xaxisPoint.X-s.Width/2, xaxisPoint.Y));

  StringFormat SF = new StringFormat();
  SF.Alignment = StringAlignment.Far;

  aGraphics.DrawString(y.ToString(), this.Font, Brushes.Black,
    new PointF(xaxisPoint.X-s.Width/2,
    xaxisPoint.Y-s.Height/2), SF);
}

// Create the x axis tick marks...
float x;
for (x=m_MinX;x<=m_MaxX;x+=m_TickX)
{
  PointF yaxisPoint = PixelPoint(new PointF(x, m_MinY));

  aGraphics.DrawLine(Pens.Black, yaxisPoint,
    new PointF(yaxisPoint.X,
    yaxisPoint.Y+s.Height/2));

  StringFormat SF = new StringFormat();
  SF.Alignment = StringAlignment.Center;

  aGraphics.DrawString(x.ToString(), this.Font,Brushes.Black,
    new PointF(yaxisPoint.X,
    yaxisPoint.Y+s.Height), SF);
}

AddLabels(aGraphics);

// Plot the stock data...
foreach (Stock aStock in m_StockList)
{
  Pen aPen = new Pen(aStock.m_Color,2);
  float startX = m_MinX;

  PointF startPoint = new PointF(m_MinX, aStock.m_Price[0]);
  PointF endPoint = new PointF(m_MinX, aStock.m_Price[0]);

  foreach(float price in aStock.m_Price)
  {
    ...
  }
```

```
        StockChart.Stock aStock = new StockChart.Stock();

        // Write ticker symbol on top of end point...
        StringFormat SF = new StringFormat();
        SF.Alignment = StringAlignment.Far;
        PointF TextStartPoint = PixelPoint(startPoint);
        TextStartPoint.Y -= this.Font.Height;
        aGraphics.DrawString(aStock.m_Ticker, this.Font,
            Brushes.Black, TextStartPoint, SF);
        aPen.Dispose();
    }
}
```

3. Build and run the application. You should see that the Portfolio Monitor has now gained labels:

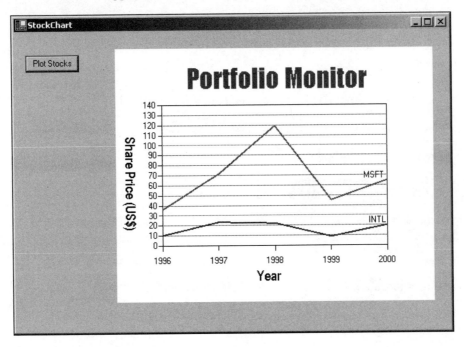

How It Works

We started by adding the AddLabels() method to the StockGraph class. This method draws labels for the x- and y-axes of the graph, and the title of the graph.

First we add a label for the y-axis. We create a Font object that we can use to draw bold Arial Narrow face text of size 14 points:

```
Font aVerticalFont=new Font("Arial Narrow",14,FontStyle.Bold);
```

Then we define a `StringFormat` object that we can use to specify that the text should be written vertically, not horizontally:

```
StringFormat aStringFormat =
    new StringFormat(StringFormatFlags.DirectionVertical);
```

We feed this `StringFormat` object, as well as the `Font` object, to the `DrawString()` method of our `Graphics` object in order to label the y-axis with **Share Price (US$)**. We also need to pass the method a brush, and a `Point` that represents the position to start writing from on the form:

```
aGraphics.DrawString("Share Price (US$)", aVerticalFont,Brushes.Black,
    new Point((m_PaintRectangle.Left-60), (m_PaintRectangle.Top+40)),
    aStringFormat);
aVerticalFont.Dispose();
```

Having finished with the `Font` object, we dispose of it. Then we create the font used for the x-axis label, and write the string `Year` near to the x-axis to label it. Note that we don't pass a `StringFormat` object to the `DrawString()` method this time, because we want the text written in the horizontal direction (which is the default):

```
Font aHorizFont=new Font("Arial Narrow", 14, FontStyle.Bold);
aGraphics.DrawString("Year", aHorizFont, Brushes.Black,
                new Point((m_PaintRectangle.Left+130),
                (m_PaintRectangle.Bottom+30)));
aHorizFont.Dispose();
```

Finally we add the title of the plot (**PortFolio Monitor**) above the graph, using a size 28 Impact font face:

```
Font aTitleFont=new Font("Impact",28);
aGraphics.DrawString("Portfolio Monitor", aTitleFont, Brushes.Crimson,
    new Point((m_PaintRectangle.Left+30),(m_PaintRectangle.Top-60)));
aTitleFont.Dispose();
```

That's the end of the `AddLabels()` method. Referring back to the `GraphPaint()` method, we add a call to the `AddLabels()` method near the end of `GraphPaint()`, and we also add some code to label the tick marks along the axes with numbers. This is the code to add each y-axis tick mark number (the code to do the same for the x-axis is very similar):

```
StringFormat SF = new StringFormat();
SF.Alignment = StringAlignment.Far;

aGraphics.DrawString(y.ToString(), this.Font, Brushes.Black,
    new PointF(xaxisPoint.X-s.Width/2,
    xaxisPoint.Y-s.Height/2), SF);
```

Notice how we have passed a `StringFormat` object to the `DrawString()` method, setting its `Alignment` property to `Far` so that the text is aligned to the right.

We write the labels for the stock tickers too:

```
StringFormat SF = new StringFormat();
SF.Alignment = StringAlignment.Far;
PointF TextStartPoint = PixelPoint(startPoint);
TextStartPoint.Y -= this.Font.Height;
aGraphics.DrawString(aStock.m_Ticker, this.Font,
    Brushes.Black, TextStartPoint, SF);
```

Notice how where we add the label depends upon the position of the final stock value, as well as the height of the Font we use to write the label in.

There is one other change that we have made that we ought to point out:

```
// Size s = new Size(12, 14);
SizeF s = aGraphics.MeasureString("H", this.Font);

m_PaintRectangle.Inflate(-(int)s.Width*6, -(int)s.Height*6);
aGraphics.DrawRectangle(Pens.Black, m_PaintRectangle);
```

We have replaced our "guessed" parameters for the Size object (which we feed to the Inflate() method to shrink the graph). By using the MeasureString() method, we can make a more informed judgement about how much space we need between the edge of the form and the edge of the graph, because we can specify that space in terms of font character width and height. Here we specify that the SizeF object corresponds to the size of an "H" character in the default font. Using the Inflate() method we then shrink the graph by adding vertical and horizontal margins around it that are 6 times the width of the "H" character wide.

Images

One of the areas where graphics support has been improved the most for GDI+ is in the handling of images. Before GDI+, loading and displaying an image was quite complicated; now it could hardly be easier.

A lot of the work is now encapsulated by the Image class in System.Drawing. The Image class is actually an abstract class, serving as the base class for two other image classes:

❑ Bitmap. When you think of images, you probably first think of bitmaps. Bitmaps are in-memory representations of the pixels on the screen. In many ways you can think of it as an in-memory copy of what is in a Graphics object or on a form. Say you have a form with a size of 100 by 100, and you use a Graphics object to draw a 10 by 10 black rectangle in the upper left corner. If you now obtain a Bitmap from the Graphics object, that bitmap contains 100 by 100 pixels, and 10 by 10 pixels in the upper left corner will be black.

❑ Metafile. This class is used to keep a log of the sequence of drawing operations on the Graphics object. So if you drew a 10 by 10 rectangle on your Graphics object, the equivalent representation in a metafile would be only one entry, representing the drawing operation. Metafiles are often used to record drawing operations so that they can be recreated later. We will not be discussing metafiles in any more depth in this chapter, since it is a fairly advanced topic.

Bitmap File Formats

Bitmaps comes in many different file formats. The native format in Windows is the .bmp format, which is almost just a direct memory dump of the contents of the bitmap. If there are 100 by 100 pixels in the bitmap, each represented by a 24-bit (3 byte) color value, there will be 100 by 100 by 3, or 30KB in the file, with 3 bytes in the file for each bit in the bitmap. So the .bmp format can take up a lot of disk space.

A number of other formats have therefore been developed to represent the bitmaps in a compressed format. Two of the most popular are the .gif format (Graphics Interchange Format) and the .jpg or .jpeg format (Joint Photographic Experts Group). You will normally use the .gif format to compress images with relatively few colors, and the .jpg image for real photos with many colors. By converting a .bmp file to a .gif or .jpg file, you can often obtain a compression of 10:1 without significant loss of quality, so it's worth considering, especially if you are dealing with a lot of graphics or working with web applications where download times are always an issue.

Loading and Saving Bitmaps

You can load and save an image by invoking a couple of static methods on the Image class. To load the image from a file you can use the FromFile() method:

```
aImage = Image.FromFile(@"..\newwroxhead.gif");
```

Image.FromFile() takes one parameter, the name of the file. It is intelligent enough to handle all of the different file formats. You can use the @ symbol to specify that the string should be used verbatim; in other words, the \n in ..\newwroxhead should not be interpreted as a newline character by the C# compiler.

The complementary function to Image.FromFile() is Image.Save(). Image.Save() comes in two flavors:

❑ Image.Save(string filename) saves the image to the file filename

❑ Image.Save(string filename, ImageFormat format) saves the image to filename, in the format specified by format (ImageFormat is an enumeration with values such as jpeg, gif, and bmp)

Displaying Images

Images are displayed using the method Graphics.DrawImage(). The DrawImage() method is also overloaded. The simplest version takes just two parameters: the image to be displayed, and a Point specifying the location of the upper left corner of the image. For example:

```
aGraphics.DrawImage(aImage, aImagePosition);
```

Another version accepts a Rectangle as a second parameter. In this instance the image will be reformatted (stretched or shrunk) to fit the size of the specified Rectangle.

Try It Out - Adding a Logo to the Portfolio Monitor

Our Wrox Portfolio Monitor is nearly complete. It just needs a final touch: a Wrox logo. Let's add it.

1. Open up the StockChart project. Make sure you have the `newwroxlogo.gif` image file stored in a directory accessible to the application. Then open the code editor for `StockGraph` and add the following method to the class (changing the directory path supplied to the `FromFile()` method if necessary):

```
void AddLogo(Graphics aGraphics)
{
  Image aImage;
  try
  {
    aImage = Image.FromFile(@"C:\\temp\newwroxlogo.gif");
    aGraphics.DrawImage(aImage, new Point(10, 10));
    aImage.Dispose();
  }
  catch
  {
    MessageBox.Show("File newwroxlogo.gif not found!");
  }
}
```

2. Near the top of the `GraphPaint()` method, add the following line:

```
protected void GraphPaint(PaintEventArgs e)
{
  Graphics aGraphics = e.Graphics;

  // Add Wrox logo to form
  AddLogo(aGraphics);

  // Calculate the location and size of the rectangle
  // within which we want to draw the graph...
  m_PaintRectangle = new Rectangle(this.ClientRectangle.Location,
                                   this.ClientRectangle.Size);

  // etc... (rest of method)
```

3. Build and run the project. You should see that the Wrox logo has appeared in the top left of the user control:

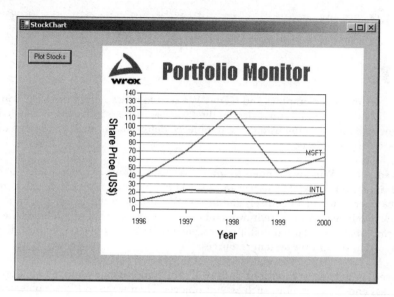

How It Works

All we have done in this Try It Out is added a method called `AddLogo()` to our `StockGraph` class, that displays an image of the Wrox logo in the top left corner of the user control:

```
void AddLogo(Graphics aGraphics)
{
```

We start by declaring an `Image` object, and then add the image contained in `newwroxlogo.gif` to this `Image` object, using the `FromFile()` method:

```
Image aImage;
try
{
    aImage = Image.FromFile(@"C:\\temp\newwroxlogo.gif");
```

Next we use the `DrawImage()` method to draw the image in the top left corner of the user control (with the top left corner of the image at pixel coordinates (10, 10)):

```
    aGraphics.DrawImage(aImage, new Point(10, 10));
    aImage.Dispose();
}
catch
{
    MessageBox.Show("File newwroxlogo.gif not found!");
}
}
```

Finally we dispose of the `Image` object. Note how we've encapsulated this functionality in a `try...catch` block, so that if there are problems with finding the image file we can tell the user this.

Then we just added a call to the `AddLogo()` method in our `GraphPaint()` method.

Summary

In this chapter we discussed graphics and GDI+. We started by exploring the basic concepts, such as how we draw by calling methods on a class in the `System.Drawing` namespace called `Graphics`. We also noted how to define position using `Point` objects, define size using `Rectangle` objects, and define color via `Color` objects.

We also looked at how Windows renders graphics. We saw that we as programmers had to be prepared to redraw our image on demand. This was most easily done in the `OnPaint()` method, which is available to be overridden in all controls and forms. We discussed the `ClipRectangle` as a means to figure out how much needed to be redrawn, and `ClientRectangle`, which holds the actual size of the control or form. Finally we learned that if you create a `Graphics` object, you must dispose of it as soon as possible in order to conserve system resources.

Then we moved on to have a closer look at drawing lines and shapes using the methods of the `Graphics` class and drawing tools, such as `Pen` objects. Then we used `Brush` objects to fill shapes and closed curves with solid, hatched or even gradient color fills. We also spent considerable time looking at different times of shapes, such as ellipses, arcs, piecharts, splines, and Bezier curves.

Since we often want to use text with our graphics, we then covered using `Font` objects with the `DrawString()` method to draw text. Finally we briefly looked at manipulating images through classes derived from the `Image` class.

Throughout the chapter we built up a small user control that plotted stock portfolio values on a graph, and used this example to illustrate the use of many of the methods and classes in the `System.Drawing` and `System.Drawing.Drawing2D` namespaces.

There is much more to GDI+ than we have had room to show here. But this should at least give you a good framework for getting started. If you are ready for more, some of the best books on the subject are probably *GDI+ Programming: Creating Custom Controls using C#* (Wrox Press, ISBN 1-86100-631-4) and *Programming Microsoft Windows with C#* (Microsoft Press, ISBN 0-73561-370-2).

Printing

In this chapter, we're going to take a look at how to "print-enable" our applications so that as well as sending their output to the screen, they can send their output to a printer attached to either the local machine, or attached somewhere on the network.

As we proceed through the chapter, we'll discuss how to invoke the following dialog boxes from our code:

- ❑   Print Preview
- ❑   Page Settings
- ❑   Print Dialog

We'll also show you coding techniques that will enable you to:

- ❑   Maintain aspect ratios as you print images
- ❑   Paginate large documents
- ❑   Add headers to documents before they are printed

We'll be gradually building up a sample application throughout the chapter that displays images and documents, and allows us to invoke the dialog boxes we mentioned above, and of course to print the images or documents. Before we can do any of this, however, we are going to need to introduce you to the most important classes associated with printing.

The System.Drawing.Printing Namespace

The System.Drawing.Printing namespace contains most of the classes that we need to support printing. There are also a few more printing-related classes in System.Windows.Forms, which we'll get to in a moment.

Of the thirty or so classes in `System.Drawing.Printing`, only one is really important for basic printing activities: `System.Drawing.Printing.PrintDocument`. This class represents the document to be printed, and is used by the printing subsystem to manage the printing process. To actually print a document we use the `Print()` method of `PrintDocument`. `PrintDocument` also has many important events associated with it, including the `PrintPage` event that is fired when the output to print for the current page is needed.

`PrintDocument` supports a few properties that are of interest. One is `PrinterSettings`. This points to a `System.Drawing.Printing.PrinterSettings` object that describes the printer that will be used. The other is `DefaultPageSettings`. This points to a `System.Drawing.Printing.PageSettings` object that describes the layout of the page. This includes settings like the page orientation, the paper size, and so on.

By and large, we don't need to worry about programmatically changing these properties. It's a better approach to tap into the built-in dialog boxes provided with Windows to give the user familiar tools to change printer and page settings with. We'll be using these three classes:

❑   `System.Windows.Forms.PrintDialog` – displays the common print dialog box:

❑ System.Windows.Forms.PageSetupDialog – displays a dialog box that allows the user to change basic page layout settings:

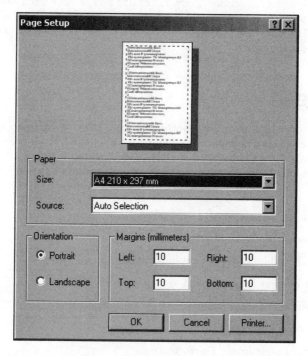

❑ System.Windows.Forms.PrintPreviewDialog – displays a dialog box that allows the user to see the print results before they commit them to the printer:

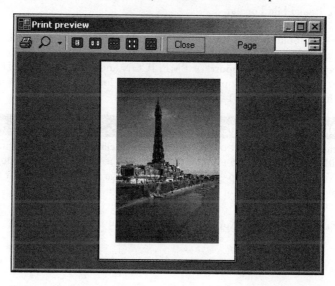

The `PrintPreviewDialog` class has a `Document` property that is set to the `PrintDocument` we want to print. The class's `ShowDialog()` method is called to invoke the print preview dialog. You should note that the `System.Windows.Forms.PrintPreviewControl` control actually provides the page view that you can see above which shows how the image will look if it's printed. In fact, all that `PrintPreviewDialog` does is encapsulate this control in a `Form` instance so that you don't have to worry about actually displaying it.

Printing Images

Because it's slightly more fun than printing boring reports or rows of numbers and charts, in the first part of this chapter we're going to demonstrate how we can create a small program that will allow us to load pictures onto a Windows Form and ultimately print them out to an installed printer of our choice. We'll be using .NET's built-in image handling code, which supports a number of different file formats. These are:

❏ BMP – Windows Bitmap format

❏ GIF – Graphics Interchange Format

❏ PNG – W3C Portable Network Graphics format

❏ JPEG – Joint Pictures Expert Group

❏ WMF – Windows Metafile

❏ EMF – Enhanced Windows Metafile

❏ EXIF – Exchangeable Image File format

❏ ICON – an icon

❏ TIFF – Tag Image File Format

One of the great things about .NET is that we get all of that for free! Prior to .NET, we'd have to go and either get a third-party library from somewhere, or write our own support for non-Microsoft formats (Windows has always had built-in support for BMP, ICON and WMF formats). However, the `System.Drawing.Image` class now provides this support for us, and also includes support for loading images from disk through its `FromFile()` method.

Try It Out – Loading and Previewing Images

Now that you've had a basic introduction to the classes associated with image printing, let's build an application that will allow us to load an image and display the print preview dialog. In the next section, we'll look at how we can manipulate page and printer settings, and in the section after that we'll look at how we can improve the appearance of the printed document.

1. Create a new C# Windows Application project. Call it PrintDemo.

2. Change the `Text` property of the newly created `Form1` to `Print Demo`, and add two new `Button` controls and a `PictureBox` control to the form. Set the `Name` property of one `Button` control to `buttonLoad` and the `Text` property to `Load`. For the other button, set its `Name` property to `buttonPreview` and its `Text` property to `Preview`. Then set the `Name` property of the `PictureBox` control to `pictureImage`, and its `Anchor` property to `Top`, `Bottom`, `Left`, `Right`. In addition, set its `BorderStyle` property to `Fixed3D` and set its `SizeMode` property to `StretchImage`. You should see the following:

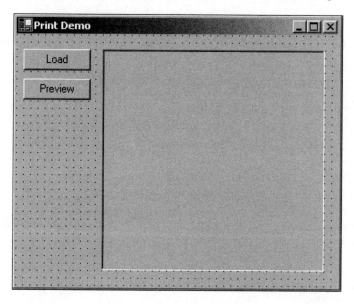

3. We need to give the user a way to load an image, so add a new `OpenFileDialog` control to the form. Change its `Name` property to `dialogOpenFile`.

4. Double-click both buttons on the form to create click handlers. Then add the code shown below:

```
public class Form1 : System.Windows.Forms.Form
{
    // fields...
    private DocumentBase _document;
    ...
    private void buttonLoad_Click(object sender, System.EventArgs e)
    {
        // show the open file dialog...
        if(dialogOpenFile.ShowDialog(this) == DialogResult.OK)
        {
            // try to load an image...
            try
            {
                // show the image...
                pictureImage.Image = Image.FromFile(dialogOpenFile.FileName);
```

```
                    // create a new document...
                    _document = new ImageDocument(pictureImage.Image);
                }
                catch (Exception ex)
                {
                    MessageBox.Show("The image could not be loaded. " + ex.Message);
                }
            }
        }

        private void buttonPreview_Click(object sender, System.EventArgs e)
        {
            // do we have an image?
            if(_document == null)
            {
                MessageBox.Show("You must load an image first.");
                return;
            }

            // preview...
            _document.ShowPrintPreviewDialog();
        }
```

5. Add a new class called `DocumentBase` to the project. Import the namespaces shown, make the class extend `PrintDocument`, and add the method shown to the class:

```
using System;
using System.Drawing;
using System.Drawing.Printing;
using System.Windows.Forms;

namespace PrintDemo
{
    public class DocumentBase : PrintDocument
    {
    ...
        public DialogResult ShowPrintPreviewDialog()
        {
            // create the new dialog...
            PrintPreviewDialog dialog = new PrintPreviewDialog();
            dialog.Document = this;

            // show...
            return dialog.ShowDialog();
        }
    ...
    }
```

6. Create a new class called `ImageDocument`. Import the same namespaces as above and make this new class extend `DocumentBase`. Also add the fields, properties and methods shown below:

```
using System;
using System.Drawing;
using System.Drawing.Printing;
using System.Windows.Forms;

namespace PrintDemo
{
    public class ImageDocument : DocumentBase
    {
        // fields...
        private Image _image;

        public Image Image
        {
            get
            {
                return _image;
            }
            set
            {
                _image = value;
            }
        }

        public ImageDocument()
        {
        }

        public ImageDocument(Image image)
        {
            this.Image = image;
        }

        // OnPrintPage - print the page...
        protected override void OnPrintPage(PrintPageEventArgs e)
        {
            // do we have an image?
            if(Image == null)
                throw new InvalidOperationException();

            // print the image...
            e.Graphics.DrawImage(Image, e.MarginBounds);
        }
    }
}
```

7. Build and run the program now. Load an image using the Load button:

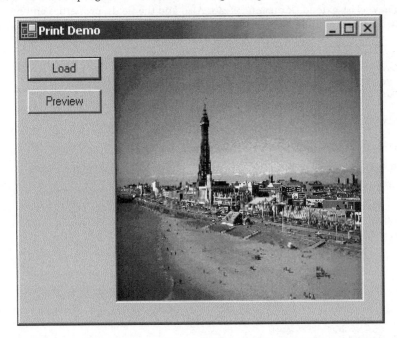

Then press the Preview button. You should see a preview of the image ready for printing:

You can click the little printer button on the toolbar to actually print the image.

How It Works

In this example, we create a new class called `DocumentBase` that extends `PrintDocument` and contains all of the data that makes up the document (what we mean by a "document" here is a `System.Drawing.Image` object). The reason that we create a new class derived from `PrintDocument` is that `PrintDocument` does not contain enough basic functionality. The extra functionality of our `DocumentBase` class includes "easier" support for actions like changing printer settings and previewing the print. The idea is to give the object to the printing subsystem, say "print this" and everything will be nicely self-contained.

We also create a new class that extends `DocumentBase` called `ImageDocument`, and this contains the data that we want to print – in this case, the image.

Let's consider what happens when we click the **Load** button. Inside the click handler, the code opens the **Open File** dialog:

```
if(dialogOpenFile.ShowDialog(this) == DialogResult.OK)
```

Then it uses the static `FromFile()` method of `System.Drawing.Image` to load the file from disk:

```
pictureImage.Image = Image.FromFile(dialogOpenFile.FileName);
```

Now we need to provide a way for `Form1` to keep track of the current image. We create an `ImageDocument` from the image, and place it into the object _document:

```
_document = new ImageDocument(pictureImage.Image);
```

Our `ImageDocument` class contains an `Image` object. We'll come back to the `ImageDocument` class in a moment. To ensure that we can cope if the user attempts to load a file that isn't a supported image type (such as a Microsoft Word document), we wrap the whole lot in a `try...catch` block.

When the user clicks the **Preview** button, assuming that there is an image in _document, the `ShowPrintPreviewDialog()` method is called on this `ImageDocument` object:

```
_document.ShowPrintPreviewDialog();
```

This method is actually defined in our `DocumentBase` class (which inherits from the `PrintDocument` class) but we can use it because our `ImageDocument` class is derived from `DocumentBase`.

The `ShowPrintPreviewDialog()` method creates a new `PrintPreviewDialog` object and then displays it using the `ShowDialog()` method. The only thing we need to do before showing the dialog is to give it a copy of the image to display. We do this using the `Document` property:

```
public DialogResult ShowPrintPreviewDialog()
{
    PrintPreviewDialog dialog = new PrintPreviewDialog();
```

```
        dialog.Document = this;

        return dialog.ShowDialog();
    }
```

You should note that the actual processes of printing to the printer and displaying the preview on the screen are *identical*. In fact, you can consider the "displaying the preview on the screen" part as being simply "printing on the screen". In the previous chapter, we saw that .NET abstracts the device (printer, screen, whatever) from us through the use of the `System.Drawing.Graphics` class. We're given a `System.Drawing.Graphics` object with the event arguments passed into the `OnPrintPage()` event handler defined in `ImageDocument`:

```
    protected override void OnPrintPage(PrintPageEventArgs e)
    {
```

`PrintDocument` will raise the `PrintPage` event if it needs to print a page. If `PrintPreviewControl` asks `PrintDocument` to raise this event, we'll get a `Graphics` object back that ultimately targets the screen. If the print button is pressed, the event will be fired but this time `PrintDocument` will provide a `Graphics` object that targets the chosen printer. We don't have to do anything to handle this difference; it is all handled for us.

We use the `DrawImage()` method of the `Graphics` object to draw the image. In this particular case, `MarginBounds` contains a rectangle that describes the printable area of the page, and `DrawImage()` will stretch the image so that it fits into this:

```
    e.Graphics.DrawImage(Image, e.MarginBounds);
```

At this point you should be able to see how we can print on the chosen printer (or the screen) by using the by-now-familiar `Graphics` object. Now let's look at how to change the settings of the page.

There is one thing that you should note before we go on. We set the `PictureBox` control's `SizeMode` property to `StretchImage` so that the image always exactly fills the available space in the control. Notice how the **aspect ratio** (ratio of image width to height) of the image is not preserved if we do this – the image can get stretched out of shape. For example, if we stretch the box containing our image horizontally, the image starts to look unnatural:

So we see that `PictureBox` does not support scaling the image with aspect ratio preservation. Don't worry about this too much at the moment, but we will be coming back to talk more about it later.

Changing Page Settings

Changing the page settings is simply a matter of using another dialog box. In this case, we'll use the class `System.Windows.Forms.PageSetupDialog`, which represents the Page Setup dialog box. To invoke the dialog, we call `ShowDialog()` on this class. Like the `PrintPreviewDialog` class, the `PageSetupDialog` class contains a `Document` property that sets the document associated with the dialog.

`PrintDocument` contains a property called `DefaultPageSettings`. This property gets and sets a `System.Drawing.Printing.PageSettings` object that describes, effectively, metrics about the paper, chosen orientation and a few other bits and pieces.

We can change this information programmatically but `PageSetupDialog` knows how to present this information and how to marshal the changes back into `DefaultPageSettings` when the user has clicked OK. If the user clicks Cancel, obviously the changes are discarded.

Try It Out – Changing Page Settings

In this Try It Out we are going to add a Settings button to our Print Demo application that will bring up a Page Settings dialog. We will also add some code that will automatically display an image in the correct orientation (landscape or portrait).

1. Open up the PrintDemo project, and add this method to `DocumentBase`:

```
public DialogResult ShowPageSettingsDialog()
{
    // create the new dialog...
    PageSetupDialog dialog = new PageSetupDialog();
    dialog.Document = this;

    // show...
    return dialog.ShowDialog();
}
```

2. To `Form1`, add a new `Button` control. Set its `Name` property to `buttonPageSettings` and its `Text` property to `Settings`.

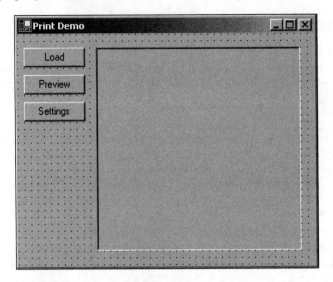

3. Double-click on the `Settings` button to create a new click event handler. Add this code:

```
private void buttonPageSettings_Click(object sender, System.EventArgs e)
{
    // do we have an image?
    if(_document == null)
    {
        MessageBox.Show("You must load an image first.");
        return;
    }

    // preview...
    _document.ShowPageSettingsDialog();
}
```

4. Open the `ImageDocument` class, and add the following code to the `Image` property:

```
public Image Image
{
    get
    {
        return _image;
    }
    set
    {
        _image = value;

        // do we have an image?
```

```
              if(_image != null)
              {
                  // are we landscape?...
                  if(_image.Size.Width > _image.Size.Height)
                      DefaultPageSettings.Landscape = true;
                  else
                      DefaultPageSettings.Landscape = false;
              }
          }
      }
```

5. Build and run the project. You'll find that if you load a landscape image and click Preview, the page will have a landscape orientation. However, you'll be able to change this default setting if you wish, along with other page settings via the page settings dialog.

How It Works

The click handler for our new button calls the ShowPageSettingsDialog() method that we add to DocumentBase. In this method we create a new PageSetupDialog, and set its Document property to the current document:

```
PageSetupDialog dialog = new PageSetupDialog();
dialog.Document = this;
```

Then we call `ShowDialog()` in order to invoke the Page Settings dialog box for our document:

```
return dialog.ShowDialog();
```

In order to orient the image correctly by default when it is previewed, we apply a little logic. We know that an image is landscape if it is wider than it is tall. We can use the `Size` property of the `Image` class to get the `Width` and `Height` values for the image, and then we can compare them to see if the image is landscape or not.

To set the page to the correct orientation, we make use of the `DefaultPageSettings` property of the `ImageDocument` class (which it inherits from `PrintDocument`). `DefaultPageSettings` has a property called `Landscape` that can be set to `true` or `false` in order to set the orientation:

```
if(_image.Size.Width > _image.Size.Height)
    DefaultPageSettings.Landscape = true;
else
    DefaultPageSettings.Landscape = false;
```

You should note that since `DefaultPageSettings` sets the page settings in the `PageSettings` object associated with the `ImageDocument`, setting `DefaultPageSettings.Landscape` also sets the `PageSettings.Landscape` property.

Print Dialogs

Aside from Print Preview and Page Settings, the other dialog box that is associated with printing is the Print dialog itself. We can invoke this dialog by calling the `ShowDialog()` method on the `System.Windows.Forms.PrintDialog` class. As with the other dialog classes the `PrintDialog` class has a `Document` property to get and set the associated document.

If we want to bypass the Print Preview dialog completely, then `PrintDocument` supports a `Print()` method that invokes the printing process straight away without displaying any dialogs.

Let's now add these printing options to our application.

Try It Out – Printing

For completeness we'll add two buttons to our `PrintDemo` application. Clicking one will invoke the Print dialog, and clicking the other will cause the document to print straight away.

1. Open the PrintDemo project, and add two buttons to Form1. Call the first one buttonPrint and set its Text property to Print. Call the second buttonPrintNow and set its Text property to Print Now!

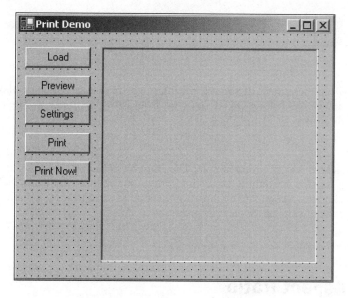

2. Double-click the Print and Print Now! buttons, and add this code to the appropriate click handlers:

```
private void buttonPrint_Click(object sender, System.EventArgs e)
{
    // do we have an image?
    if(_document == null)
    {
        MessageBox.Show("You must load an image first.");
        return;
    }

    // create the new dialog...
    PrintDialog dialog = new PrintDialog();
    dialog.Document = _document;

    if (dialog.ShowDialog() == DialogResult.OK)
    {
        _document.Print();
    }
}

private void buttonPrintNow_Click(object sender, System.EventArgs e)
{
    // do we have an image?
    if(_document == null)
```

```
    {
        MessageBox.Show("You must load an image first.");
        return;
    }


    // print...
    _document.Print();
}
```

3. Build and run the project. If you click **Print**, the print dialog will be displayed and you can print the image by clicking **OK**. If you click **Print Now!** the image will be printed directly on the default printer.

How It Works

The code that we added was all pretty simple. The **Print Now!** button basically just calls the `PrintDocument.Print()` method, while the **Print** button invokes the Print Dialog by calling `DocumentBase.ShowDialog()`. Note how we must set the `Document` property of the `PrintDialog` to the document we want to print:

```
dialog.Document = _document;
```

Preserving Aspect Ratio

We mentioned before that the images appear to be stretched out of shape when displaying them on the screen or when printing. That's because the `DrawImage()` method doesn't automatically preserve the aspect ratio of the image that it's working with.

To preserve the aspect ratio of an image when we scale it, we need to create a "best fit" rectangle. This rectangle is designed to fit inside the container (in our ultimate case, this is the page), while preserving the aspect ratio of the image. This rectangle is then centered to the middle of the container. We can do this through a few simple calculations.

When thinking about this problem, it's logical to assume four cases: landscape image inside landscape page, landscape image inside portrait page, portrait image inside landscape page, and portrait image inside portrait page.

Although this looks like four distinct cases it is actually just two cases. It doesn't matter whether the image is landscape or portrait – we use one algorithm for landscape pages and one for portrait pages and everything works fine.

We can account for the image aspect ratio by deriving a best-fit rectangle that is the biggest that can be placed in the printable area of the page, and placing the image inside this best-fit rectangle. Any space that is inside the printable area but outside the best-fit will be left white.

Let's now apply this technique to our sample application.

Try It Out – Preserving Aspect Ratio

In this Try It Out we are going to add a method to our ImageDocument class that will enable us to print an image while maintaining its image aspect ratio.

1. To ImageDocument, add the following method:

```
protected Rectangle GetBestFitRectangle(Rectangle toContain,
                                        Size objectSize)
{
    // are we landscape, or portrait ?
    bool containerLandscape = false;
    if(toContain.Width > toContain.Height)
        containerLandscape = true;

    // what's the aspect ratio of the image?
    float aspectRatio = (float)objectSize.Height / (float)objectSize.Width;

    // where's the middle of the container...
    int midContainerX = toContain.Left + (toContain.Width / 2);
    int midContainerY = toContain.Top + (toContain.Height / 2);

    // mode...
    int x1 = 0, x2 = 0, y1 = 0, y2 = 0;
    if(containerLandscape == false)
    {
        // OK, make the width equal the container...
        x1 = toContain.Left;
        x2 = toContain.Right;

        // what's the adjusted height?
        int adjustedHeight =
            (int)((float)toContain.Width * aspectRatio);

        // move...
        y1 = midContainerY - (adjustedHeight / 2);
        y2 = y1 + adjustedHeight;
    }
    else
    {
        // make the height equal the container...
        y1 = toContain.Top;
        y2 = toContain.Bottom;

        // adjusted width...
        int adjustedWidth = (int)((float)toContain.Height / aspectRatio);

        // move...
        x1 = midContainerX - (adjustedWidth / 2);
        x2 = x1 + adjustedWidth;
    }

    // return...
    return new Rectangle(x1, y1, x2 - x1, y2 - y1);
}
```

2. Make these changes to the `OnPrintPage()` method in `ImageDocument`:

```
// OnPrintPage - print the page...
protected override void OnPrintPage(PrintPageEventArgs e)
{
    // do we have an image?
    if(Image == null)
        throw new InvalidOperationException();

    // calc the bounds appropriately...
    Rectangle bestFit = GetBestFitRectangle(e.MarginBounds, Image.Size);

    // draw the image...
    e.Graphics.DrawImage(Image, bestFit);

    // debugging rectangles...
    e.Graphics.DrawRectangle(Pens.Black, bestFit);
    e.Graphics.DrawRectangle(Pens.Black, e.MarginBounds);
}
```

3. Build and run the project. You'll find that the image is properly centered in the middle of the page. For example, here is a portrait image in landscape orientation:

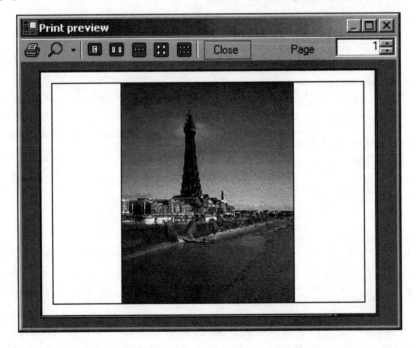

Here is the same picture in portrait orientation:

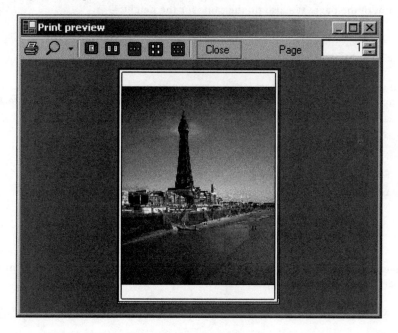

How It Works

We add a method to `ImageDocument` called `GetBestFitRectangle()` that enables us to print while maintaining aspect ratio. This method accepts a `Rectangle` (called `toContain`) representing the printing bounding box, and a `Size` object (called `objectSize`) that represents the image size. It makes more sense to add this to `ImageDocument` as this class is related to image printing and we're unlike to want this method when printing text. Inside `OnPrintPage()`, we call `GetBestFitRectangle()` and then pass the image and this rectangle to `DrawImage()`. We also draw on rectangles representing the printable extent of the page, and a bounding rectangle around the image for debugging purposes.

The first thing we do in `GetBestFitRectangle()` is work out if the page has a landscape or portrait orientation. We've already seen this idea earlier in the chapter:

```
bool containerLandscape = false;
if(toContain.Width > toContain.Height)
    containerLandscape = true;
```

Once we've done that, we need the aspect ratio of the image. To find it, we divide the width by the height.

```
float aspectRatio = (float)objectSize.Height / (float)objectSize.Width;
```

Dividing the width of the page in half and adding it to the left side of the page gives us the x-coordinate of the mid-point of the page. We also do the same for the height:

```
int midContainerX = toContain.Left + (toContain.Width / 2);
int midContainerY = toContain.Top + (toContain.Height / 2);
```

Here's where we split depending on whether or not we have a landscape or a portrait container. We also set up variable for holding the top-left and bottom-right coordinates of the new rectangle:

```
int x1 = 0, x2 = 0, y1 = 0, y2 = 0;
if(containerLandscape == false)
{
```

In landscape orientation, we make the image "stick" to the vertical edges of the page:

```
x1 = toContain.Left;
x2 = toContain.Right;
```

Once we have the width of the page, we set the height equal to the width multiplied by the aspect ratio. This is the part that preserves the aspect ratio:

```
int adjustedHeight = (int)((float)toContain.Width * aspectRatio);
```

Finally, we just have to orientate the rectangle around the midpoint. As the left and right edges are the sides of the page, we just have to move the top edge. The top edge is equal to the mid y-coordinate of the page, minus half the height of the rectangle. The bottom edge is equal to the top edge plus the height:

```
y1 = midContainerY - (adjustedHeight / 2);
y2 = y1 + adjustedHeight;
}
else
{
```

When dealing with portrait pages, the situation is just flipped around. Rather than sticking to the left and right edges, we stick to the top and bottom edges. This gives us the height, and we calculate the width using the aspect ratio again, but this time we reverse the operation and divide rather than multiply:

```
y1 = toContain.Top;
y2 = toContain.Bottom;

int adjustedWidth = (int)((float)toContain.Height / aspectRatio);

x1 = midContainerX - (adjustedWidth / 2);
x2 = x1 + adjustedWidth;
}
```

Finally, we return a `Rectangle` representing the "best fit" box containing the scaled image back to the caller (the `OnPrintPage()` method in our case). The `OnPrintPage()` method then displays the properly-scaled image, along with the "best fit" rectangle.

Printing Multiple Pages

In the previous example, we saw how the most important printing classes work, and created some code for scaling images to a page while preserving aspect ratio. However, in most business applications you're more likely to be printing dull multi-page documents like reports, rather than exciting things like vacation photos!

In this section, we're going to take a look at how you handle printing multiple pages. We'll build a new class called `CodeDocument`, set it to extend `DocumentBase` and write code in there to load a `.cs` or `.vb` source code document from disk ready for printing.

Pagination

Printing a multiple page document requires us to deal with "pagination". This is the process in which we divide a document up into pages, depending on the size of the font that we're drawing the text with and the size of the paper stock used for printing. In this section, we're going to learn how to paginate and print multiple pages. In the next section, we're going to add a header to each page.

Pagination is quite a curious process in .NET. Basically, we have to arrange for `OnPrintPage()` to be called exactly once per printed page. During processing of that method, you'll have the opportunity to tell the printing engine that you want to print another page. This is done by setting the `HasMorePages` property of the `PrintPageEventArgs` that are passed into `OnPrintPage()`to `True`. This will prompt .NET to call back into the event handler to get the information for the next page. All you need then is a way of keeping track of the current page being printed.

Try It Out – Printing Multiple Pages

In this Try It Out, we're going to paginate and print a C# or VB.NET source code file in multiple pages, with the line number printed against each source code line.

1. We'll need a font to use when printing. To `DocumentBase`, add this field:

```
public class DocumentBase : PrintDocument
{
    // fields...
    public Font Font = new Font ("Verdana", 10, GraphicsUnit.Point);
```

2. To the project, add a new class called `CodeDocument` that extends `DocumentBase`. Add some namespace import declarations, as well as the fields and properties shown below:

```
using System;
using System.IO;
using System.Drawing;
using System.Drawing.Printing;
```

```
using System.Collections;

...
    public class CodeDocument : DocumentBase
    {
        // fields...
        private string[] _lines;
        private int _pageNumber;
        private int _currentLine;

        public CodeDocument()
        {
        }

        public CodeDocument(string[] lines)
        {
            Lines = lines;
        }

        public string[] Lines
        {
            get
            {
                return _lines;
            }
            set
            {
                _lines = value;
            }
        }
    }
```

3. To load a source code document from disk, we'll create a static `Load()` method in `CodeDocument`:

```
public static CodeDocument Load(string filename)
{
    // open the file...
    FileStream stream = null;
    try
    {
        stream = new FileStream(filename, FileMode.Open);
        StreamReader reader = new StreamReader(stream);

        // read each line in...
        ArrayList readLines = new ArrayList();
        while(true)
        {
            string line = reader.ReadLine();
            if(line == null)
                break;

            // add it to the array...
            readLines.Add(line);
```

```
        }

        // copy...
        string[] lines = new string[readLines.Count];
        readLines.CopyTo(lines, 0);

        // return...
        return new CodeDocument(lines);
    }
    finally
    {
        // close...
        if(stream != null)
            stream.Close();
    }
}
```

4. The `BeginPrint` event will be fired before printing begins. We can overload `OnBeginPrint()` in `CodeDocument` to respond to this event and we can configure the print process here. We also need to add the `OnPrintPage()` method:

```
protected override void OnBeginPrint(PrintEventArgs e)
{
    // reset the page counters...
    _pageNumber = 0;
    _currentLine = 0;
}


protected override void OnPrintPage(PrintPageEventArgs e)
{
    // anything?
    if(_lines == null)
        return;

    // adjust the page number...
    _pageNumber += 1;

    // where does the page start...?
    float y = e.MarginBounds.Top;

    // how big is the line number width?
    SizeF lineNumberSize =
        e.Graphics.MeasureString(string.Format("{0}: ",
        _lines.Length), Font, e.MarginBounds.Width);
    float normalLineHeight = lineNumberSize.Height;

    // print this page...
    int linesOnThisPage = 0;
    while(true)
    {
        // get the line...
```

```
        string line = _lines[_currentLine];

    // where...
    RectangleF rectangle =
        new RectangleF(e.MarginBounds.Left +
        lineNumberSize.Width, y,
        e.MarginBounds.Width - lineNumberSize.Width,
        e.MarginBounds.Bottom - y);
    RectangleF lineRectangle =
        new RectangleF(e.MarginBounds.Left, y,
        lineNumberSize.Width, e.MarginBounds.Bottom - y);

    // now, measure the text...
    SizeF lineSize = e.Graphics.MeasureString(line, Font, rectangle.Size);
    if(lineSize.Height < normalLineHeight)
        lineSize.Height = normalLineHeight;

    // does this line fit on this page?
    if(y + lineSize.Height > e.MarginBounds.Bottom && linesOnThisPage > 0)
        e.HasMorePages = true;
    else
    {
        // draw the line number and line...
        e.Graphics.DrawString(string.Format("{0}:",
            _currentLine + 1), Font, Brushes.Black,
            lineRectangle);
        e.Graphics.DrawString(line, Font, Brushes.Black,
            rectangle);

        // measure the text...
        y += lineSize.Height;

        // flag...
        linesOnThisPage++;
    }

    // next...
    if(e.HasMorePages == false)
    {
        _currentLine++;
        if(_currentLine == _lines.Length)
            break;
    }
    else
        break;
    }
}
```

5. Now open the Code Editor for `Form1`. `Form1` can already store and work with objects inherited from `DocumentBase`. All we need do is tweak the Load button event handler code so that if we're loading a `.cs` or `.vb` file we'll create a new `CodeDocument`, otherwise we'll create an `ImageDocument` as we have been doing. Make the following change to `buttonLoad_Click()` on `Form1` check to see if the extension of the file we have is `.cs` or `.vb`, and add the namespace reference shown:

```
using System.IO;
...
    public class Form1 : System.Windows.Forms.Form
    {
    ...
        private void buttonLoad_Click(object sender, System.EventArgs e)
        {
            // show the open file dialog...
            if(dialogOpenFile.ShowDialog(this) == DialogResult.OK)
            {
                // try and load an image...
                try
                {
                    // what kind of document?
                    FileInfo info = new FileInfo(dialogOpenFile.FileName);
                    string extension = info.Extension.ToLower();
                    if(extension == ".cs" || extension == ".vb")
                        _document = CodeDocument.Load(dialogOpenFile.FileName);
                    else
                    {
                        // show the image...
                        pictureImage.Image = Image.FromFile(dialogOpenFile.FileName);

                        // create a new document...
                        _document = new ImageDocument(pictureImage.Image);
                    }
                }
                catch(Exception ex)
                {
                    MessageBox.Show("The document could not be loaded. " + ex.Message);
                }
            }
        }
    }
```

6. Build and run the project now and load a `.cs` or `.vb` file. Click the **Preview** button and you'll find that the document will be paginated and be spread across a number of pages.

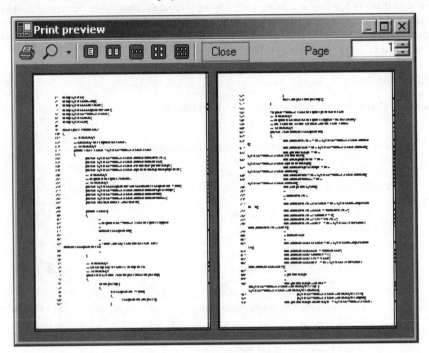

You can change the orientation of the page and everything will still work properly.

How It Works

We start off by modifying the **Load** button handler so that it checks to see if the file to be loaded is a C# or VB.NET file (with file extensions of `.cs` and `.vb` respectively). If it does, the `Load()` method of our new `CodeDocument` class is called:

```
try
{
    // what kind of document?
    FileInfo info = new FileInfo(dialogOpenFile.FileName);
    string extension = info.Extension.ToLower();
    if(extension == ".cs" || extension == ".vb")
        _document = CodeDocument.Load(dialogOpenFile.FileName);
    else
    {
        // show the image...
        pictureImage.Image = Image.FromFile(dialogOpenFile.FileName);

        // create a new document...
        _document = new ImageDocument(pictureImage.Image);
    }
}
```

The static `Load()` method in `CodeDocument` takes a filename as a parameter, opens and loads the file into memory and then creates a new instance of `CodeDocument` that will be returned to the user.

```
public static CodeDocument Load(string filename)
{
    // open the file...
    FileStream stream = null;
    try
    {
        stream = new FileStream(filename, FileMode.Open);
        StreamReader reader = new StreamReader(stream);
```

Once we've opened the file, we create a new `System.Collections.ArrayList` and start walking through the file. We add each line to the `ArrayList`. If we get a null value back from `ReadLine()`, we assume we've reached the end of the document and we quit:

```
        // read each line in...
        ArrayList readLines = new ArrayList();
        while(true)
        {
            string line = reader.ReadLine();
            if(line == null)
                break;

            // add it to the array...
            readLines.Add(line);
        }
```

When we've finished, we create a new string array and copy the contents of the `ArrayList` to the array. We then return this array back to the caller:

```
        // copy...
        string[] lines = new string[readLines.Count];
        readLines.CopyTo(lines, 0);

        // return...
        return new CodeDocument(lines);
    }
    finally
    {
        // close...
        if(stream != null)
            stream.Close();
    }
}
```

We use a `try...finally` block in the code to properly handle any file exceptions when loading the source from disk. Working with files is fraught with problems, so this is a sound plan. Notice how we don't implement a `catch` clause here. If an exception should occur, we don't actually want to do anything with it. Instead, we want the exception handler maintained by the caller to deal with the error. The `finally` block gives us the opportunity to close the file stream should it be open when we leave the method – and we can leave either by an exception, or by the `return` call.

So, we can load the source code file into memory. All we need to do now is print it out, and we deal with this aspect in the `OnBeginPrint()` and `OnPrintPage()` methods.

In our override of `OnBeginPrint()`, we set the `_currentLine` field of `CodeDocument`, representing the current line of the document, to be zero and we also set `_pageNumber` to be zero. Because we're storing `_currentLine` in a field, on each call into `OnPrintPage()`, this variable will report the next line to be printed. This means that if we print 50 lines on the first page (starting with line zero), the second time `OnPrintPage()` is called, `_currentLine` will be set to 50 and so we'll know that we have to print starting at line 50.

Let's take a look at the override of `OnPrintPage()` now. We start off by checking that there is something to print, and if so we increment the `pageNumber` counter:

```
// anything?
if(_lines == null)
    return;

// adjust the page number...
_pageNumber += 1;
```

For each page, we start printing at the top. `y` is used to record the top y-coordinate of the next line to be printed. We use the `MarginBounds` property supplied through `PrintPageEventArgs` to determine where the top of the printable area is:

```
float y = e.MarginBounds.Top;
```

Measuring the size of a string takes precious processor power, and if not optimized use of this routine can cause performance problems. Here, we're going to assume that the space we have to allocate on the left-hand side of the page for line numbers will never be larger than the size of the number of lines we have. We're generating the largest possible string and assuming that this will accommodate all of the line numbers that we ever need to print for this document:

```
SizeF lineNumberSize = _
    e.Graphics.MeasureString(string.Format("{0}: ", _
    _lines.Length), Font, e.MarginBounds.Width);
```

After measuring the size of the largest potential line number, we store the height of this in `normalLineHeight`. If we have a string that is empty, `MeasureString()` will claim that it is zero pixels tall, in which case we need to assume that the line is actually `normalLineHeight` tall, otherwise the next line will be drawn on top of it:

```
float normalLineHeight = lineNumberSize.Height;
```

Now we drop into a loop. We'll quit this loop when we've filled up the printable area of the page, or when we've run out of lines to draw. We'll use `linesOnThisPage` to keep track of how many lines we've printed on this page so far.

```
int linesOnThisPage = 0;
while(true)
{
    string line = _lines[_currentLine];
```

We now need two rectangles – one into which we'll draw the line and one into which we'll draw the line number. To build the rectangle, we'll assume the top edge is aligned with `y` and the bottom edge is aligned with the bottom of the printable area of the page. Imagine a shrinking rectangle moving down the page as we print more lines on it. `lineRectangle` (containing the line number), only needs to be as wide as `lineNumberSize.Width`, while `rectangle` (containing the line), needs to have its left edge aligned with the right edge of `lineRectangle`.

```
RectangleF rectangle =
    new RectangleF(e.MarginBounds.Left +
    lineNumberSize.Width, y,
    e.MarginBounds.Width - lineNumberSize.Width,
    e.MarginBounds.Bottom - y);
RectangleF lineRectangle =
    new RectangleF(e.MarginBounds.Left, y,
    lineNumberSize.Width, e.MarginBounds.Bottom - y);
```

Now that we have the rectangles, we measure the text. If the height of the line is less than `normalLineHeight` (usually meaning that it is a blank line), we adjust the height appropriately:

```
SizeF lineSize = e.Graphics.MeasureString(line, Font, rectangle.Size);
if(lineSize.Height < normalLineHeight)
    lineSize.Height = normalLineHeight;
```

Next we check to see if the line will fit on the page. If it will not, we need to move to a new page. Note that we do not increment the line counter as we have not printed the line. There's an important caveat here – if this is the first line to draw onto the page and it won't fit, we don't want to start a new page. If we do this, we'll set up an infinite loop because every time we try to write the line, it won't fit, so we'll start a new page, and so on. If we need a new page, we set `e.HasMorePages` to true.

```
if(y + lineSize.Height > e.MarginBounds.Bottom && linesOnThisPage > 0)
    e.HasMorePages = true;
else
{
```

If we don't need a new line, we use `DrawString()` to draw the text. We then move `y` down to the y-coordinate of the next line to be printed and increment `linesOnThisPage`:

```
e.Graphics.DrawString(string.Format("{0}:",
    _currentLine + 1), Font, Brushes.Black,
    lineRectangle);
e.Graphics.DrawString(line, Font, Brushes.Black,
    rectangle);

y += lineSize.Height;

linesOnThisPage++;
}
```

If we don't need a new page, we'll move the `_currentLine` index down to the next line. If this is the last line (in which case, `_currentLine` will equal `_lines.Length`), we quit the loop. `HasMorePages` will be `false` at this point and the printing process stops naturally. If `HasMorePages` is `true`, we quit the loop and wait until `OnPrintPage()` is called again to start printing the next page in the list:

```
if(e.HasMorePages == false)
{
    _currentLine++;
    if(_currentLine == _lines.Length)
        break;
}
else
    break;
}
```

Adding a Header

Most reports contain a header of some kind, so let's quickly run through how to add a header to each page of the document.

Adding a header (or footer) is pretty straightforward – you just have to allocate the same amount of space on the document for the details. We're already using `y` to signal where the next line should be drawn onto the report page. Instead of starting `y` at the top of the printable page, we start the header there instead and then start `y` at the bottom of the header. The pagination code that we've already written will handle this eventuality, so everything will continue working fine.

Try It Out – Adding a Header to the Document

1. Make these code changes to the `OnPrintPage()` method on `CodeDocument`. I've omitted some code for brevity:

```
protected override void OnPrintPage(PrintPageEventArgs e)
{
    // anything?
```

```
if(_lines == null)
    return;

// adjust the page number...
_pageNumber += 1;

// format the header text and measure it...
string headerText = string.Format("Page {0}", _pageNumber);
SizeF headerSize = e.Graphics.MeasureString(headerText, Font,
    e.MarginBounds.Width);

// draw on the page number...
e.Graphics.DrawString(headerText, Font, Brushes.Black, e.MarginBounds);

// now, draw the date...
StringFormat alignRightFormat = new StringFormat();
alignRightFormat.Alignment = StringAlignment.Far;
e.Graphics.DrawString(DateTime.Now.ToShortDateString(),
    Font, Brushes.Black, e.MarginBounds, alignRightFormat);

// draw a separation line between the header and the doc body...
float sepLineY = (float)e.MarginBounds.Top +
                 ((float)1.5 * headerSize.Height);
e.Graphics.DrawLine(Pens.Black, e.MarginBounds.Left,
    (int)sepLineY, e.MarginBounds.Right, (int)sepLineY);

// where does the page start...?
float y = e.MarginBounds.Top + (2 * headerSize.Height);

// how big is the line number width?
SizeF lineNumberSize =
    e.Graphics.MeasureString(string.Format("{0}: ",
    _lines.Length), Font, e.MarginBounds.Width);
float normalLineHeight = lineNumberSize.Height;
...
}
```

2. Build and run the project. You'll now find that each page has a header comprising the page number and the current date:

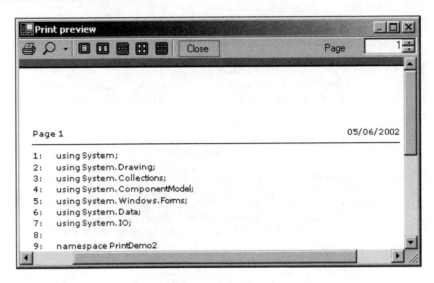

How It Works

All we've done here is add some text to the top of the document. The first bit of text that we draw is the page number:

```
protected override void OnPrintPage(PrintPageEventArgs e)
{
    if(_lines == null)
        return;

    _pageNumber += 1;

    string headerText = string.Format("Page {0}", _pageNumber);
    SizeF headerSize = e.Graphics.MeasureString(headerText, Font,
        e.MarginBounds.Width);

    e.Graphics.DrawString(headerText, Font, Brushes.Black, e.MarginBounds);
```

To draw the date, we want to align the text to the right-hand edge of the page. This is done by constructing a StringFormat object and setting its Alignment property to Far. (This is deliberately non-specific as to left and right edges to accommodate right-to-left reading locales.)

```
StringFormat alignRightFormat = new StringFormat();
alignRightFormat.Alignment = StringAlignment.Far;
e.Graphics.DrawString(DateTime.Now.ToShortDateString(),
    Font, Brushes.Black, e.MarginBounds, alignRightFormat);
```

To divide the header and the report, we add a separation line. We want a complete line of space between the header and the report body, so we draw the line midway between this:

```
float sepLineY = (float)e.MarginBounds.Top +
    ((float)1.5 * headerSize.Height);
e.Graphics.DrawLine(Pens.Black, e.MarginBounds.Left,
    (int)sepLineY, e.MarginBounds.Right, (int)sepLineY);
```

Finally, when we come to write the report body, we start y off below the header line. We use a value of twice the height of the header to add the proper amount of space:

```
float y = e.MarginBounds.Top + (2 * headerSize.Height);
```

Summary

In this chapter, we took a detailed look at how to make your .NET applications print program output to a printer attached to the local computer, or to the network. Luckily for us, Windows and .NET abstracts a lot of the difficulty of this task, making printing to the printer as easy as drawing on the screen. In fact, the same graphics rendering commands are issued irrespective of what we're actually drawing or printing on. In .NET, this abstraction is done through the System.Drawing.Graphics class, as we saw in the previous chapter.

We kicked off by looking at how to use the PrintPreviewDialog and PrintDocument classes to preview an image on the screen. We later added functionality to configure the page settings in terms of paper size and orientation through the PageSettingsDialog class and later learned how to directly print using the PrintDialog class. Rather than using PrintDocument objects directly, we created a new class derived from PrintDocument and rolled in simple helper methods to make common functions more easily accessible.

We then saw how you can inherit from this new class in order to create other new classes that are each intended for handling different types of document to print. For example, although we started off by looking at the example of printing images, most of you will be working on printing reports from your applications. We rounded off the chapter by developing pagination code that enables us to print large documents that span multiple pages.

Linking to a Database

All computer software is in the business of taking some data, manipulating it, and doing something with the results. For example, we might write an application that goes through a list of orders from customers and produces an invoice for each one. Alternatively, we might write an application that listens for keyboard input and moves blocks around on the screen for a puzzle game.

A common requirement for software is the "database". This is a store of data that contains some or all of the data that the software application needs. A database can contain a vast variety of data, from a customer database, to a product catalog, to telephone billing information. Virtually anything can be contained within a database, and database technology today is very well developed.

Think of a database as just a chunk of data sitting on a computer somewhere, and a "database management system" or "DBMS" as a piece of software that you can connect your application to in order to get at the database. Once connected, you can get data back, change data, delete data, or create new data.

> The distinction between a "database" and a "DBMS" is very important. Most marketers refer to a "DBMS" as a "database", but in this chapter we stick to the strict definition above.

In this chapter we're going to look at how to connect to a DBMS from our .NET applications, how to manipulate data in the database from our code, and how to retrieve and display database data.

Database Connectivity in .NET

Database connectivity in Microsoft .NET is the end of a very long road that's had potentially more acronyms associated with it than any other Microsoft strategy. Starting at ODBC, we've had OLE DB, DAO, ADO, UDA, and in Microsoft .NET we have a technology called ADO.NET.

Microsoft has always been very keen on this idea of **unified data access** (UDA). Different vendors write their DBMS solutions in different ways. These differences vary from subtle to grotesque, and what effectively can happen without a good unified solution is that you write your application to talk to "DBMS A" and everything works fine until you try and get your application to talk to "DBMS B".

A unified strategy will allow your customer to use whatever DBMS package they feel will fit with your applications. To do this, Microsoft posited the idea of ODBC – Open Database Connectivity. This was the first step on a road to a unified strategy.

It worked – almost. What developers found was that the promise of a unified strategy where an application would still work fine when the DBMS was switched was largely a fantasy. In fact, in this author's opinion, this is *still* a fantasy. Moving a non-trivial application from one DBMS package to another *should* work, but either way you need to invest considerable time, effort, and money into making sure that it actually *does* work. You'll find that although an application works fine on SQL Server, moving it over to Oracle can break it, even though we're supposed to have an idealized universal data access method. What a unified strategy does give us is the ability to make these kinds of switches in a far more cost-effective manner than we could before.

As we mentioned, the actual evolution from ODBC to the current incarnation – ADO.NET – is largely irrelevant. All you need to know about ADO.NET is that it allows you to connect your application to a DBMS package, and through that connection you can get at and manipulate a database.

The unified data access story has got a little more complex with .NET than it used to be. Previously, Microsoft wanted you to connect to a single "unified layer" and that layer would take care of abstracting the connectivity to whichever DBMS you were trying to use. What Microsoft has finally realized is that this "one size fits all" strategy makes it very hard to take advantage of the specific differences between DBMS packages. What they were trying to do before was go down to the lowest common denominator.

What they have done with ADO.NET is create different "providers". These are like "mini-layers" glued to the main ADO.NET layer. Each of these mini-layers can take advantage of the specific features available in each database. What it means is that you do have to target a specific provider, rather than just a single "one-size-fits-all" ADO.NET API. However, the only thing that's really different between providers is the namespaces used and the names of the classes. Once you learn how to use one of them, adapting your skills for a different provider is very straightforward.

At the time of writing, Microsoft supports providers that can connect directly to Microsoft SQL Server and to Oracle, and also supports providers that can connect to any ODBC and OLE DB data source. COM Interop is required for the ODBC and OLE DB providers.

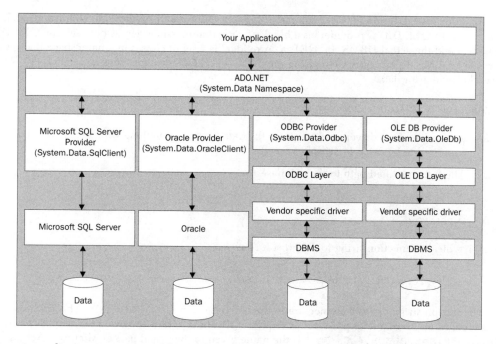

There is no direct connection to Microsoft Access, mainly because Microsoft Access is not a high-performance enterprise (read as "big business" if you're unfamiliar with the term) DBMS in the same way that Microsoft SQL Server and Oracle are. There's no real motivation to create a highly optimized provider for connecting to Microsoft Access, because if you need that level of performance they expect you to move up to Microsoft SQL Server. Therefore, we'll be using the OLE DB provider, implemented in the System.Data.OleDb namespace of ADO.NET, to connect to our database.

Connecting to a Database

To connect to the database, all we have to do is define a "connection string" and pass that connection string over to a new instance of System.Data.OleDb.OleDbConnection. We'll then be able to use that new object to get data back from the database as well as make changes to the database.

A connection string is basically a path to a database – it tells OleDbConnection where to find the DBMS driver that will ultimately manage the connection, and also contains driver-specific information that the driver can use to find the database. It comprises of a number of elements separated by semicolons. In order to connect to a database, the DBMS has to support OLE DB, and your individual DBMS provider will be able to tell you this. The structure of the OLE DB connection string will also vary from provider to provider. However, the first part of the connection string typically gives the name of the OLE DB "provider" that will be used for the database connection.

Note that this OLE DB provider is a separate thing to a .NET data provider, but confusingly shares the same name. In OLE DB, a "provider" is a block of code that marshals access between the OLE DB subsystem and the actual DBMS. In .NET, a "provider" is a set of classes in a namespace that gives access to a DBMS. In our case, we're using the .NET "OLE DB" provider to ask the OLE DB "Microsoft Access" provider for data.

For Microsoft Access, our connection string comprises:

❑ The name of the driver used to access the data (that is, something which tells OLE DB that it's supposed to be using Microsoft Access)

❑ The fully qualified path to the database

❑ A username

❑ A password

Here's a typical connection string for Microsoft Access:

```
Provider=Microsoft.Jet.OLEDB.4.0;Data Source=C:\My.mdb;User ID=;Password=;
```

This connection string opens a connection to the database stored at `C:\My.mdb`. This database is unsecured, so no username or password is required. Also notice how the provider name is given as `Microsoft.Jet.OLEDB.4.0`. "Jet" is the name given to the actual part of Microsoft Access that performs the database management activities. This connection string is in the same format as an ADO connection string.

In the first part of this discussion we're going to look at how we can connect to the database. We're not going to bring any data back, so this won't be terribly exciting. We will use an Open File dialog to allow the user to select the database they want to work with.

Before we begin you will need to make sure that you have the Northwind sample database installed. This comes as part of Microsoft Access, but is not installed by default. If it's not installed, Windows Installer will install it for you.

The sample database is stored in the Samples folder of your Microsoft Office installation folder, so it can typically be found at `C:\Program Files\Microsoft Office\Office\Samples\Northwind.mdb`. Look for the file and, if it isn't there, use Windows Explorer to search for it.

Try It Out – Connecting to a Database

1. Create a new Visual C# Windows Application project, and call the new project CustomerEditor. Change the Text property to Customer Editor.

2. Add a `MainMenu` control to the form, naming it `menuMain`. Click the form and change the `Menu` property to `menuMain`. Click the menu and type in &Data. Now right-click and open the Properties window. In this enter the **Name** property as `menuData`. Then click the box below this menu item, and type &Connect.... Name this child menu item `menuDataConnect`. The form should then look like the following:

3. Now add an `OpenFileDialog` control and set its `Name` property to `dialogOpenFile`.

4. The .NET OLE DB provider is implemented in the `System.Data.OleDb` namespace. Add a reference to this namespace to the code listing for `Form1` (`Form1.cs`).

```
using System;
using System.Drawing;
using System.Collections;
using System.ComponentModel;
using System.Windows.Forms;
using System.Data;
using System.Data.OleDb;

namespace CustomerEditor
{
```

5. Throughout the life of the form, we'll want to hold the current database connection in a field called `_connection`. Add this field to `Form1`:

```
public class Form1 : System.Windows.Forms.Form
{
    // Fields...
    private OleDbConnection _connection;
```

6. Back in the designer select the `MainMenu` control and then double-click on the **Connect...** menu option to add a `Click` event handler. Add this code:

```
private void menuDataConnect_Click(object sender, System.EventArgs e)
{
    Connect();
}
```

7. Add the `Connect()` method. In it we need to show the **Open File** dialog and then create a new database connection based on whatever Microsoft Access file we choose. Add this code:

```
public void Connect()
{
   // Display the dialog...
   if(dialogOpenFile.ShowDialog(this) == DialogResult.OK)
   {
      // Try to connect...
      try
      {
         // Create a new connection string...
         string connectionString = string.Format(
"Provider=Microsoft.Jet.OLEDB.4.0;Data Source={0};User ID=;Password=;",
         dialogOpenFile.FileName);

         // Create a connection...
         OleDbConnection newConnection =
            new OleDbConnection(connectionString);

         // Try and open it...
         newConnection.Open();

         // Store it for use...
         Connection = newConnection;
      }
      catch(Exception ex)
      {
         // Report the problem...
         HandleException("A connection could not be made.", ex);
      }
   }
}
```

8. Also add the `HandleException()` method:

```
public void HandleException(string message, Exception ex)
{
   // Display a message box...
   MessageBox.Show(this, string.Format("{0}\n{1}:{2}",
               message, ex.GetType().ToString(), ex.Message));
}
```

9. Next, add the `Connection` property:

```
public OleDbConnection Connection
{
   get
   {
      return _connection;
```

```
      }
      set
      {
         // Disconnect...
         Disconnect();

         // Set...
         _connection = value;
      }
   }
```

10. Next, add the `Disconnect()` method:

```
public void Disconnect()
{
   // Do we have a connection?
   if(_connection != null)
   {
      // Is it open?
      if(_connection.State != ConnectionState.Closed)
         _connection.Close();

      // Clear it...
      _connection = null;
   }
}
```

11. Finally, find the `Dispose()` method and add a call to `Disconnect`.

```
protected override void Dispose( bool disposing )
{
   // Do we have a connection?
   Disconnect();

   // Standard dispose...
   if( disposing )
   {
      if (components != null)
      {
         components.Dispose();
      }
   }
   base.Dispose( disposing );
}
```

12. Run the project now. If you attempt to open a file that's not an .mdb file, you'll see an exception message like this:

However, if you do open an .mdb file, no message will appear. In a moment, we'll look at how to load data once we've made a connection.

How It Works

We're going to assume that you're familiar with how to work with menus and the Open File dialog, so we'll concentrate here on looking at what happens with the actual database connection code.

After we display the Open File dialog and the user clicks the OK button, we have to construct a new OLE DB connection string that can connect to SQL Server. We'll assume that Provider, User ID, and Password remain the same (in our case, User ID and Password are both blank), and just the Data Source member changes. We'll use string.Format() to insert the full name of the selected file into the string.

```
public void Connect()
{
    ...
        // Create a new connection string...
        string connectionString = string.Format(
"Provider=Microsoft.Jet.OLEDB.4.0;Data Source={0};User ID=;Password=;",
        dialogOpenFile.FileName);
```

Once we have that, we create a new OleDbConnection object and pass in the string to the constructor. At this point, no database communication has been attempted.

```
        // Create a connection...
        OleDbConnection newConnection =
            new OleDbConnection(connectionString);
```

If anything is going to go wrong, it's on this line. If the file cannot be opened for any reason, an exception will be thrown. We can handle that exception and display a message box and then allow the user to try the connection process again. After this point, we can get data from and send data to the database.

```
        // Try to open it...
        newConnection.Open();
```

When the connection has been successfully opened, we set the `Connection` property. This stores the connection for later use.

```
            // Store it for use...
            Connection = newConnection;
        }
        catch(Exception ex)
        {
            // Report the problem...
            HandleException("A connection could not be made.", ex);
        }
    }
}
```

Let's look at the `Connection` property now. This property is used whenever we need to instruct `Form1` to use a different connection. If we do this, though, we have to close the connection. Closing the connection is *very* important when working with databases. Databases only support a limited number of open connections at any one time. When you've finished using the connection, you have to tell the connection object explicitly to close the connection. This makes the connection available to other applications that need access to the database. Relying on the garbage collection to close the connection is not sufficient – garbage collection will close it (usually – it may not run on application exit, though the connection will be closed) eventually but before that happens you could be using many needed resources.

> **This is very sound programming practice, and you should always take care to make sure that any resources you use, including database connections, are properly closed when you've finished using them.**

The `Connection` property then just abstracts access to the `_connection` field. When this property is set, we call `Disconnect` first.

```
    public OleDbConnection Connection
    {
        get
        {
            return _connection;
        }
        set
        {
            // Disconnect...
            Disconnect();

            // Set...
            _connection = value;
        }
    }
```

A connection object like `OleDbConnection` can be in a number of "states". If you look in the MSDN documentation, you'll discover that six separate connection states are defined. However, at the time of writing, just two are implemented: `Open` and `Closed`. On using the `Disconnect()` method, we check the connection object's `ConnectionState` property and if it reports that the connection is open, we close it.

```
public void Disconnect()
{
    // Do we have a connection?
    if(_connection != null)
    {
        // Is it open?
        if(_connection.State != ConnectionState.Closed)
            _connection.Close();

        // Clear it...
        _connection = null;
    }
}
```

Finally, to round off this design pattern, you'll recall that we added a `Disconnect` call to the `Dispose()` method. The Framework calls `Dispose()` when the form is no longer needed. As the form is no longer needed, we'll assume that the connection is no longer needed either and so we use the common `Disconnect()` function to get rid of it and make the connection available to other applications.

Loading and Displaying Data

We've seen a simple design pattern to provide for opening and closing a database connection. Now we can look at how to load and display data.

We're going to be loading and displaying "customer" information in this section. In the Northwind database, this information is stored in the `Customers` table. Use Microsoft Access to take a look at this table and you'll see a basic grid of information.

Customer ID	Company Name	Contact Name	Contact Title	Address
ALFKI	Alfreds Futterkiste	Maria Anders	Sales Representative	Obere Str. 57
ANATR	Ana Trujillo Emparedados y helados	Ana Trujillo	Owner	Avda. de la Constitución 2222
ANTON	Antonio Moreno Taquería	Antonio Moreno	Owner	Mataderos 2312
AROUT	Around the Horn	Thomas Hardy	Sales Representative	120 Hanover Sq.
BERGS	Berglunds snabbköp	Christina Berglund	Order Administrator	Berguvsvägen 8
BLAUS	Blauer See Delikatessen	Hanna Moos	Sales Representative	Forsterstr. 57
BLONP	Blondel père et fils	Frédérique Citeaux	Marketing Manager	24, place Kléber
BOLID	Bólido Comidas preparadas	Martín Sommer	Owner	C/ Araquil, 67
BONAP	Bon app'	Laurence Lebihan	Owner	12, rue des Bouchers
BOTTM	Bottom-Dollar Markets	Elizabeth Lincoln	Accounting Manager	23 Tsawassen Blvd.
BSBEV	B's Beverages	Victoria Ashworth	Sales Representative	Fauntleroy Circus

This kind of table layout is a very common thing to find when working with databases, mainly because modern relational database systems work in terms of rows and columns like this. Each row represents a customer, and each column tells us something about that customer.

Using DataGrids, DataSets and DataAdapters

What we can do relatively quickly from this point is get a view very similar to that in our application. The .NET Framework provides a class called System.Windows.Forms.DataGrid, which as its name suggests displays data in a grid. All we need to do is load all of the rows and columns from the Customers table and pass it to a DataGrid to display.

The architects of ADO.NET created the DataSet (implemented in System.Data.DataSet) as a kind of base currency for moving data from the DBMS to your application and from your application back to the DBMS (although, technically, the DataSet is a great general-purpose device for moving data from one application to another). The DataSet is just a big bucket into which you can pour tables of data – providing that those tables are structured into the classic row/column metaphor that we've already introduced.

In terms of classes:

❑   A DataSet contains a collection of tables stored in System.Data.DataTable objects. This table collection is accessed through the DataSet class' Tables property.

❑   A DataTable contains a collection of column definitions (that is, name, size, data type, and so on) as a collection of System.Data.DataColumn objects. This collection is accessed through the DataTable class' Columns property. This is simply schema information – no actual data from the database table is stored here.

❑   A DataTable also contains a collection of rows, and it's this that contains the actual data. These are stored as a collection of System.Data.DataRow objects, accessed through the DataTable class' Rows property.

A DataSet can contain multiple DataTable objects, each one containing a discrete set of data. The DataSet adds a further layer of flexibility by being able to contain DataTable objects constructed from a number of sources. We can use one or more databases at the same time, we can load an XML file into a DataTable, we can create one programmatically, or we can use third-party class libraries to get data from some other data source and build a DataTable from it.

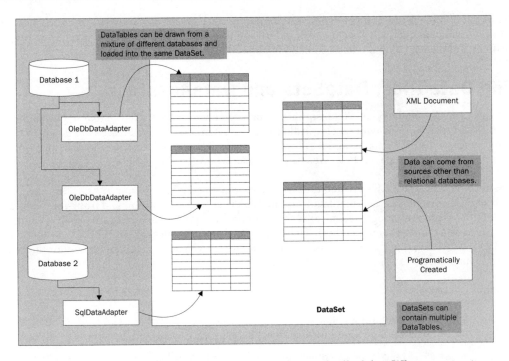

The DataGrid class encapsulates functionality that understands all of this. When we give it a DataSet through its DataSource property, it understands how to iterate through the tables, then iterate through the rows of the table and then iterate through the columns of the table in order to construct the view of customer data.

Finally, to get data from our connection into a DataSet, we have to use an adapter class, which for OLE DB connection is OleDbDataAdapter. Essentially, the adapter is used to hold SQL commands (represented by the wrapper OleDbCommand class) that we can use to manipulate the contents of the database. We fill the DataSet with data from the database by calling the Fill() method on the adapter.

There are three main types of command we use with an adapter:

❑   TableDirect – we give it the name of a table and it assumes that we want all of the data from that table

❑   Text – a SQL command string (more later)

❑   StoredProcedure – a special kind of SQL command

To create an OleDbCommand object, we call the CreateCommand() method on the connection object. We can set the type of command to TableDirect or Text through the CommandType property of the OleDbCommand class. We can also set the text contained in the OleDbCommand itself, by specifying a value for the CommandText property.

Let's now make use of these classes to load and display data from our database in a DataGrid.

Try It Out – Loading Customer Data

1. To the Designer of `Form1` add a `DataGrid` control.

2. Set the `Name` property of this control to `datagridCustomers` and also set the `Dock` property to `Fill`. This will make the control fill all of the available space on the form.

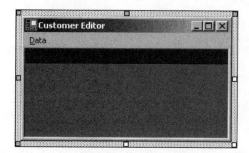

3. To the Data menu, add a new option called **&Load**. Set its `Name` property to `menuDataLoad`.

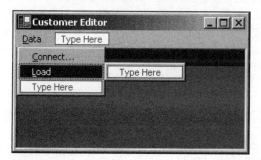

4. Double-click on the **Load** menu option to create a new `Click` event handler. Add this code:

```
private void menuDataLoad_Click(object sender, System.EventArgs e)
{
    LoadData();
}
```

5. Next add this method:

```
public void LoadData()
{
    // Do we have a connection?
    if(_connection == null)
    {
        MessageBox.Show(this, "You must connect to a database.");
        return;
    }
```

```
// Setup...
OleDbCommand command = null;
OleDbDataAdapter adapter = null;
try
{
    // Create a command...
    command = _connection.CreateCommand();

    // Configure the command...
    command.CommandText = "Customers";
    command.CommandType = CommandType.TableDirect;

    // Create an adapter...
    adapter = new OleDbDataAdapter(command);

    // Create and fill a dataset...
    DataSet dataset = new DataSet();
    adapter.Fill(dataset);

    // Show the dataset...
    dataGridCustomers.DataSource = dataset;
}
catch(Exception ex)
{
    // Report the problem...
    HandleException("The data could not be loaded.", ex);
}
finally
{
    // Cleanup...
    if(adapter != null)
        adapter.Dispose();
    if(command != null)
        command.Dispose();
}
}
```

6. Run the project now and connect to the Northwind database. Once connected, select Data | Load and you'll see this:

Click on the little + button, and you'll see this:

Now click the Table link and you'll see the customer data.

	CustomerID	CompanyName	ContactName	ContactTitle	Address	City	
▶	ALFKI	Alfreds Futterkiste	Maria Anders	Sales Representative	Obere Str. 57	Berlin	
	ANATR	Ana Trujillo Emparedados y helados	Ana Trujillo	Owner	Avda. de la Constitución 2222	México D.F.	
	ANTON	Antonio Moreno Taquería	Antonio Moreno	Owner	Mataderos 2312	México D.F.	
	AROUT	Around the Horn	Thomas Hardy	Sales Representative	120 Hanover Sq.	London	
	BERGS	Berglunds snabbköp	Christina Berglund	Order Administrator	Berguvsvägen 8	Luleå	
	BLAUS	Blauer See Delikatessen	Hanna Moos	Sales Representative	Forsterstr. 57	Mannheim	
	BLONP	Blondel père et fils	Frédérique Citeaux	Marketing Manager	24, place Kléber	Strasbourg	
	BOLID	Bólido Comidas preparadas	Martín Sommer	Owner	C/ Araquil, 67	Madrid	
	BONAP	Bon app'	Laurence Lebihan	Owner	12, rue des Bouchers	Marseille	
	BOTTM	Bottom-Dollar Markets	Elizabeth Lincoln	Accounting Manager	23 Tsawassen Blvd.	Tsawassen	

How It Works

In our code, we're just adding a single `DataTable` to a `DataSet` using an `OleDbDataAdapter`. To use an adapter, we need a command. In our case, we're using `TableDirect`. We ask the connection to give us a new command, give it the table that we want and then pass that new command to a new `OleDbDataAdapter`.

```
public void LoadData()
{
    ...

    // Setup...
    OleDbCommand command = null;
    OleDbDataAdapter adapter = null;
    try
    {
        // Create a command...
        command = Connection.CreateCommand();

        // Configure the command...
        command.CommandText = "Customers";
        command.CommandType = CommandType.TableDirect;
```

```
        // Create an adapter...
        adapter = new OleDbDataAdapter(command);
```

At this point, the adapter is configured and knows which database it's connected to (through the connection), and what data it's supposed to be getting back (through the command). We can now create a new `DataSet` and fill it with data.

```
        // Create and fill a dataset...
        DataSet dataset = new DataSet();
        adapter.Fill(dataset);

        // Show the dataset...
        datagridCustomers.DataSource = dataset;
    }
    catch(Exception ex)
    {
        // Report the problem...
        HandleException("The data could not be loaded.", ex);
    }
    finally
    {
```

When we've finished populating the `DataGrid`, we need to clean up our resources. This means disposing of the adapter and the command, as we do here. We do this in a `finally` block so that this happens if an exception is thrown, or if the method exits properly.

```
        // Cleanup...
        if(adapter != null)
          adapter.Dispose();
        if(command != null)
          command.Dispose();
    }
}
```

If you recall the image that we got when we first clicked the little plus button on the newly populated `DataGrid`, we saw this:

This list is actually a list of tables contained in the `DataSet`. As we only have one table loaded, we only get one item. Obviously, if we had more tables here, we'd see a bigger list.

Modifying the Database

Now that we can load data into the application, let's see how we can edit that data and save changes back.

Not surprisingly, the `DataGrid` does support editing of the data (providing that its `ReadOnly` property is set to `False`, which it is by default). Therefore, we don't have to do any clever user interface tricks to get that part working. What we do have to do, though, is handle moving the data from the user interface back to the database.

So far, the work that `OleDbDataAdapter` does under the hood has largely been abstracted. What's happening when we create one of these commands and configure it to get all of the data from the table is that it builds a SQL command (represented by the `OleDbCommand` class). This command is used to select rows from the target table – and in this case, we're selecting "all rows from the `Customers` table".

To change existing rows, delete rows, or insert new rows, we have to construct different commands. In fact, we have to construct UPDATE, DELETE, and INSERT commands and make all of these available to `OleDbCommand`. Or rather "we" don't have to do anything – we can ask a class called `OleDbCommandBuilder` to do this for us. We pass an instance of an `OleDbDataAdapter` object to the constructor of this class, and this action binds the adapter to the command builder. When bound to an `OleDbDataAdapter`, the builder will examine the SELECT command and infer new UPDATE, DELETE, and INSERT commands automatically. Finally, to execute the command in the database, we call the `Update()` method on the adapter.

Let's show you how this works in practice through our sample application.

Try It Out – Saving Changes to the Database

1. To the Designer of `Form1`, add a new menu item called **&Save Changes**. Set its `Name` property to `menuDataSaveChanges`.

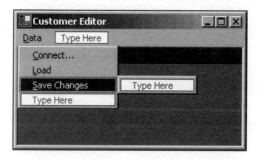

203

2. Double-click on the new menu item to create a `Click` event handler. Add this code:

```
private void menuDataSaveChanges_Click(object sender, System.EventArgs e)
{
  SaveChanges();
}
```

3. Next, add the `SaveChanges()` method:

```
public void SaveChanges()
{
  // Do we have a Connection?
  if(_connection == null)
  {
    MessageBox.Show("You must connect to a database.");
    return;
  }

  // Get the dataset...
  DataSet dataset = (DataSet)dataGridCustomers.DataSource;
  if(dataset == null)
  {
    MessageBox.Show("You must load a DataSet.");
    return;
  }

  // Create...
  OleDbCommand command = null;
  OleDbDataAdapter adapter = null;
  try
  {
    // Create the command...
    command = _connection.CreateCommand();

    // Populate...
    command.CommandText = "Customers";
    command.CommandType = CommandType.TableDirect;

    // Create an adapter...
    adapter = new OleDbDataAdapter(command);

    // Now, create a command builder...
    OleDbCommandBuilder builder = new OleDbCommandBuilder(adapter);

    // Update...
    adapter.Update(dataset);

    // Tell the user...
    MessageBox.Show("Changes have been saved.");
  }
  finally
```

```
    {
       // Cleanup...
       if(adapter != null)
          adapter.Dispose();
       if(command != null)
          command.Dispose();
    }
  }
```

To test this out, run the project, connect to the database, and load the customers. Now open Access and look at the Customers table. In this example, we're going to change the Contact Name of Alfreds Futterkist from Maria Anders to Darren Clarke. Here's the original data:

Here's the same data loaded into our editor:

As we edit the information, notice how the icon in the left-margin of the DataGrid control turns from an arrowhead into a pencil:

After changing the information, flip back to Microsoft Access. Notice how the information has not changed. That's because although we've changed the in-memory copy of the data in our application, we haven't committed the changes back to the database. To do this, select Data | Save Changes from the menu.

Now if you flip back to Access, you'll notice that the information has changed there too. That's because Access listens for changes to the data and automatically updates its own view of the data if and when the data changes.

Customer ID	Company Name	Contact Name	Contact Title	Address
ALFKI	Alfreds Futterkiste	Darren Clarke	Sales Representative	Obere Str. 57
ANATR	Ana Trujillo Emparedados y helados	Ana Trujillo	Owner	Avda. de la Constitución 2222
ANTON	Antonio Moreno Taquería	Antonio Moreno	Owner	Mataderos 2312
AROUT	Around the Horn	Thomas Hardy	Sales Representative	120 Hanover Sq.

Record: 1 of 91

How It Works

Let's start by looking at the `SaveChanges()` method. Here we create an adapter, and populate it with a `TableDirect` command:

```
public void SaveChanges()
{
    // Do we have a Connection?
    ...

    // Get the dataset...
    ...

    // Create...
    OleDbCommand command = null;
    OleDbDataAdapter adapter = null;
    try
    {
        // Create the command...
        command = _connection.CreateCommand();

        // Populate...
        command.CommandText = "Customers";
        command.CommandType = CommandType.TableDirect;

        // Create an adapter...
        adapter = new OleDbDataAdapter(command);

        // Now, create a command builder...
        OleDbCommandBuilder builder = new OleDbCommandBuilder(adapter);
```

Then we create the new `OleDbCommandBuilder`, and we pass in the adapter as a parameter to the constructor. It's this action that binds the two together.

When we have a properly configured adapter and command builder, we call `Update()` and pass in the `DataSet`. This is the same `DataSet` that's been edited by the `DataGrid` control.

```
        // Update...
        adapter.Update(dataset);

        // Tell the user...
        MessageBox.Show("Changes have been saved.");
    }
    finally
    {
```

Of course, as before when we've finished using the adapter and the command, we need to clean up their resources using `Dispose()`.

You may be wondering why we've created the command and the adapter twice. It would seem logical to keep both of these in memory in the same way that we keep the connection in memory.

In fact, this may not be such a smart plan. Just like a DBMS has a limited number of connections available, a DBMS also has a limited number of *commands* available. By keeping commands open in memory (which is exactly what we would be doing if we held the command used in `LoadData()` in a field for use in `SaveChanges()`), we're hogging the capacity of the database for our own purposes.

In some cases, this might be acceptable. Like most things, you're looking at a tradeoff. By not keeping the command in memory, you're making `SaveChanges()` do more work – that is, creating the command in the database again. It might be that you have an application where a method like `SaveChanges()` is being called a lot. In this case, it might actually be better to keep the command around in memory to make this routine more efficient. In our situation here, a few extra milliseconds to establish the command again seems to be worth it.

Because connecting to a database is a very common operation, ADO.NET implements connection pooling. This means that ADO.NET creates a number of instances of connection objects, and gives us one of these when we need one. When a connection is "closed" by calling the `Close()` method, what actually happens is that the connection object is disassociated with that particular database connection, but the connection object instance is not destroyed, and becomes available to connect to another database. This saves on the overhead of continually creating new connection object instances and then destroying them.

Relationships Between Tables

One thing we haven't looked at so far is the relationships between data in tables. If you look at the `Customers` table in Access, you'll notice that there is a little plus (+) sign on the left margin of the table view against every row. If we click this button, we can drill down and see the orders against the particular customer. This information is drawn from the **Orders** table:

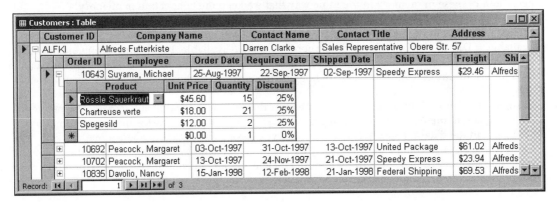

In fact, each order also has a plus button, we can drill down again to see the products that were included as part of the order. This further data has been drawn from the Order Details table:

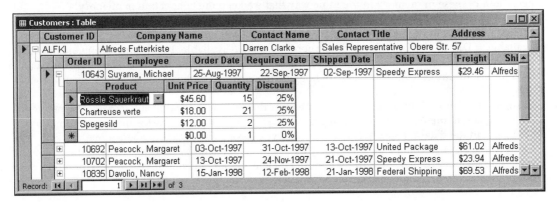

Being able to get at this sort of information in our application would be very useful. What we need to do is create three separate adapters and create three separate tables inside the DataSet. All we need to do then is tweak the DataSet slightly to define the relationships between the three tables and then pass it over to the DataGrid control to display.

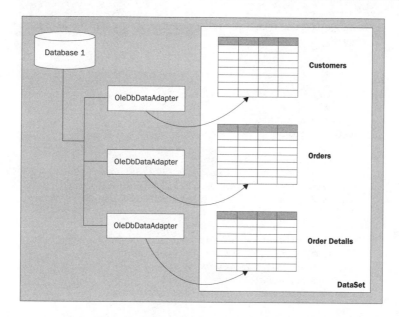

Relationships between tables are defined using DataRelation objects. These are constructed by providing a name and a list of columns from the parent table and a list of columns from the child tables that define the relationship. (In our case, because the tables are keyed from a single ID column, we only need to provide a column and not a list of columns.) To find the columns, we only need to know the name. The DataTable exposes a collection of DataColumn objects through the Columns property. This collection is indexed through either an integer ordinal (0 for the first column, 1 for the second column, and so on), or by the name of the column.

Therefore, to add relationships between tables, all we have to do is identify the column on each table that defines the relationship, and then tell the DataSet about it by adding a new DataRelation object to its Relations collection using the Add() method.

In our database, the CustomerID column defines the relationship between Customers and Orders. Both tables contain a CustomerID column. Searching through the Orders table for a given CustomerID yields just those orders that "relate" to the specified customer. Likewise, the OrderID column defines the relationship between Orders and Order Details. Searching through Order Details for a given OrderID yields the details for a given order.

Try It Out – Adding Relationships Between Tables

1. For this exercise, we're going to rewrite the LoadData() method. Find the method and replace it with this new implementation:

```
public void LoadData()
{
    // Do we have a connection?
    if(_connection == null)
    {
```

```
        MessageBox.Show(this, "You must connect to a database.");
        return;
    }
```

```
    // Setup...
    try
    {
        // Create a dataset...
        DataSet dataset = new DataSet();

        // Create and fill the tables...
        DataTable customers = CreateAndFill(dataset, "Customers");
        DataTable orders = CreateAndFill(dataset, "Orders");
        DataTable orderDetails = CreateAndFill(dataset, "Order Details");

        // Establish customers/orders relationship...
        DataRelation customersToOrders =
            new DataRelation("OrdersForCustomers",
            customers.Columns["CustomerID"],
            orders.Columns["CustomerID"]);
        dataset.Relations.Add(customersToOrders);

        // Establish orders/order details relationship...
        DataRelation ordersToOrderDetails =
            new DataRelation("OrderDetailsForOrder",
            orders.Columns["OrderID"],
            orderDetails.Columns["OrderID"]);
        dataset.Relations.Add(ordersToOrderDetails);

        // Show the dataset...
        dataGridCustomers.DataSource = dataset;
        dataGridCustomers.DataMember = customers.TableName;
    }
    catch(Exception ex)
    {
        // Report the problem...
        HandleException("The data could not be loaded.", ex);
    }
}
```

2. To make this method work, we need to build `CreateAndFill()`. Add this method to the code:

```
protected DataTable CreateAndFill(DataSet dataset, string tableName)
{
    // Create the new table...
    DataTable table = new DataTable(tableName);

    // Add it to the dataset...
    dataset.Tables.Add(table);

    // Fill the table...
```

```
        Fill(table);

        // Return the table...
        return table;
    }
```

3. Next, add the `Fill()` method that this method uses:

```
    protected void Fill(DataTable table)
    {
        // Set up command and adapter...
        OleDbCommand command = null;
        OleDbDataAdapter adapter = null;
        try
        {
            // Create the command...
            command = Connection.CreateCommand();
            command.CommandText = table.TableName;
            command.CommandType = CommandType.TableDirect;

            // Create an adapter...
            adapter = new OleDbDataAdapter(command);

            // Fill...
            adapter.Fill(table);
        }
        finally
        {
            if(adapter != null)
                adapter.Dispose();
            if(command != null)
                command.Dispose();
        }
    }
```

4. We now need to fix the `SaveChanges()` method. If we don't do anything then nothing will happen when we try to save. Alter the following line in the `SaveChanges()` method:

```
        // Update...
        adapter.Update(dataset.Tables["Customers"]);
```

5. Run the project and load the data. The first thing you'll notice is that the Customers table is displayed straight away. You'll also notice plus signs next to each row. Click one and you'll get a list of relationships – although in this case we just have one relationship defined.

If you click on this relationship, you'll get a list of the orders specifically related to Alfreds Futterkiste.

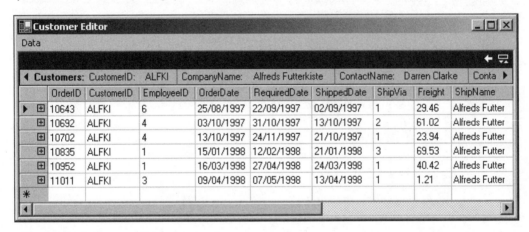

We personally find it a bit of a shame that the DataGrid control doesn't employ the "embedded table" metaphor used in Access. You'll notice however that the customer details for the row is displayed above the order data, and that every row in the CustomerID column is set to ALFKI, the ID of Alfreds Futterkiste.

You can further drill into the details for each order by using the plus button again and clicking on the relationship.

One thing you'll notice is that in Access, the actual name of the product is displayed, whereas here we're just seeing the ID of the product. We'll look at this problem in a moment but for now let's take a look at how this works.

How It Works

Let's start with the `LoadData()` method. As we mentioned before, the trick here is to create three separate tables inside the `DataSet`. We're using a helper method called `CreateAndFill()` to do this.

```
try
{
    // Create a dataset...
    DataSet dataset = new DataSet();

    // Create and fill the tables...
    DataTable customers = CreateAndFill(dataset, "Customers");
    DataTable orders = CreateAndFill(dataset, "Orders");
    DataTable orderDetails = CreateAndFill(dataset, "Order Details");
```

The `CreateAndFill()` method takes the `DataSet` and the name of the target table. It creates the new `DataTable` object, adds it to the `DataSet` and then hands it over to `Fill()`, where it will be filled with data. This is very similar to what the adapter was doing before. If you recall, we gave it a new `DataSet` object and it automatically created and added a new table to it. Here, because we need multiple tables, and because we need those tables to have a specific name (it was called `Table` before, but we want ours to be named as `Customers`, `Orders`, and `Order Details`), we do this manually.

Next we create `DataRelation` objects that represent the relationships between data columns:

```
    // Establish customers/orders relationship...
    DataRelation customersToOrders =
        new DataRelation("OrdersForCustomers",
        customers.Columns["CustomerID"],
        orders.Columns["CustomerID"]);
    dataset.Relations.Add(customersToOrders);
```

```
// Establish orders/order details relationship...
DataRelation ordersToOrderDetails =
    new DataRelation("OrderDetailsForOrder",
    orders.Columns["OrderID"],
    orderDetails.Columns["OrderID"]);
dataset.Relations.Add(ordersToOrderDetails);
```

Note how we use the Add() method to add the DataRelation to the Relations collection of the DataSet. Then we hand the new DataSet over to the DataGrid control for presentation:

```
dataGridCustomers.DataSource = dataset;
dataGridCustomers.DataMember = customers.TableName;
```

One thing that's worth noting is that we make a tweak to display the **Customers** table first, rather than relying on the user to select the **Customers** table when the data was loaded. We do this by setting the DataMember property of the DataGrid control to the name of the table that we wanted to load – in this case, Customers.

The Fill() method is just a generic version of the method we wrote in the original version of LoadData(). Rather than using a specific name for the target table, we use the TableName property of the supplied DataTable. The parameter we passed to the constructor of each DataTable populates this property:

```
try
{
    // Create the command...
    command = Connection.CreateCommand();
    command.CommandText = table.TableName;
    command.CommandType = CommandType.TableDirect;

    // Create an adapter...
    adapter = new OleDbDataAdapter(command);

    // Fill...
    adapter.Fill(table);
}
```

So, that's all we need to do in order to load the three tables in the DataSet. All we need to do now is establish relationships between them to get close to the functionality available in Access.

The Tables property provides access to the collection of DataTable objects that the DataSet is holding. We can select out the table we want by name through the indexer to this collection.

```
// Update...
adapter.Update(dataset.Tables["Customers"]);
```

This fixes the `SaveChanges()` method. Basically, when we wrote this method it just passed the entire `DataSet` over to the `Update()` method of the adapter. If we don't specifically specify a table, this method will walk through all of the tables looking for ones that need updating. As the adapter only understands how to update the Customers table, if the Orders table changes, the adapter won't be able to do the update and nothing will happen.

The `Tables` property of the `DataSet` provides access to a collection of `DataTable` objects. We can use this to specifically pass in the stored `Customers` table.

Using Custom Queries

What we want to look at now is how to solve the issue that if we look at details for an order, we don't get very helpful information. Unless the user has committed the entire product database to memory, "ProductID 28" isn't going to be as helpful as "Rössle Sauerkraut".

With Access, we can define "queries" simply as a predefined way of getting data from the database. For example, if we want to find the name of a product when we have an ID, we need to take the `ProductID` from Order Details and take it over to the Products table to find what it relates to and from there we can get the name of the product. All we have to do then is define a query that does this for us automatically.

In Access, tables and queries are interchangeable. This means that we can give `CreateAndFill()` the name of a query rather than the name of a table.

> **In other DBMSs (like SQL Server), you may find that "queries" are called "views", for example.**

Northwind defines a query called Order Details Extended. If you look at the Northwind Database window, and select Queries from the list on the left, you'll be able to find it.

Double-click on this query and you'll see a view containing the data. Frustratingly, Access tries to be really helpful at this point and won't display the ID of the product. Where you see the names of the products under the Product column, in our application this will actually be shown as a list of IDs.

Order ID	Product	Product Name	Unit Price	Quantity	Discount	Extended Price
10248	Queso Cabrales	Queso Cabrales	$14.00	12	0%	$168.00
10248	Singaporean Hokkien Fried Mee	Singaporean Hokkien Fried Mee	$9.80	10	0%	$98.00
10248	Mozzarella di Giovanni	Mozzarella di Giovanni	$34.80	5	0%	$174.00
10249	Manjimup Dried Apples	Manjimup Dried Apples	$42.40	40	0%	$1,696.00
10249	Tofu	Tofu	$18.60	9	0%	$167.40
10250	Manjimup Dried Apples	Manjimup Dried Apples	$42.40	35	15%	$1,261.40

Record: 1 of 2155

You'll also notice that the last column, Extended Price, is a calculated column. What's happening here is that Access is taking the unit price for each line, multiplying it by the quantity and applying a discount percentage. All very helpful information!

> **Access does give us the ability to create our own queries. However, this activity is beyond the scope of this book. There's lots of information on how to do this in the Microsoft Access documentation.**

Let's now use the Order Details Extended query in our sample application.

Try It Out – Using a Custom Query

1. To use the Order Details Extended query in our application, we just need to pass the name Order Details Extended to CreateAndFill() rather than Order Details:

```
public void LoadData()
{
  // Do we have a connection?
  if(_connection == null)
  {
    MessageBox.Show(this, "You must connect to a database.");
    return;
  }

  // Setup...
  try
  {
    // Create a dataset...
    DataSet dataset = new DataSet();

    // Create and fill the tables...
    DataTable customers = CreateAndFill(dataset, "Customers");
    DataTable orders = CreateAndFill(dataset, "Orders");
    DataTable orderDetails = CreateAndFill(dataset, "Order Details Extended");

    // Establish customers/orders relationship...
```

```
    ...
    }
    catch(Exception ex)
    {
        // Report the problem...
        HandleException("The data could not be loaded.", ex);
    }
}
```

2. Run the project and you'll see that the new information is available in our application:

OrderID	ProductID	ProductName	UnitPrice	Quantity	Discount	ExtendedPrice
10643	39	Chartreuse verte	18	21	0.25	283.5
10643	46	Spegesild	12	2	0.25	18
10643	28	Rössle Sauerkraut	45.6	15	0.25	513

(Customer Editor window — Data menu. Customers: CustomerID: ALFKI, CompanyName: Alfreds Futterkiste, ContactName: Darren Clarke. Orders: OrderID: 10643, CustomerID: ALFKI, EmployeeID: 6.)

How It Works

As we mentioned before, Access tables and queries are *equivalent*. This means that we can select information from a query using the same code that was once selecting information from a table. By changing the name of the table used with the `orderDetails` from `Order Details` to `Order Details Extended`, we told Access that we want information from the query and not from the view.

Summary

In this chapter, we looked at how we can connect an application to a database. We started off by learning about Microsoft's ongoing development of unified data access technologies. Today, with Microsoft .NET, we use ADO.NET to connect to our databases to retrieve and to change data.

Our first example examined how we could access the Customers table from the Northwind sample database and display it using the .NET Framework's `DataGrid` control. We then adapted this example to include editing of the data and saving of any changes back to the Access database.

In the second half of the chapter, we look at how we could define relationships between a number of tables loaded from the Northwind database, and how the `DataGrid` would automatically give the user interface widgets to manipulate the view to see the underlying data in a drill-down fashion.

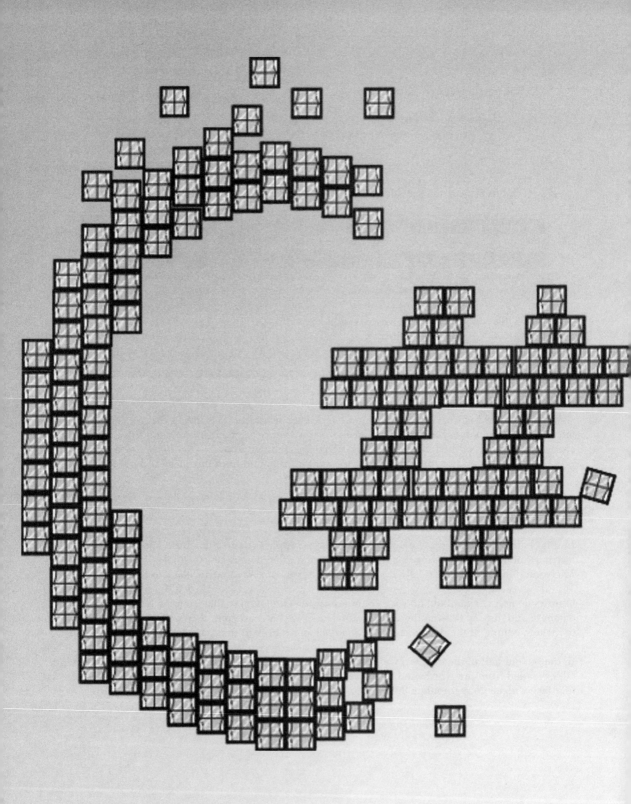

File and Registry Operations

In the previous chapter we discussed how to store data in a database. In this chapter we will look at two alternative places to store data: the file system and the Registry. You should consider using a file system to store data instead of a database in the following scenarios:

- ❏ For loading or storing large singular documents containing lots of information. This includes text documents, images, audio, video, spreadsheets, and design models.

- ❏ For loading or storing executables, assemblies, HTML, ASP and other programming-related files.

- ❏ For importing and exporting data between disparate systems or applications. You may use the import/export solution to move data between different data systems, or you may simply use a data file as a container when transferring data from one place to another.

Likewise, the Registry is often used to store application configuration data. Since different users have access to different parts of the Registry, it is a convenient place to store user preferences, for example.

In this chapter we have divided the file and Registry discussion into four sections. First we will explore the classes used to read and write data, especially text, to the file system. To round off that discussion we will create a simple text editor.

Then we will take a step back and look at how we can navigate the file system. As an example we will create an application that allows the user to investigate and browse the complete directory tree of a machine.

In the third section of this chapter we will discuss **serialization** – the act of storing the state of the application's objects to a file. We will demonstrate how to serialize object state into XML. Finally, we will take a look at the Registry. We will discuss how the Registry is structured, and which classes can be used to access it. We will show how to store and retrieve a user setting. So, let's start by considering how we can read and write data to file from our Windows applications.

Reading and Writing Files

Reading and writing to files is performed via a number of classes that support the concept of a data stream. So what is a "stream"?

Streams

To move data across a network or between files, the data must be streamed; in other words, packets of data are passed sequentially from one data store to another. Therefore, a **stream** is essentially a flow of data.

In .NET, the concept of a stream is abstracted into several classes. The (abstract) base class for all stream classes is the Stream class in the System.IO namespace. The .NET Framework provides concrete classes derived from Stream that allow you to stream across files, networks, and sockets. We can stream encrypted data, and we can **buffer** the stream too.

Buffering Stream Data

When a stream is buffered, the data directed to the stream is first passed to an area of memory known as a buffer. When the buffer is filled with data, it is **flushed**; in other words, the contents of the buffer are streamed to the destination of the stream. Then the buffer is gradually filled with data again until it is flushed again. This cycle continues until there is no more data to be passed to the stream.

The advantage of the buffered approach to streaming is that the source and destination of the stream do not have to be connected throughout the streaming process: the connection only needs to be available each time the buffer is flushed. Since maintaining connections is a resource-intensive activity, buffering can improve the performance of a system.

Stream Classes

A summary of the stream classes available to us is shown in the table below:

Class	Description
FileStream	This is the class used for reading and writing data to a file (especially binary data), and it offers additional functions to open, search, and close files on disk.
NetworkStream	This class (in the System.Net.Sockets namespace) allows you to access a TCP/IP socket.
MemoryStream	This class allows you to create an expandable area of memory which you can access using the stream's methods. It also lets you treat a pre-allocated area of memory as a stream.
BufferedStream	This is a utility class that can be used to add buffering to a stream, if it does not already have a buffer.
CryptoStream	This utility class, in the System.Security.Cryptography namespace, will encrypt or decrypt information that is sent through it.

Since we are only interested in file handling and the Registry in this chapter, the only one of these classes that we will look at more closely is the FileStream class. However, there are several points that you should note about stream objects in general:

❑ If you have a program that accesses files through a Stream object, you can easily modify the program to write over the network or to an in-memory file, simply by choosing a NetworkStream or a MemoryStream as the interface to the data source.

❑ You can put stream objects in series. For example, if you insert a CryptoStream in front of a FileStream, all of the text you read and write from or to a file will be encrypted. You can also use the BufferedStream class in conjunction with another stream class. This technique is generally referred to as wrapping one stream around another.

The FileStream Class

As we noted in the previous section, the FileStream class is mainly used to read and write binary data to and from files. Therefore, the first step to reading or writing binary data is to instantiate a FileStream object.

Creating a FileStream Object

To construct a FileStream using its constructor you must supply two or more of the following parameters.

Parameter	Description
String *path*	The name (and path) of the file you want to access.
FileMode *mode*	Specifies how an existing file should be opened, or how a new file should be created. Values for FileMode are listed in the table below.
FileAccess *access*	Specifies access privileges for the file. Options include Read (read-only), Write (write-only) and ReadWrite (both read and write access, which is the default).
FileShare *share*	Specifies how much access you want to give other processes to the file you are working on. Values include None, Read (which is the default), Write, and ReadWrite.
int *bufferSize*	Specifies the required buffer size. Normally you can just keep the default setting, which is 4096 bytes.

You should note that there are actually more parameters available to us than this, but those described above are the most commonly used. A complete description of all FileStream properties and methods is available in the Visual Studio help files, or online at http://msdn.microsoft.com.

The `FileMode` enumeration, which specifies how the file should be opened, can take the following values:

FileMode Value	Description
Append	Opens the file if it exists and seeks to the end of the file, or creates a new file.
Create	Creates a new file. If the file already exists, it will be overwritten.
CreateNew	Creates a new file. If the file already exists, an `IOException` will be thrown.
Open	Opens an existing file. If the file does not exist, a `FileNotFoundException` will be thrown.
OpenOrCreate	Opens a file. If the file does not exist, a new file will be created.
Truncate	Opens an existing file, and set its length to zero. If the file does not exist, a `FileNotFoundException` will be thrown.

As you can see, the `FileStream` constructor supplies a number of sensible default values. It's therefore quite easy to instantiate a `Filestream` object for use in the most common situations. Some simple ways of instantiating `FileStream` are shown below.

```
FileStream fs = new FileStream(@"c:\temp\demo.dat", FileMode.Create);
```

This first example creates the file `demo.dat` in the `c:\temp` directory. Once the file is open we can both read from and write to it.

```
FileStream fs1 = new FileStream(@"c:\temp\demo.dat", FileMode.OpenOrCreate);
```

Here, it will attempt to open the file, but if the file does not exist, it will create it. Again we have both read and write access to it.

The line below opens the file (which must exist) for reading only:

```
FileStream fs2 = new FileStream(@"c:\temp\demo.dat",
                        FileMode.Open,
                        FileAccess.Read);
```

The final example below will attempt to open the `demo.dat` file, but if the file does not exist, it will create it. It will then move to the end of the file, and allow us to append to it. We will not be able to read from the file:

```
FileStream fs3 = new FileStream(@"c:\temp\demo.dat",
                        FileMode.Append,
                        FileAccess.Write);
```

You should almost always enclose the instantiation of `FileStream` objects within a `try...catch` block, as many situations can cause instantiation to fail. Some of these are listed below:

❑ **The file name is invalid, or the file doesn't exist.**
If you allow the user to specify the file name, be prepared for this to happen! If this happens, exceptions derived from `System.IO.IOException` should be thrown.

❑ **The file is locked.**
The file may be locked by another process or program, so that your program cannot gain access to it. In this case a `System.UnauthorizedAccessException` should be thrown.

❑ **We don't have the appropriate file access permissions.**
Finally, the user running the application may not have sufficient security permissions to access the file. This will mean that a `System.Security.SecurityException` or a `System.IO.IOException` will be thrown.

Reading and Writing Binary Data

Having instantiated a `FileStream` object, we can then use its `ReadByte()` and `WriteByte()` methods to read and write binary data from or to file. Here's an example where we transfer data between files. First we create input and output `FileStream` objects:

```
// create input stream
FileStream inpStr = new FileStream(@"c:\temp\source.dat",
                            FileMode.Create,
                            FileAccess.Read);

// create output stream
FileStream outStr = new FileStream(@"c:\temp\destination.dat",
                            FileMode.Create,
                            FileAccess.Write);
```

Then we create a loop, and inside it we read in a byte of data from the source file:

```
int iData;
do
{
    // read in a byte from the source file
    iData = inpStr.ReadByte();
```

If the value of the byte data isn't –1 (which indicates the end of the file), we write the byte out on the console and we also write it in the destination file using `WriteByte()`:

```
    // check to see if we've reached the end of the file...
    if(iData != -1)
    {
        // write the byte to the console
        Console.Write((char)iData);
        // write the byte to the destination file
        outStr.WriteByte((byte)iData);
    }
```

```
    }
    while(iData != -1);
    inpStr.Close();
    outStr.Close();
```

Finally, we stop looping if the end of the file has been reached, and since we don't need them anymore we use the `Close()` method to close both streams, so that we conserve system resources.

Reading and Writing Text

Although the stream classes are full of methods used to read and write data, and to open or close files, you are unlikely to directly use the I/O operations available on a stream in your program. This is because they are too low-level (they only work on individual bytes). You are more likely to want to perform higher-level operations, such as reading and writing text.

For transferring text, you will probably find it more convenient to create a **Reader** or **Writer** object instead, attach it to the stream, and use the methods in the Reader or Writer object. Your program can now make a call to one of its methods – such as `WriteLine()` which writes a line of text – and the Writer object will in turn make the appropriate low level calls to the stream. Therefore, we can think of these Reader and Writer classes as utility classes that interface between a stream and your code, as shown in the figure below:

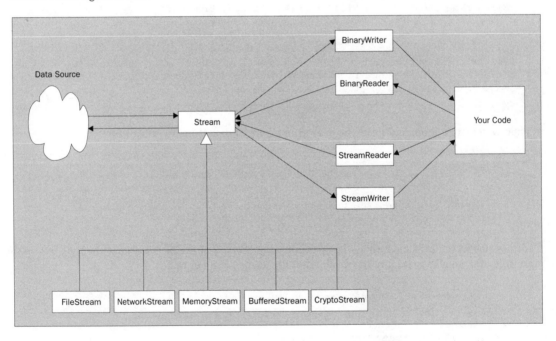

The data source could be anything from a file to a network socket. You will also notice from the figure the names of some specific Writer and Reader classes:

❑ `StreamReader` and `StreamWriter`. Both of these classes are derived from the abstract `TextReader` class. We can use them to read and write text to and from a stream.

❑ `BinaryReader` and `BinaryWriter`. These classes have methods that make it easier to read and write *formatted* binary data of different types, such as floats, doubles, and decimals, as well as arrays of data.

A big advantage of using Writer and Reader classes is that they understand different encoding schemes. Let's take a closer look at this issue.

Character Encoding

Traditionally, each text character was represented by a single byte value; this character set was called ASCII. However, to allow for more characters, Windows 2000 (and higher) represents all characters as a 16-bit value following a standard called Unicode.

Unfortunately, the Unicode standard is not universally adopted, so sometimes you may want to store your text in a different format. In this case, we run into a problem: Unicode represents standard ASCII values in two bytes with the most significant byte set to 0. This makes it easy to convert to the standard one-byte version of ASCII; you just remove the 0-byte. However doing this causes big problems for earlier programs written using the standard C input/output library, which interpret a 0 character as an end of line. Such a program would see the text as being a set of characters with only one character per line.

In order to overcome this problem, the default encoding scheme used by the `StreamWriter` class is actually something called UTF-8. The UTF-8 encoding specifies the use of between 1 and 6 non-zero characters to represent a two-byte Unicode character. Further, it specifies that original ASCII character values (from 0 to 127) must be represented by a one-byte value (also between 0 and 127). That way a file containing only regular ASCII text will be stored in the same way using UTF-8 encoded Unicode as it would have been using only ASCII representation.

Now let's get back on track, and look at how we can use the `StreamReader` and `StreamWriter` classes to transfer text between files. First, we'll discuss how to instantiate and use a `StreamReader`.

Using StreamReader Objects

The `StreamReader` constructor takes one or more of the following parameters:

Parameter	Description
Stream *stream*	An open stream, for example a `FileStream` as discussed above.
Encoding *encoding*	The desired encoding scheme. Possible values include `Unicode`, `BigEndianUnicode`, `UTF8`, `UTF7` and `ASCII`. `BigEndianUnicode` and `UTF7` are other types of encoding schemes. Further discussions of encoding can be found in the online help, by searching for the `System.Text.Encoding` class.

Table continued on following page

Parameter	Description
int *bufferSize*	Specifies the minimum required buffer size (normally you can just keep the default setting).
string *path*	Instead of specifying a stream, you can directly specify a filename. The StreamReader will then open a stream behind the scenes and use it to read from the file.
bool *detect*	Specifies if you want the StreamReader to automatically detect the encoding format used in the file (which is the default behavior).

The constructor arguments must include either a stream or a path. Once you have a StreamReader, you can use various methods, including:

Method	Description
Read()	Reads the next character in the text stream
ReadLine()	Reads a line from the text stream and returns it in a string variable
ReadToEnd()	Reads the stream, from the current position to the end of the stream, into one single string
Close ()	Closes the StreamReader and the underlying stream

We've covered quite a lot of classes and methods so far, so it's about time we put them to some good use. For our first Try It Out example of the chapter, we will build a simple text file viewer, and use it to demonstrate the use of streams and StreamReader objects. After this, when we've looked more closely at StreamWriter objects, will extend this application into a text editor.

Try It Out – Creating a Text File Viewer

In this example we are going to create a text viewer application called NotePadDotNet, which reads in text from a file using a StreamReader object.

1. Create a new C# Windows Application project called NotePadDotNet.

2. Drag a TextBox onto the form. Using the Properties window, set the properties of the TextBox to: MultiLine=true; AutoSize=true; Dock=Fill; ScrollBars=Both. This makes the textbox fill the form, and if you resize the form, you automatically resize the textbox as well. Remove any entry for the **Text** property of the TextBox. Also change the Text property of the form itself to NotePadDotNet.

3. Drag a `MainMenu` onto the form. Create the File menu shown below, with an Open menu item, and use the menu's Properties window to name the menu item `menuFileOpen`.

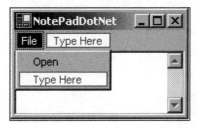

4. Drag an `OpenFileDialog` onto the form.

5. Switch to the form code editor and add the following namespace references:

```
using System.IO;
using System.Text;
using System.Collections.Specialized;
```

6. Add the `ReadFile()` method below to the form class:

```
void ReadFile(string filePath)
{
    const int MaxTextSize = 65535;

    FileStream fileStream = new FileStream(filePath,FileMode.Open,
                                           FileAccess.ReadWrite);
    StreamReader streamReader = new StreamReader(fileStream);

    //Or even simpler:
    //StreamReader aStreamReader = new StreamReader(filePath);

    //Read file into a string collection
    StringCollection stringCollection = new StringCollection();
    int noBytesRead = 0;
    string oneLine;
    while ((oneLine = streamReader.ReadLine())!=null)
    {
        noBytesRead+=oneLine.Length;
        if (noBytesRead>MaxTextSize) break;
        stringCollection.Add(oneLine);
    }
    streamReader.Close();

    // copy string collection into an array supported by the textbox
    string[] stringArray = new string[stringCollection.Count];
    stringCollection.CopyTo(stringArray,0);
    textBox1.Lines = stringArray;
}
```

7. Switch to the form designer and double-click on the File | Open menu item. This should create an event handler for the clicked event, and bring you back to the form code editor. Enter the following code into the handler:

```
private void menuFileOpen_Click(object sender, System.EventArgs e)
{
    //Open dialog box to get file name
    OpenFileDialog openFileDialog1 = new OpenFileDialog();

    openFileDialog1.InitialDirectory = "c:\\" ;
    openFileDialog1.Filter = "Text files (*.txt)|*.txt|All files (*.*)|*.*" ;
    openFileDialog1.FilterIndex = 1 ;
    openFileDialog1.RestoreDirectory = true ;

    if(openFileDialog1.ShowDialog() == DialogResult.OK)
    {
        //Read in the file
        try
        {
            ReadFile(openFileDialog1.FileName);
        }
        catch (Exception ex)
        {
            MessageBox.Show(ex.Message,"Error reading file");
        }
    }
}
```

8. Build and run the application. Select File | Open and select a text file. The contents of the file should appear in the form:

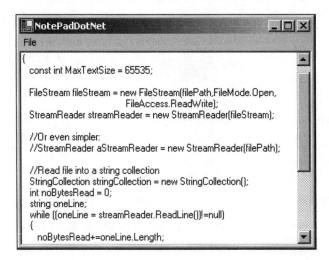

How It Works

Let's turn our attention to the code. First we import the `System.IO` namespace, where the stream classes reside. The `System.Collections.Specialized` namespace holds the `StringCollection` class.

Next we implement the read method `ReadFile()`:

```
void ReadFile(string filePath)
{
    const int MaxTextSize = 65535;
    FileStream fileStream = new FileStream(filePath,FileMode.Open,
                                    FileAccess.ReadWrite);
    StreamReader streamReader = new StreamReader(fileStream);
```

Here we create a `FileStream` object, and then instantiate the `StreamReader` by passing the constructor this `FileStream` object.

The `TextBox` control represents lines of text as an array of strings. So the next part of the code reads in the text one line at a time and places it in a `StringCollection`. The `StringCollection` is a handy utility class, which functions like an expandable array of strings – we can't allocate a fixed array up front, because we do not know how many lines are in the text.

```
StringCollection stringCollection = new StringCollection();
int noBytesRead = 0;
```

The next step is to use the `ReadLine()` method on the `StreamReader` and a `while` loop to iterate through lines of text, reading them in. A further complication is that the `TextBox` cannot handle more than 65535 characters, so we break the loop if that limit is reached:

```
string oneLine;
while ((oneLine = streamReader.ReadLine())!=null)
{
    noBytesRead+=oneLine.Length;
    if (noBytesRead>MaxTextSize) break;
    stringCollection.Add(oneLine);
}
streamReader.Close();
```

Finally we close the `StreamReader` by calling the `Close()` method. Then we create an array, fill it with the contents of the `StringCollection`, and hand it to the textbox:

```
string[] stringArray = new string[stringCollection.Count];
stringCollection.CopyTo(stringArray,0);
textBox1.Lines = stringArray;
```

We use an `OpenFileDialog` control to allow the user to pick the file to open. If the user presses **OK**, we can use the `FileName` property of the `OpenFileDialog` as the name of the file:

```
try
{
    ReadFile(openFileDialog1.FileName);
}
catch (Exception ex)
{
    MessageBox.Show(ex.Message,"Error reading file");
}
```

Notice that we have enclosed the call to our ReadFile() method in a try...catch block. There are many reasons why file access may not be possible, so it's good coding to be prepared for this.

Using StreamWriter Objects

The StreamWriter constructor takes almost the same parameters as the one for the StreamReader, but instead of having a detect parameter, we have a boolean append parameter. If we specify the filename, we can using this append parameter to specify whether we want the StreamWriter to start writing to the file from the start, or whether you want it to append to the file. If the file exists and append is false, the file is overwritten. If the file exists and append is true, the data is appended to the file. Otherwise, a new file is created.

Once you have instantiated a StreamWriter, you can use these methods on the object:

Method	Description
Write()	Writes text to the stream.
WriteLine()	Writes text to the stream followed by an "end of line" marker (in other words a line of text).
Flush()	Flushes the buffer to the data source. If you want to make sure that data is pushed all the way to the receiver (to the disk in this case), and not just sitting in some buffer, you should call the Flush() method.
Close()	Closes the StreamWriter and the underlying Stream. The StreamWriter will automatically get flushed when Close() is called.

The Write() and WriteLine() methods support string formatting, like this:

```
StreamWriter sw = new StreamWriter(@"c:\temp\demo.txt");
sw.WriteLine("The time is now {0,0:hh} o'clock.", DateTime.Now);
sw.Close();
```

This is equivalent to what you may have seen before when writing to the console (using Console.WriteLine() or formatting strings (using String.Format()). The first parameter to the WriteLine() method is a string containing a placeholder identified with curly braces {}. The next parameter is the value that should be inserted into the first string at the position specified by the placeholder.

Notice that the placeholder also contains characters in the format:

```
{i,w:fp}
```

The placeholder always contains a zero-based index *i*. This index indicates which of the value parameters should be inserted at a particular placeholder, since there may be more than one placeholder. In addition, the placeholder may contain formatting instructions that follow the *w:fp* format where:

- ❑ *w* indicates the minimum width of the field. If you set *w* to a positive number, the text will be right justified within the specified width. If *w* is a negative number, the text will be left justified.

- ❑ *f* is one or more characters specifying how the data should be formatted. For example if we use C here, it assumes that the value to be shown is numeric, and specifies that it should be shown as a currency.

- ❑ *p* is a precision specifier. You can, for example, specify the number of digits after the decimal point.

Formatting options are quite elaborate, and you can find more information about it in the Visual Studio .NET help under *Formatting Overview*. Some examples are given below:

```
sw.WriteLine("{0,3:F1} + {1,4:F2} = {2,4:F2}",
             10.45,12.43,22.88);
sw.WriteLine("{0,10:C2}", 11.25);
sw.WriteLine("{0,0:P}", 0.1125);
```

This results in the following text:

```
10.5 + 12.43 = 22.88
    $11.25
11.25 %
```

The first line illustrates the F (fixed point decimal) specifier. The number after the F specifies the number of digits after the decimal point. The following line uses the C (currency) specifier, which will render the number with the local specific pre- or postfix currency symbol. As you can see, the $11.25 is pushed to the right. This is because we specified a minimum width of 10 characters. Finally the P (percentage) specifier will display the number as a percentage.

Let's now show how we can make use of StreamWriter, by adapting the previous Try It Out so that we can edit and save text files.

Try It Out – Creating a Text Editor

In this example we are going to extend the functionality of our text file viewer from the previous Try It Out, so that we can edit and save text files too. In other words, we will create a text editor. We want to follow standard text editor behavior:

- ❑ If we just open up the application and start writing, we must be prompted for a filename before the file can be saved.

❑ If the filename is already known, no prompt is necessary when saving. However, if we select the **Save As...** menu item, we should still be prompted for a file name.

❑ The application should note if any changes have been made to the text since it was last saved. If so, the user should be prompted to save before the application closes.

To write the text to file, we will use a `StreamWriter` object.

1. Open up the NotePadDotNet form code editor, and add a private member variable to the form class to hold the name of the file we are working on, as well as the methods shown below:

```
private System.ComponentModel.Container components = null;

private string m_FileName = "";

public Form1()
```

```
void SetModified(bool bModified)
{
    textBox1.Modified = bModified;
}

bool IsModified()
{
    return textBox1.Modified;
}

private void SaveFile(string filePath)
{
    try
    {
        StreamWriter aStreamWriter = new StreamWriter(filePath,false);
        int I;
        for (I=0;I<textBox1.Lines.Length;I++)
        {
            aStreamWriter.WriteLine(textBox1.Lines[I]);
        }
        aStreamWriter.Close();
    }
    catch (Exception e)
    {
        MessageBox.Show(e.Message,"Error Saving File");
    }
}

private void SaveFileWithName(string filePath)
// Saves file to the supplied filePath
// if filePath is empty then opens up the saveFileDialog first.
{
    if (filePath!=null)
    {
```

```
        SaveFile(filePath);
        m_FileName = filePath;
        SetModified(false);
    }
    else
    {
        //Open dialog to select the file name
        SaveFileDialog saveFileDialog1 = new SaveFileDialog();

        saveFileDialog1.Filter =
            "Text files (*.txt)|*.txt|All files (*.*)|*.*";
        saveFileDialog1.FilterIndex = 1 ;
        saveFileDialog1.RestoreDirectory = true ;

        if(saveFileDialog1.ShowDialog() == DialogResult.OK)
        {
            SaveFile(saveFileDialog1.FileName);
            m_FileName = saveFileDialog1.FileName;
            SetModified(false);
        }
    }
}
```

2. In the `menuFileOpen_Click()` method, add the following highlighted code:

```
    try
    {
        ReadFile(openFileDialog1.FileName);
        //Remember file name
        m_FileName = openFileDialog1.FileName;
        SetModified(false);
    }
    catch (Exception ex)
    {
        MessageBox.Show(ex.Message,"Error reading file");
    }
```

3. Switch to the form designer view, and add **Save**, and **Save As** menu items to the **File** menu of the form. Use the menu's Properties window to name the menu items as `menuFileSave` and `menuFileSaveAs` respectively. Also drag a `SaveFileDialog` onto the form.

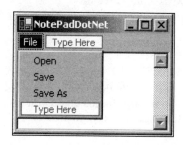

4. Double-click on the File | Save and File | Save As menu items to create event handlers for both. In the form code editor, modify these to include a call to `SaveFileWithName()`:

```
private void menuFileSave_Click(object sender, System.EventArgs e)
{
    SaveFileWithName(m_FileName);
}

private void menuFileSaveAs_Click(object sender, System.EventArgs e)
{
    SaveFileWithName(null);
}
```

5. Switch back to design mode and click on the form title bar. In the Properties window, click the lightning arrow, find the `Closing` event and double-click that. Fill in the event handler as follows:

```
private void Form1_Closing(object sender,
                     System.ComponentModel.CancelEventArgs e)
{
    if (IsModified())
    {
        //Ask the question
        DialogResult aDialogResult;
        aDialogResult=MessageBox.Show(
            "Would you like to save the file "+m_FileName,
            "Save File?",MessageBoxButtons.YesNoCancel);

        //Cast event so we can access the Cancel property
        CancelEventArgs aCancelEventArgs=(CancelEventArgs)e;

        //Take action:
        switch (aDialogResult)
        {
            case DialogResult.Yes:
                SaveFileWithName(m_FileName);
                aCancelEventArgs.Cancel=false;
                break;
            case DialogResult.No:
                aCancelEventArgs.Cancel=false;
                break;
            case DialogResult.Cancel:
                aCancelEventArgs.Cancel=true;
                break;
        }
    }
}
```

6. Build and run the application. Verify that you can now read in a file, edit it and save it either to the same or a new file name. Also notice that if you try to close the editor after having edited some text, you will be asked to save first.

How It Works

We start off by adding the private member variable m_FileName, which is used to hold the name of the file, so that we know what name to save it under if the user selects **File | Save**. In a similar way, the two methods which set and return the value of the Modified flag of our textbox are used to find out if we need to save the text when exiting the application.

The real work is done in the SaveFile() method. We start by creating a StreamWriter. Setting the second parameter to false indicates that we want to write the file from the start, rather than append to a file if the file already exists.

Then we write out the text one line at a time using the StreamWriter.WriteLine() method. Notice how this code is also encapsulated in a try...catch block:

```
try
{
    StreamWriter aStreamWriter= new StreamWriter(filePath,false);
    int I;
    for (I=0;I<textBox1.Lines.Length;I++)
    {
        aStreamWriter.WriteLine(textBox1.Lines[I]);
    }
    aStreamWriter.Close();
}
catch (Exception e)
{
    MessageBox.Show(e.Message,"Error Saving File");
}
```

The code in SaveFileWithName() is concerned with finding the name of the file to save. The filePath parameter will be null if m_FileName is empty (a file has not already been read in) or if the user selected the **File | Save As** menu item.

We also modify the menuFileOpen_Click() method so that we can keep track of the opened file in the m_FileName field, and we reset the Modified flag property of the TextBox:

```
try
{
    ReadFile(openFileDialog1.FileName);
    //Remember file name
    m_FileName = openFileDialog1.FileName;
    SetModified(false);
}
```

Finally the code in the Form1_Closing() event handler is called when the application is being closed. The event handler calls IsModified() to find out if something needs to be saved. IsModified() just returns the value of the textbox's Modified flag.

```
bool IsModified()
{
    return textBox1.Modified;
}
```

Depending on the user's choice, we either save and exit, just exit, or interrupt the closing of the form. The event handler decides if the form should close by setting the `Cancel` property of the supplied `CancelEventArgs` parameter.

Accessing Directory Information

In this section we are going to introduce the classes that we can use to browse folders and files.

First up we have the `Directory` and `File` classes. These two classes contain a bunch of static methods to access directories and files. They are convenient if you only want to do a few simple file system operations. We will not be covering these classes in any more depth in this chapter.

Then we have the `DirectoryInfo` and `FileInfo` classes. These implement roughly the same methods as `Directory` and `File`. The difference is that `DirectoryInfo` and `FileInfo` must be instantiated, and each instance of `DirectoryInfo` or `FileInfo` corresponds to an actual directory or file on the system. This is more convenient and more efficient if you are doing slightly more complex operations, so we will look more closely at these in a moment.

`DirectoryInfo` and `FileInfo` are both derived from the base class `FileSystemInfo`. Sometimes it is useful to get a list of `FileSystemInfo` objects representing all entries (both directories and files) in a directory. You can then iterate through the list and write out different information depending on the actual type of the entry in the list.

Finally, we have the `Path` class. `Path` is a utility class with a lot of useful static methods for manipulating file and directory names, including:

- ❑   `GetExtension()`
- ❑   `GetFileName()`
- ❑   `GetFileNameWithoutExtension()`
- ❑   `GetFullPath()`
- ❑   `GetPathRoot()`

These methods all return different fragments of a complete file path. The `Combine()` and `ChangeExtension()` methods are helpful when concatenating two file names or changing a file extension. The `GetTempPath()` and `GetTempFileName()` methods can be used to create temporary files.

Let's now take a closer look at the `DirectoryInfo` and `FileInfo` classes.

The DirectoryInfo Class

To instantiate an instance of a DirectoryInfo, you must pass in a valid directory path to the constructor:

```
DirectoryInfo dirInfo = new DirectoryInfo(@"c:\wrox\");
```

The DirectoryInfo object created gives you access to a set of properties and methods. Some of these properties include:

Property	Description
CreationTime	Time when the directory was created
LastAccessTime/ LastModifiedTime	Time when the directory was last accessed or modified
Name, FullName, Root, Extension	The full name, or parts of the full name, of the directory
Parent	Reference to a DirectoryInfo object representing the parent directory

Here are some of the methods:

Method	Description
Create() and CreateSubDirectory()	Creates a directory
Delete()	Deletes the directory
MoveTo()	Moves and/or renames a directory
GetDirectories()	Returns an array of DirectoryInfo objects representing all directories contained in this directory
GetFiles()	Returns an array of FileInfo objects representing all files contained in this directory
GetFileSystemInfos()	Returns an array of FileSystemInfo objects representing all files and directories in the directory

We can use these methods like this:

```
DirectoryInfo[] dirs = dirInfo.GetDirectories();
FileSystemInfo[] fSIs = dirInfo.GetFileSystemInfos();
FileInfo[] filesInDirInfo = dirInfo.GetFiles();
```

Here the first line retrieves all of the directories contained in the dirInfo directory, and the second line returns the FileSystemInfo objects for all of the files and directories in dirInfo. The last line retrieves all of the files in dirInfo.

The FileInfo Class

The `FileInfo` class has properties and methods that are very similar to the `DirectoryInfo` class (after all, they both derive from `FileSystemInfo`). The `FileInfo` class has an additional `Length` property, indicating the size of the file.

A brief list of `FileInfo` methods is provided below:

Method	Description
`CreateText()` and `AppendText()`	These methods open a `StreamWriter` object on the file and allow you to either create the file from scratch or append text to it
`OpenText()`	Opens a `StreamWriter` object that reads from an existing file
`Open()`, `OpenRead()`, `OpenWrite()`	These methods all allow you to open a `FileStream` with different access attributes
`CopyTo()`	Copies an existing file to a new file

As with `DirectoryInfo`'s methods, these methods are pretty easy to use. One technique you'll see quite a lot is to iterate through an array of `FileInfo` objects returned by a call to `DirectoryInfo.GetFiles()`:

```
foreach (FileInfo file in filesInDirInfo)
{
    // do something with each file, like copy each file to new directory...
    file.CopyTo(newDirName);
}
```

There is probably no better way to illustrate the use of these file- and directory-related classes than by an example.

Try It Out – Viewing Directory Trees

The following program represents the solution to a real problem in the author's company. No matter how big your company's file server is, sooner or later you will run out of space. The problem is now, who is using all the space – who is the "SpaceHog"? The program we will build in this example will iterate through a directory and all of its files and subdirectories. At each level it will record the total amount of space taken up by all underlying files and subdirectories. You can do this by right-clicking on files and directories in Windows Explorer, but Explorer recalculates space usage every time at every level, which makes the process very arduous.

1. Start a new Windows Application project called **SpaceHog**.

2. Drag a `TreeView`, a `Label`, a `TextBox` and a `Button` onto the form. Position them, and set their `Text` properties so that they display the text shown in the screenshot below. Also change the form's `Text` property to `SpaceHog`.

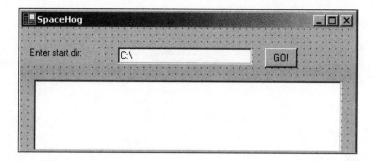

3. Double-click on the `Button` to create the event handler. Enter the following code:

```
private void button1_Click(object sender, System.EventArgs e)
{
    BuildTreeView(textBox1.Text);
}
```

4. Add the `FileSizeString()` method below:

```
string FileSizeString(long fileSize)
//Return a string representing file size in bytes, KB, MB or GB
{
    const long OneMB = 1024 * 1024;
    const long OneGB = OneMB * 1024;
    string unit;
    double dispSize;
    if (fileSize < 1024)
    {
        unit = "bytes";
        dispSize = fileSize;
    }
    else if (fileSize < OneMB)
    {
        unit = "KB";
        dispSize = fileSize / 1024;
    }
    else if (fileSize < OneGB)
    {
        unit = "MB";
        dispSize = fileSize / OneMB;
    }
    else
    {
        unit = "GB";
        dispSize = fileSize / OneGB;
    }
    return string.Format(" ({0,4:F}", dispSize) + unit + ")";
}
```

5. Then add the `AddDirectory()` method:

```
long AddDirectory(DirectoryInfo dir, TreeNode tNode)
// Create a complete representation of the supplied directory, including
// all files and subdirectories.
{
    //Get list of all entries in directory
    FileSystemInfo[] fSIs = dir.GetFileSystemInfos();
    FileSystemInfo fSI;
    int i;
    long directorySize = 0;

    // Iterate list
    for(i=0;i<fSIs.Length;i++)
    {
        fSI = fSIs[i];
        // If it's a file...
        if (fSI.GetType()==typeof(FileInfo))
        {
            FileInfo fInfo = (FileInfo)fSI;
            string s = fInfo.Name + FileSizeString(fInfo.Length);
            TreeNode newTreeNode = new TreeNode(s);
            tNode.Nodes.Add(newTreeNode);
            directorySize+=fInfo.Length;
        } // if it's a directory...
        else if (fSI.GetType()==typeof(DirectoryInfo))
        {
            DirectoryInfo dirInfo = (DirectoryInfo)fSI;
            TreeNode dirTreeNode = new TreeNode(dirInfo.Name);
            long dirSize = AddDirectory(dirInfo,dirTreeNode);
            dirTreeNode.Text+=FileSizeString(dirSize);
            tNode.Nodes.Add(dirTreeNode);
            directorySize+=dirSize;
        }
        else // should never come here
            MessageBox.Show("Ooops");

    }
    return directorySize;
}
```

6. The final method to add is `BuildViewTree()`:

```
private void BuildTreeView(string dirName)
// Build a TreeNode containing complete directory information
// Add this TreeNode to the treeView control
{
    DirectoryInfo dirInfo = new DirectoryInfo(dirName);
    TreeNode tNode = new TreeNode(dirName);
    long totalSize = AddDirectory(dirInfo,tNode);
```

```
        tNode.Text+=FileSizeString(totalSize);
        treeView1.Nodes.Clear();
        treeView1.Nodes.Add(tNode);
    }
```

7. Add the import of the `System.IO` namespace at the top of the file:

```
using System.IO;
```

8. Build and run the **SpaceHog** application. Enter a valid directory into the textbox and press the button. Beware that **SpaceHog** will iterate the whole directory and all subdirectories – so you may not want to enter **c:** if you have a large hard disk and just want to see how the app works. (A real-world application would have code to report progress, and allow you to abandon the process, but this has been removed here to make the example simpler.) You can now drill down to find out exactly where the space is being wasted.

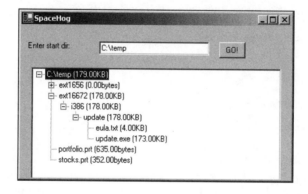

How It Works

Let's first look at `BuildTreeView()`. It gets called by the button click event handler with a directory name (`dirName`). The first line creates a `DirectoryInfo` to represent this top-level directory:

```
private void BuildTreeView(string dirName)
{
    DirectoryInfo dirInfo = new DirectoryInfo(dirName);
```

The second line instantiates a `TreeNode`, which is an object that represents a node in a `TreeView` control. In the third line we call `AddDirectory()`, and this is where the real work gets done. Upon return from `AddDirectory`, the `Nodes` collection on `TreeNode` we passed in will have been filled with other `TreeNodes` representing all files and subdirectories.

```
    TreeNode tNode = new TreeNode(dirName);
    long totalSize = AddDirectory(dirInfo,tNode);
```

AddDirectory() also returns the combined size of the directory, and this information is added to the text property of our top-level tree node. We now clear the current nodes collection and add our node to the TreeView control, so that it will be displayed:

```
    tNode.Text+=FileSizeString(totalSize);
    treeView1.Nodes.Clear();
    treeView1.Nodes.Add(tNode);
}
```

The heart of our program is the AddDirectory() method. AddDirectory() is a recursive function, which means that it will call itself repeatedly during its execution. Recursive functions are very useful when dealing with directory structures.

We start by calling GetFileSystemInfos() on the DirectoryInfo object passed into the method. This returns a list of FileSystemInfo objects. We can now iterate through this list:

```
long AddDirectory(DirectoryInfo dir, TreeNode tNode)
{
    FileSystemInfo[] fSIs = dir.GetFileSystemInfos();
    FileSystemInfo fSI;
    int i;
    long directorySize = 0;

    for(i=0;i<fSIs.Length;i++)
    {
```

We use the GetType() method to find out if a given entry is a FileInfo or a DirectoryInfo.

If it is a FileInfo, we create a TreeNode (newTreeNode) containing the filename and filesize and add this newTreeNode to the top level TreeNode. We also increase the top-level directorySize by the size of the file:

```
        fSI = fSIs[i];
        if (fSI.GetType()==typeof(FileInfo))
        {
            FileInfo fInfo = (FileInfo)fSI;
            string s = fInfo.Name+FileSizeString(fInfo.Length);
            TreeNode newTreeNode = new TreeNode(s);
            tNode.Nodes.Add(newTreeNode);
            directorySize+=fInfo.Length;
        }
```

If it is a DirectoryInfo, we also create a new TreeNode (dirTreeNode). But in this case we call the AddDirectory() function again to have it fill the supplied dirTreeNode with info about all subdirectories and files. Once AddDirectory() returns, it will have filled dirTreeNode with lots of other nodes. We add dirTreeNode to the top level TreeNode and increase directorySize by the size returned from AddDirectory():

```
    else if (fSI.GetType()==typeof(DirectoryInfo))
    {
        DirectoryInfo dirInfo=(DirectoryInfo)fSI;
        TreeNode dirTreeNode=new TreeNode(dirInfo.Name);
        long dirSize=AddDirectory(dirInfo,dirTreeNode);
        dirTreeNode.Text+=FileSizeString(dirSize);
        tNode.Nodes.Add(dirTreeNode);
        directorySize+=dirSize;
    }
```

Finally, a word about `FileSizeString()`. This method is only there to provide a more convenient read out of file sizes. For instance, instead of "15,728,640 bytes", it will return "15.00 MB".

Serializing Objects

In Chapter 5 we discussed how to use databases to store information, such as program state (data associated with an application), in tables. However, we don't have to store program state in a database; we could save it to a file, too. The act of storing the values of application objects to disk is called **serialization**, because the objects are serially stored one after another in logical order in a file, rather than in separate tables in a database. When the data is retrieved it is said to be **deserialized**.

Serialization is useful in a couple of situations:

❑ If you want to store the complete state of a complex application or dataset for later reuse

❑ If you want to transport application data between different applications

.NET supports two types of serialization:

❑ **Binary serialization**
Using binary serialization, the data will be packed into the file in a binary format. Binary serialization is more flexible and more compact than XML serialization. But it cannot be used if you want to exchange information with other non-.NET programs.

❑ **XML serialization**
Using XML serialization, an object's public properties will be represented as XML elements and attributes. This can be exchanged with other .NET as well as non-.NET programs. In addition it's much easer to see what is going on than with binary serialization, as XML is just structured text.

In the following chapter we will only deal with XML serialization, since it is simpler to understand, and useful for inter-application communication (including Web Services).

If you are unfamiliar with XML, you will probably wish to learn more about it before continuing with this section. We recommend that you read Wrox'Beginning XML, 2nd Edition (ISBN 1-861005-59-8) or Professional XML, 2nd Edition (ISBN 1-861005-05-9) from Wrox Press for more information.

XML Serialization

XML serialization (and deserialization) is handled by the `XmlSerializer` class found in the `System.Xml.Serialization` namespace. The first step to using this class is to instantiate an `XmlSerializer` object.

Creating an XmlSerializer

To create the `XmlSerializer`, we pass into the constructor the type of the object we want to have serialized. So say we had an object of type `dataType` that we wanted to serialize/deserialize. We could use the following code:

```
XmlSerializer xmlSer = new XmlSerializer(typeof(dataType));
```

The next step is determined by whether we want to serialize or deserialize the object.

Serializing Data

To serialize the object `objToSer` of type `dataType` we would call the `Serialize()` method, passing in an instance of the object you want to serialize and an object to receive the output:

```
xmlSer.Serialize(str, objToSer);
```

The output `str` object can be a `Stream`, a `TextWriter` or an `XmlWriter` object. Notice how we have a choice of output objects. While we will only be working with output objects that write to a file, we can use the same method to serialize our data over the network to another machine or server. Typical examples include near-realtime updates of inventory data from a warehouse computer to a central inventory system, purchase orders issued from an Enterprise Resource Planning (ERP) system to an external supplier, or an invoice generated from a web server sent to the back-end billing and shipping system.

Deserializing Data

The procedure for deserialization is almost the same as the one for serialization, expect that we call the `Deserialize()` method instead:

```
newObj = (dataType)xmlSer.Deserialize(str);
```

Notice how we must cast the deserialized object `newObj` to the correct type.

Let's now make use of the `XmlSerializer` in a Try It Out.

Try It Out – Serializing Stock Portfolios

You may remember that the Graphics chapter ended with a small application (**StockChart**), which displayed the performance of a stock portfolio. Over the next few Try It Outs we will gradually develop a small program that we can use to serialize and deserialize a portfolio like our stock one. Ultimately you could imagine that this program could be used to manage portfolios, and store them serialized in different files. We could then move the deserialization code into the **StockChart** application, and use that to display the data.

1. Create a new project called **StockFeeder**. Drag a `MainMenu` control onto the form and create a **File** menu with two menu items: **FeedStocks**, and **ReadStocks**. Set the names of these two menu items to `menuFileFeedStocks`, and `menuFileReadStocks`. Also change the `Text` property of the form to `StockFeeder`.

2. Double-click on the **FeedStocks** menu item, and enter the following code in the event handler:

```
private void menuFileFeedStocks_Click(object sender, System.EventArgs e)
{
    Stock aStock = new Stock();
    aStock.m_Ticker = "MSFT";
    aStock.m_Color = Color.Red;
    aStock.m_Price = new float[5]{36.1F,71.3F,119.35F,45.2F,64.9F};

    SerializeStock(aStock);
}
```

3. Add the `SerializeStock()` method too (you may want to change the directory if you don't have a `c:\temp` folder on your machine):

```
void SerializeStock(Stock aStock)
{
    StreamWriter sr = new StreamWriter(@"c:\temp\stocks.prt");
    XmlSerializer xsr = new XmlSerializer(typeof(Stock));

    xsr.Serialize(sr,aStock);
    sr.Close();
}
```

4. At the top of the file, just under the namespace declaration, add the definition for the `Stock` class:

```
public class Stock
{
    public Color m_Color = Color.Blue;
    public String m_Ticker = "NNNN";
    public float[] m_Price;
};
```

5. Finally, at the start of the file, include the import of these three namespaces (we only need the first two for this example, but we will need the third later):

```
using System.IO;
using System.Xml.Serialization;
using System.Text;
```

6. Build and run the application. Select File | FeedStocks. Then open your text editor and read in the contents of the file `c:\temp\stocks.prt`. The file should contain the following:

```
<?xml version="1.0" encoding="utf-8"?>
<Stock xmlns:xsd="http://www.w3.org/2001/XMLSchema"
xmlns:xsi="http://www.w3.org/2001/XMLSchema-instance">
  <m_Color />
  <m_Ticker>MSFT</m_Ticker>
  <m_Price>
    <float>36.1</float>
    <float>71.3</float>
    <float>119.35</float>
    <float>45.2</float>
    <float>64.9</float>
  </m_Price>
</Stock>
```

How It Works

Ignoring the graphics-related code that we discussed in the previous chapter, the real work is done in the `SerializeStock()` method:

```
void SerializeStock(Stock aStock)
{
    StreamWriter sr = new StreamWriter(@"c:\temp\stocks.prt");
    XmlSerializer xsr = new XmlSerializer(typeof(Stock));
```

The first line instantiates a `StreamWriter` in order to create and write to a file called `c:\temp\stocks.prt`. The second line instantiates an `XmlSerializer`, and tells it that is expected to serialize objects of type `Stock`. The actual serialization is performed by `Serialize()`, and then the `StreamWriter` is closed:

```
    xsr.Serialize(sr,aStock);
    sr.Close();
}
```

Now we will take a closer look at the `stocks.prt` file. I hope you can see the close resemblance between the structure of the `Stock` class and the contents of the file.

The first `<Stock>` tag indicates that it is a stock element, and that the schema will follow a certain standard for representing different data types:

```
<Stock xmlns:xsd="http://www.w3.org/2001/XMLSchema"
xmlns:xsi="http://www.w3.org/2001/XMLSchema-instance">
```

The next tag is the `<m_Color />` tag:

```
    <m_Color />
```

You will notice that this is an empty tag. Why? This is because XmlSerializer can only serialize the primitive data types, user-defined classes, and arrays of these. It cannot serialize the Color type, because it does not know how to represent it in a textual format (don't worry, we will solve this problem a little later).

The following tag is the ticker symbol, represented as the <m_Ticker> element:

```
<m_Ticker>MSFT</m_Ticker>
```

Finally we have the m_Price array. This is represented as one element with a number of child elements. The child elements are named <float> after their data type:

```
<m_Price>
  <float>36.1</float>
  ...
  <float>64.9</float>
</m_Price>
```

Finally there is the end tag, delineating the end of the Microsoft stock.

```
</Stock>
```

Let's take a moment to reflect upon what we've achieved here. The SerializeStock() code is very general, yet it was able to persist a structured textual representation of our object to file, along with any other objects owned by our object (for example the array of price points).

Controlling XML Serialization

While we have successfully serialized our Stock object to file, there are a few issues regarding the serialization that we have largely ignored so far.

First, we noted that the value of m_Color was not serialized because the XmlSerializer cannot serialize enumerated types. To solve this problem, we just make m_Color a private member variable, and expose it as a string.

Second, the XML element names created by serialization correspond directly to object field and class names. For instance, the m_Price field is converted into an <m_Price> XML element. While convenient for us, there are several disadvantages to this approach:

❑ We know what data <m_Price> corresponds to, but someone else who isn't so familiar with our application probably won't. In order to aid understanding of the contents of the file, we should make the names of elements and attributes as clear and descriptive as possible (within reason – we don't really want our file cluttered with elements and attributes that have incredibly long names either).

❑ If we only transfer information between our own applications we may not care too much about the XML representation. But, if you intend to use an XML file to pass data between your application and someone else's, the structure and names of the XML elements in the file could well be dictated by an agreement between you and the owner of the other application. The resulting XML element names will probably not correspond fully to the names of your classes or fields.

This suggests that we need a way to control the names of XML elements (and attributes too) as they are added to the file during serialization. You probably won't be too surprised to hear that .NET provides us with several ways to do this.

The first technique is to attach C# attributes to the members of our class, to specify how they are serialized by the XmlSerializer. To do this, inside the C# attribute we call the constructor for a class that represents an XML element or attribute. These classes include the following from the System.Xml.Serialization namespace:

❑ System.Xml.Serialization.XmlElementAttribute – Represents an XML element when using XmlSerializer

❑ System.Xml.Serialization.XmlRootAttribute – Represents a root element

We would call the constructors for these classes in a C# attribute to pin down whether the following class or field should be an element or a root element respectively. For instance:

```
[XmlRootAttribute()]
public class Stock
{
...
```

Here, we have identified the Stock class as the root element in the XML file. We can also use the XmlAttributes.XmlArray(arrayName) property from this namespace to specify that a public member variable array will be represented by a list of child elements inside an element called arrayName, like this:

```
[XmlArray("Prices")]
```

Several other classes from other namespaces are also useful for controlling serialization:

❑ System.Xml.XmlElement – Represents a public member variable as an XML element

❑ System.Xml.XmlNode.XmlAttribute – Represents a public member variable as an XML attribute

To control the names of elements or attributes, we just input the name we would like used in the XML file into the constructor. For example, we can use the following to specify that the ticker symbol should be represented as an XML attribute, rather than an element:

```
[XmlAttribute("Ticker")]
```

The second technique is to pass information directly to the XmlSerializer() constructor, specifying how a class should be streamed. For instance, to make it clearer that we are dealing with stock portfolios, we might want to specify that the root element should be called <Portfolio> instead of <Stock>. To do this, we would use XmlRootAttribute() to specify that the root element should be called <Portfolio>:

```
XmlSerializer xsr = new XmlSerializer(typeof(Stock[]),
                              new XmlRootAttribute("Portfolio"));
```

Let's now improve our previous Try It Out, by incorporating these changes which allow us better control over XML serialization.

Try It Out – Controlling Stock Portfolio Serialization

We will now complete our stock feeder example by implementing the improvements discussed above, adding extra stocks to make it a "real" portfolio, and adding deserialization code.

1. Switch to the code editor and modify the declaration of the Stock class so that it looks like this:

```
public class Stock
{
   private Color m_Color;

   public string ColorName
   {
      get {return m_Color.Name;}
      set {m_Color = Color.FromName(value);}
   }
   [XmlAttribute("Ticker")]
   public String m_Ticker = "NNNN";
   [XmlArray("Prices")]
   public float[] m_Price;
};
```

2. Add this method to serialize a portfolio (an array of stocks):

```
void SerializePortfolio(Stock[] aPortfolio)
{
   StreamWriter sr = new StreamWriter(@"c:\temp\portfolio.prt");
   XmlSerializer xsr = new XmlSerializer(typeof(Stock[]),
                                    new XmlRootAttribute("Portfolio"));
   xsr.Serialize(sr,aPortfolio);
   sr.Close();
}
```

3. Extend the menuFileFeedStocks_Click() method to create a portfolio of both MSFT and INTL stock. Also change the Color property to ColorName and change the property to be a string.

```
private void menuFileFeedStocks_Click(object sender, System.EventArgs e)
{

   Stock aStock = new Stock();
   aStock.m_Ticker = "MSFT";
   aStock.ColorName = "Red";
   aStock.m_Price = new float[5]{36.1F,71.3F,119.35F,45.2F,64.9F};

   Stock bStock = new Stock();
   bStock.m_Ticker = "INTL";
```

```
    bStock.ColorName = "Blue";
    bStock.m_Price = new float[5]{10.3F,23.34F,22.2F,8.78F,20.19F};

    Stock[] Portfolio = new Stock[2]{aStock,bStock};

    SerializePortfolio(Portfolio);
}
```

4. Switch to the form designer and drag a `Label` control onto the form. Set its `Text` property to `Share Prices:`. Below the `Label` drag a `ListBox` control onto the form. Set its `Size` property to 300 by 200:

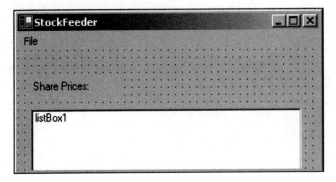

5. Select the **File | ReadStock** menu item and double-click to create the event handler. Then add the following code:

```
private void menuFileReadStocks_Click(object sender, System.EventArgs e)
{
    Stock[] aPortfolio = DeserializePortfolio();
    DisplayPortfolio(aPortfolio);
}
```

6. Add the following two extra methods to the form code:

```
Stock[] DeserializePortfolio()
{
    FileStream fs=new FileStream(@"c:\temp\portfolio.prt",FileMode.Open);

    XmlSerializer xs=new XmlSerializer(typeof(Stock[]),
                                       new XmlRootAttribute("Portfolio"));
    Stock[] aPortfolio;
    aPortfolio = (Stock[])xs.Deserialize(fs);
    fs.Close();
    return aPortfolio;
}
```

```
private void DisplayPortfolio(Stock[] aPortfolio)
{
    foreach (Stock s in aPortfolio)
    {
        StringBuilder sb = new StringBuilder();
        sb.Append(s.m_Ticker+","+s.ColorName);
        foreach (float f in s.m_Price)
        {
            sb.Append(" ,");
            sb.Append(f.ToString());
        }
        listBox1.Items.Add(sb);
    }
}
```

7. Build and run the application. Then select **File | FeedStocks**, and open the file `c:\temp\portfolio.prt`. It should look like this:

```xml
<?xml version="1.0" encoding="utf-8"?>
<Portfolio xmlns:xsd="http://www.w3.org/2001/XMLSchema"
xmlns:xsi="http://www.w3.org/2001/XMLSchema-instance">
  <Stock Ticker="MSFT">
    <Prices>
      <float>36.1</float>
      <float>71.3</float>
      <float>119.35</float>
      <float>45.2</float>
      <float>64.9</float>
    </Prices>
    <ColorName>Red</ColorName>
  </Stock>
  <Stock Ticker="INTL">
    <Prices>
      <float>10.3</float>
      <float>23.34</float>
      <float>22.2</float>
      <float>8.78</float>
      <float>20.19</float>
    </Prices>
    <ColorName>Blue</ColorName>
  </Stock>
</Portfolio>
```

Notice how the root element is now called `Portfolio`, the `Ticker` is now an attribute (called `Ticker` instead of `m_Ticker`), the color is now serialized through the `ColorName` property, and the price list is now nested inside the `Prices` element.

8. Finally, select File | ReadStocks. The screen should display the contents of the two stocks like this:

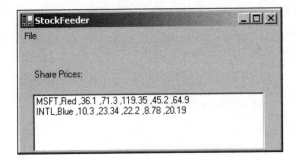

How It Works

We have already discussed many of the changes we have made to the application. But take a look at how symmetrical the `SerializePortfolio()` and the `DeserializePortfolio()` methods are. The first takes an array of `Stock` objects and serializes them to a disk file. The second reads the file and creates the array of objects. Very simple, yet very powerful.

One thing to note is the use of the `StringBuilder` class in the `DisplayPortfolio()` method. You should always use the `StringBuilder` over the += operator for performance reasons if you need to concatenate more than three or four strings.

Manipulating the Registry

In this section, we are going to discuss how to manipulate data in the Registry via C# code.

Since its introduction with Windows 95, the Registry is probably one of the most contentious pieces of Windows infrastructure. At its introduction back in '95, the Registry was touted as the replacement for .ini files as the primary vehicle and central location for storing user preferences, general program configuration, and of course COM component registration.

But with central control comes vulnerability and lack of flexibility. If, for some reason, entries in the Registry are destroyed, you will quite often have to reformat your hard disk and reinstall all software from scratch. Another problem is that it is quite difficult to move a program's configuration settings from one machine to another if the settings are only stored as Registry entries.

In the light of this Microsoft is now suggesting that most program configuration settings should be stored in an XML-based configuration file, and the Registry is intended to store small pieces of information (1-2 KB maximum). If you want to replicate configuration settings from one machine to another, all you have to do is to copy the configuration file. If you need to store a lot of configuration information, you should use an XML file to store the data, and place a reference to the file in the Registry.

The Registry's Structure

The Registry is hierarchical, much like a file system. Each entry in the structure is called a **key**. A key may contain any number of **subkeys**. It may also contain data entries called **values**. A top-level key is also sometimes called a **hive**.

You can inspect and make changes to the Registry by using one of two programs: `regedt32.exe` and `regedit.exe`. `regedit.exe` comes will all versions of Windows from 95 and up, whereas `regedt32.exe` is only supplied with Windows NT, 2000 and XP. `regedit.exe` is a little more intuitive to use, but `regedt32.exe` gives the user access to security information.

We will use `regedit.exe`. To do this, simply select Run... from the program start menu and type in `regedit.exe`. You should see something like this:

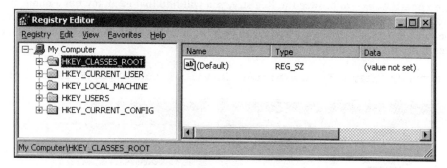

At the top level you should see at least five keys. They are all predefined by Microsoft, and there are rules about what information should go under which keys:

❑ **HKEY_CLASSES_ROOT (HKCR)**
This contains information about file types, and about which application should be used by default to open a particular file type. Another very important set of information stored here is the registration of all COM components on the system.

❑ **HKEY_CURRENT_USER (HKCU)**
This contains configuration settings that are particular to the current user. Applications that want to store information related to a particular user should do it under the subkey `Software\<application name>`.

❑ **HKEY_LOCAL_MACHINE (HKLM)**
This contains information about all software and hardware installed on the machine. An application should store information pertinent to all users under the subkey `Software\<application name>`.

❑ **HKEY_USERS (HKUSR)**
This contains information about all users (not just the current user).

❑ **HKEY_CURRENT_CONFIG (HKCF)**
This contains details about the current hardware configuration.

As you can probably understand, you must have administrator privileges to modify some of the keys in HKCR, HKLM, HKUSR, and HKCF.

You may find two additional keys:

❑ **HKEY_DYN_DATA**
This key is only supported under Windows 98/ME. It is intended to store "dynamic" information that changes often. This area is often used to exchange information between a low-level device driver and a Win 32 application.

❑ **HKEY_PERFORMANCE_DATA**
This contains performance information for running applications.

If you use `regedit.exe` to browse the Registry, you will find that each key has a name and a default value. Additional values with separate names can be stored under the key. Each value has a name, a data type, such as REG_DWORD, and REG_SZ, as well as the value itself. Below is a screenshot showing the values under the key:

`\HKEY_CURRENT_USER\Software\Microsoft\VisualStudio\7.0\FileMRUList`

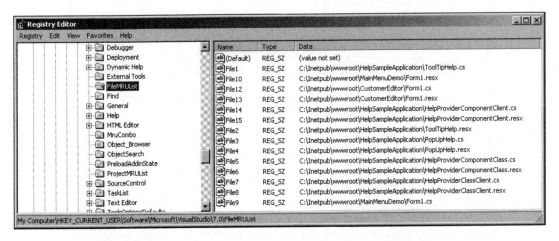

As you can see it stores a list of the most recently used files in Visual Studio .NET by the current user (me). Except for the default value, which is empty, all other values have a name (like `File1`), they are all of type REG_SZ (indicating a text string), and they each point to a different file.

Classes for Working with the Registry

You only need two .NET classes to work with the Registry, both found in the `Microsoft.Win32` namespace. They are:

❑ `Registry`

❑ `RegistryKey`

Let's take a closer look at them.

> In this section we will be discussing how to make simple changes in the Registry.
> Please beware that the Registry must remain intact for the machine, Windows, and all
> applications to work properly. You should never change Registry settings manually
> unless you really know what you are doing! Further, you should take care to type
> Registry paths accurately. If you want to be on the safe side, you can export the
> Registry using the **File | Export** menu item in `regedit.exe`. Then you can restore
> the Registry later (using **File | Import**).

The Registry Class

This simple class just has seven static read-only properties, one for each of the seven possible top-level
Registry keys. In other words:

Property	Description
ClassesRoot	Gives access to the HKEY_CLASSES_ROOT (HKCR) key
CurrentConfig	Gives access to the HKEY_CURRENT_CONFIG (HKCF) key
CurrentUser	Gives access to the HKEY_CURRENT_USER (HKCU) key
DynData	Gives access to the HKEY_DYN_DATA key
LocalMachine	Gives access to the HKEY_LOCAL_MACHINE (HKLM) key
PerformanceData	Gives access to the HKEY_PERFORMANCE_DATA key
Users	Gives access to the HKEY_USERS (HKUSR) key

The RegistryKey Class

The `RegistryKey` class is more interesting. As the name implies, it represents a key in the Registry. It
provides a couple of properties and a set of methods to work with:

Property	Description
Name	The name of the key (read-only)
SubKeyCount	Number of subkeys under this key (read-only)
ValueCount	Number of values under this key (read-only)

As you can see, the properties are all read-only. To add, set, and remove subkeys and values, you must use the following methods:

Method	Description
Close()	Closes the key and flushes it to disk
CreateSubKey()	Creates a new subkey or opens an existing subkey
DeleteSubKey()	Deletes the specified subkey
DeleteSubKeyTree()	Deletes the specified subkey and all child subkeys recursively
DeleteValue()	Deletes the specifed value
Flush()	Writes all Registry keys and subkeys into the registry
GetSubKeyNames()	Retrieves an array of strings that contains all the subkey names
GetValue()	Gets the specified value
GetValueNames()	Retrieves an array of all value names under this key
OpenSubKey()	Returns the specified subkey
SetValue()	Sets the specified value

Simple Registry Operations

To perform any access to the Registry, we need to start by picking one of the seven entry properties in the `Registry` class. From then on we can work our way down the hierarchy one level at a time. Here's some sample code:

```
RegistryKey rkCU = Registry.CurrentUser;
RegistryKey rkSoftware = rkCU.OpenSubKey("Software");
RegistryKey rkMicrosoft = rkSoftware.OpenSubKey("Microsoft");
RegistryKey rkVisualStudio = rkMicrosoft.OpenSubKey("VisualStudio");
RegistryKey rk70 = rkVisualStudio.OpenSubKey("7.0");
RegistryKey rkFileMRUList = rk70.OpenSubKey("FileMRUList");
```

This code will drill down to:

```
HKEY_CURRENT_USER\Software\Microsoft\VisualStudio\7.0\FileMRUList
```

Alternatively you can go directly to the key you want:

```
RegistryKey rkFileMRUList =
    Registry
        .CurrentUser
            .OpenSubKey(@"Software\Microsoft\VisualStudio\7.0\FileMRUList");
```

Once you have a Registry key, you can look for its values. If you know the name of a value, you can call `GetValue()` directly. Alternatively you can call `GetValueNames()`. This will return an array of strings containing the value names. An example is shown below:

```
//Get array of value names in FileMRUList key
string[] fileNameValues = rkFileMRUList.GetValueNames();

//If the array is not empty...
if (fileNameValues.Length>0)
{
    //Get the first value name into fileName1
    string fileName1 = fileNameValues[0];

    //Then use fileName1 to lookup the value, by calling GetValue and
    //display value name and value
    MessageBox.Show(fileName1+"="+rkFileMRUList.GetValue(fileName1),
                    "The first file in the MRU list");
}
```

This results in a message box with the title **The first file in the MRU list**, which displays the value of this file.

You can also modify the current entry by calling the `SetValue()` method on the key. However, since modifying the Registry is serious business, you can only write to a value in a key if the key has been opened with write access. You specify the writability in the second parameter to the `OpenSubKey()` call. If we want to modify the filename we found in the code above, we must open another key with write access, and then call `SetValue()`:

```
fileName1 = ...
RegistryKey rkWritableFileMRUList = rk70.OpenSubKey("FileMRUList",true);
rkWritableFileMRUList.SetValue(fileName1,@"c:\temp\myfile.txt");
```

Finally, you can add new keys and subkeys by calling `CreateSubKey()`. As with `OpenSubKey()`, you can either pass in a relative or an absolute path for the location of the key. The example below shows how to create a `Colors` key under `HKCU\Software\Wrox\StoreMyColor`.

```
RegistryKey ColorKey =
        Registry
            .CurrentUser
                .CreateSubKey(@"Software\Wrox\StoreMyColor\Colors");
```

Note that if the key already exists its values will not be overwritten.

Try It Out – Store My Color

To give a simple demonstration of Registry access, let's make a program that uses the Registry to store the user's preference for the background color of the form.

Since the preference will be different for different users, and it only applies to our program, it makes sense that we store it under the following key:

HKCU\Software\Wrox\StoreMyColor\Colors

1. Create a new Windows Application project called **StoreMyColor**.

2. Drag a `ComboBox` onto the form. Remove the text from the `ComboBox`'s `Text` property, and change the form's `Text` property to `StoreMyColor`.

3. With the `ComboBox` selected, click the lightning tab on the Properties window, and then double click on the `SelectedValueChanged` event to create an event handler. Add one line to the event handler, so that it looks like this:

```
private void comboBox1_SelectedValueChanged(object sender,
                                            System.EventArgs e)
{
    this.BackColor=Color.FromName(comboBox1.SelectedItem.ToString());
}
```

4. Insert the following three methods:

```
void FillCombo()
    // Fills the combo box with the names of all colors
    // Uses reflection to get those.
{
    Type ct = typeof(Color);
    PropertyInfo[] cMembers = ct.GetProperties();
    foreach(PropertyInfo pi in cMembers)
    {
        if (pi.PropertyType == typeof(Color) && pi.Name!="Transparent")
        {
            comboBox1.Items.Add(pi.Name);
        }
    }
}

void RetrieveColor()
{
    // Retrieves color from registry and sets it in combo box and screen
    RegistryKey ColorKey =
        Registry
            .CurrentUser
                .CreateSubKey(@"Software\Wrox\StoreMyColor\Colors");
    string colorName = (string)ColorKey.GetValue("BackColor");
    try
    {
        Color c = Color.FromName(colorName);
        comboBox1.SelectedItem = colorName;
        this.BackColor = c;
    }
    catch
    {
```

```
            //color may be invalid which would cause exception..
        }
    }

void StoreColor(string colorName)
    // Stores selected color in the registry
{
    RegistryKey ColorKey =
        Registry
            .CurrentUser
                .CreateSubKey(@"Software\Wrox\StoreMyColor\Colors");
    ColorKey.SetValue("BackColor",colorName);
    ColorKey.Close();
}
```

5. Insert calls to `FillCombo()` and `RetrieveColor()` in the form's constructor, and a call to `StoreColor()` in the form's `Dispose()` method:

```
public Form1()
{
    InitializeComponent();
    FillCombo();
    RetrieveColor();
}

protected override void Dispose( bool disposing )
{
    if( disposing)
    {
        if (comboBox1.SelectedIndex>-1)
            StoreColor(comboBox1.SelectedItem.ToString());
        if (components != null)
    ...
```

6. Finally, insert a reference to the `Microsoft.Win32` and `System.Reflection` namespaces at the top of the file:

```
using Microsoft.Win32;
using System.Reflection;
```

7. Build and run the application. Select a color from the combo box and see that the form changes background color. Close and reopen the application, and notice that the new color has been retained.

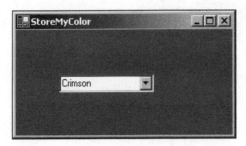

Also open up the Registry editor and verify the existence of a Registry key holding the color value:

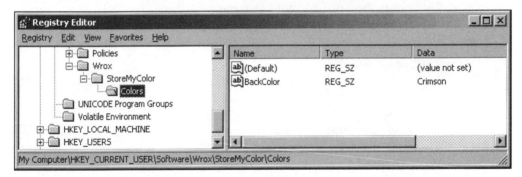

How It Works

We start by setting up an event handler that will get called each time the user selects a new color on the combo box.

In the `FillCombo()` method we use reflection to get a list of available standard colors.

> *Reflection is a technique by which we can programmatically access names, types and signatures of all private and public member variables, properties, and methods in a class. If you wish to know more about reflection in C#, refer to* Professional C#, 2nd Edition *by Wrox Press, ISBN 1-86100-704-3.*

These standard colors are available as static properties on the `Color` structure, and the code just iterates through these properties, checks whether they are of type `Color`, and then adds their names to the `ComboBox` list. There is only one exception. Since a form cannot have the color `Transparent`, that color is not added to the `ComboBox`:

```
Type ct = typeof(Color);
PropertyInfo[] cMembers = ct.GetProperties();
foreach(PropertyInfo pi in cMembers)
```

```
    {
        if (pi.PropertyType == typeof(Color) && pi.Name!="Transparent")
        {
            comboBox1.Items.Add(pi.Name);
        }
    }
}
```

If we had wanted to, we could have instantiated a `ColorDialog` instead, and used that to pick the color.

The `RetrieveColor()` method is called when we want to retrieve the color name from the Registry. Instead of moving slowly down the hierarchy, we access the key directly by giving the full path starting from HKCU. Notice the use of `CreateSubKey()` instead of `OpenSubKey()`. `CreateSubKey()` will create (and open) the subkey if it does not already exist. If it does exist, it will just open it, and will not destroy its contents:

```
RegistryKey ColorKey =
    Registry
        .CurrentUser
            .CreateSubKey(@"Software\Wrox\StoreMyColor\Colors");
```

Even if we are assured that we can get a key (not taking into account any possible security issues), the key may not contain a valid color name. The following code, which sets the background color, is therefore enclosed in a `try...catch` block:

```
Color c = Color.FromName(colorName);
comboBox1.SelectedItem = colorName;
this.BackColor = Color.FromName(colorName);
```

The `StoreColor()` method works in a similar fashion. We use `CreateSubKey()` again to make sure a key is created if it does not already exist. We then use `SetValue()` to store the color. Finally we close the key:

```
RegistryKey ColorKey =
    Registry
        .CurrentUser
            .CreateSubKey(@"Software\Wrox\StoreMyColor\Colors");
ColorKey.SetValue("BackColor",colorName);
ColorKey.Close();
```

The calls to `FillCombo()` and `RetrieveColor()` are inserted into the constructor after the call to `InitializeComponent()`, so the combo box is filled and the color retrieved before the form becomes visible.

Likewise, the `Dispose()` method includes the call to `StoreColor()`, so the settings are saved just before the application closes.

Summary

We have covered quite a lot of ground in this chapter. The emphasis has been on ways to store and retrieve data that does not really belong in a database.

We first looked at regular file I/O. We discussed the use of streams to transfer data, and the use of Reader and Writer objects to read and write text to file. We also noted that the same mechanisms used for writing to a disk could also be used for writing over, say, a network connection.

We then took a closer look at the .NET classes we can use to navigate the PC's directory and file structure, namely `FileInfo` and `DirectoryInfo`.

In the third part of the chapter we discussed serialization. Serialization allows us to stream the contents of objects and write them to file. A simple use of this is to store the data for later reload. A more advanced use is to transfer data between two applications. While we did not demonstrate it, it should be easy to appreciate how the **StockFeeder** application could be coupled with the **StockChart** application from the previous chapter, if we wanted to serialize and deserialize the data supplied to the chart.

Finally we looked at the Registry, which is mostly used to store user or application configuration data. We discussed how the Registry is structured, and created an example that showed where to store the background color of a simple app.

In the next chapter we are going to look at how to create Windows applications based upon a document/view structure.

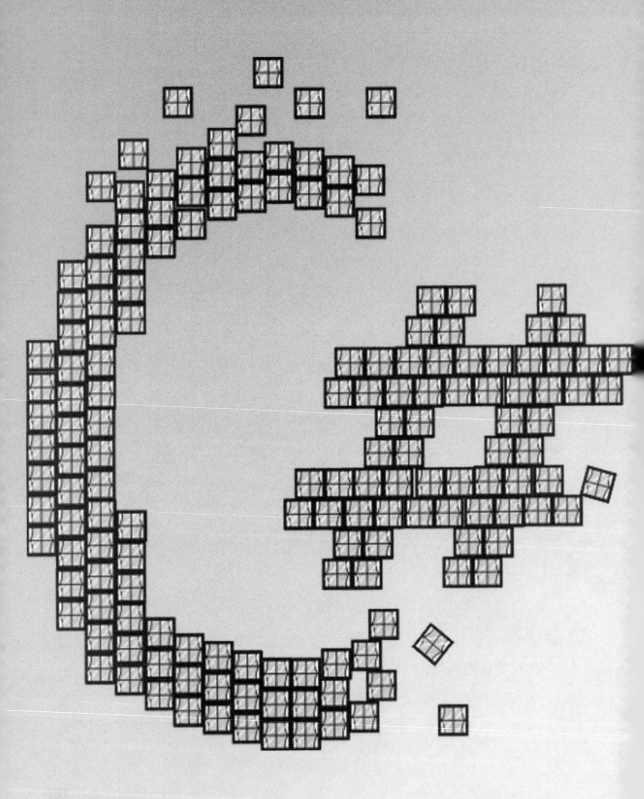

Using the Document/View Model

In this chapter, we're going to be taking a look at a very common requirement of software applications – dealing with more than one document at the same time. For example, when using the latest versions of Microsoft Word, although we have a separate top-level window that appears on the Task Bar at the bottom of the screen for each document, each of those windows are driven by a single application process.

Enabling Windows applications with this functionality is a matter of applying a couple of very simple design patterns.

First, it is desirable to deal with form (GUI) interactions in one class (the "view"), and interactions with any data sources in another class (the "document"). Separating application code into document and view classes like this makes it easier to write, reuse and maintain.

Second, we need to include a class in our application that keeps track of the documents, and manages the view and editing process of each one.

Third, we must deal with the problems associated with saving and opening files that may lead to loss of data. There are some basic rules in Windows applications that you'll find in most applications (and you'll really notice them if an application doesn't follow them). For example, in a well-designed Windows application, if you have an untitled document and select File | Save from the menu, that application will ask you to provide a filename for the file. On future selections of this option, because we now have a filename for the file, the file will be saved without you being prompted for the filename. Another "rule" like this is that if you have a document that has some changes in it that haven't been saved, and you select the Open, or New menu option or attempt to quit the program, you'll be asked if you would like to save the file to prevent you from losing any changes.

In this chapter we will discuss these issues further, and show you how to design and implement a Windows application that can handle multiple documents at once, based on the document/view model.

What is the Document/View Model?

In this chapter, the kind of application that we're going to consider is called **document/view**. In this type of application, the document is managed separately from the view. In other words, we split the code that handles the presentation of a document (the view) from the code that handles the manipulation of the document (the document itself).

To illustrate this, consider a word processing application and imagine that this application supports a class called WordDocument. This class does *not* handle any presentation of the document – it's just a bucket into which we can pour the document and run document-specific activities. For example, we may want to save or load the document, run a spell check, create labels, print, and so on. All of these activities are distinct from the actual activity of presenting the document to the user, and allowing the user to edit the contents of it.

A separate class called WordDocumentView could handle these presentation and editing aspects. This class might contain a property called Document that maintains a reference to the document that's being displayed. All of the logic to present the document, and present an editing interface is implemented in WordDocumentView.

But why would we want to adopt such a model? This document/view separation is very useful in situations where you want to be able to manipulate a document without having to have all of the presentation overhead, or even in situations where displaying the presentation overhead is an impossibility. Consider an e-commerce web site. After the order has been captured, an invoice has to be created and printed. The web site wishes to use the powerful features of our word processing application to layout and print the document. The problem is that the web site does not want to have to suffer with the overhead of the view portion of our application. The customer can never see it (it's on the server machine, which is probably remote to the customer's machine) – in fact we don't want the customer to see it anyway because we don't want the view edited by the customer.

Indeed, if we have a good document/view separation, the application can create an instance of WordDocument without *requiring* an instance of WordDocumentView to be available. The web site can then programmatically generate the invoice and print it. Specifically, we can leverage the power of the word processing application to reuse all this rich functionality, but we don't have to strangle our computer by running all this useful presentation code. Imagine a tiny progress bar displaying the status of a document print, rather than having to load the document, display it to the user and then show them a dialog box in the middle of the screen showing the print process.

What About MDI?

When talking about multiple documents in an application you'll often hear the acronym **MDI** mentioned. This stands for "Multiple Document Interface" and is the opposite of SDI or "Single Document Interface".

MDI was used a lot with versions of Windows prior to Windows 95. In MDI, several document windows were contained within a master application window. However, Microsoft researchers discovered that users found this split artificial and confusing. For instance, in the following screenshot, I have three document windows containing three views of a SQL Server installation here in my office.

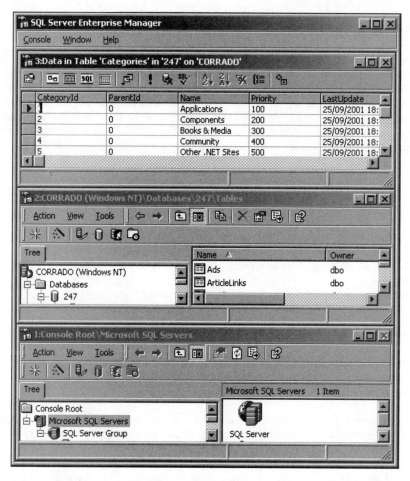

As you can see, the windows are bunched up together and constrained in this fairly artificial "master" window. Other problems include the fact that the familiar Alt+Tab method of navigating through windows doesn't work with MDI, because the only one of these windows you can navigate to is the master window itself. (However, in some cases, the Ctrl+Tab combination may allow you to navigate between child windows of the MDI application instead.) So from Windows 95, Microsoft announced that MDI would be deprecated and that it should not be used for Windows applications.

However, Microsoft's story on MDI has never been consistent; legacy support has continued to be included with Windows (as it should be), and different developer teams at Microsoft have continued to use the paradigm. Some Windows applications do still support MDI; notably the Microsoft Management Console – a standard application used for administering server applications on Windows. Microsoft Access is an MDI application, whereas Microsoft Word behaves in accordance with the official guidelines. Microsoft Excel isn't an MDI application, but there are some subtle differences between the way windows are handled in this compared to other Microsoft Office applications.

Although you can create MDI applications with .NET, in this book we're going to go down the recommended document/view route and avoid MDI.

Creating a Document/View Application

Now that we understand the advantages of creating an application based upon the document/view model, let's move on and discuss how we might actually implement one. The easiest and clearest way to do this is obviously to develop a sample application based upon document/view. Therefore we are going to create a basic text editor application (like Windows Notepad) that supports multiple document windows. We'll call the document class `TextDocument` and the view class `TextDocumentView`. As you might expect, `TextDocumentView` will extend `System.Windows.Forms.Form`. There are several issues we need to consider as we implement the text editor application:

- ❑ How do we manage multiple documents?
- ❑ How do we create new windows in the application?
- ❑ How do we allow the user to edit a document?
- ❑ How do we allow the documents to be loaded and saved?
- ❑ How do we allow the user to navigate from window to window?

Over the course of the rest of the chapter we'll consider all of these issues.

Managing Multiple Document Windows

The first thing we'll look at doing is handling multiple document windows. We need a way of creating the first window, allowing the user to create new windows and, ultimately, quitting the application once all of the windows have been closed.

A good way to approach this problem is to create a "coordination" class that will manage the document windows. The responsibility of this class is to provide an entry point into the application, and to maintain a list of open document windows. It will also listen for `Closed` events on the document windows and remove them from the list of open windows as the user closes each one. Ultimately, when the number of items in this list reaches zero, we can assume that all of the windows have been closed and that we can quit the application.

Try It Out – Creating the Infrastructure for the Text Editor Application

For our first Try It Out of the chapter we'll create the skeletons for the basic classes that we'll need for our text editor application, including a `TextDocumentView` class, a `TextDocument` class, and a `DocumentManager` class. We'll also add the functionality needed to allow the user to open new document windows via a main menu option.

1. Create a new Visual C# Windows Application project. Call it TextEditor.

2. Delete the default `Form1` Windows Form using Solution Explorer, and create a new class called `DocumentManager` by right-clicking on the **TextEditor** project and selecting Add | Add Class.

3. In a similar way, create another new class called TextDocument, and a new Windows Form called TextDocumentView.

4. Open up the Code Editor for DocumentManager. To the top of the listing, add namespace references to System.Collections and System.Windows.Forms:

```
using System.Windows.Forms;
using System.Collections;
```

5. Into the DocumentManager class, add a _current field and a _documents field, a Current property and a Documents property, and three methods: Main(), RegisterDocumentView(), and ViewClosed().

```
public class DocumentManager
{
    // fields...
    private static DocumentManager _current;
    private ArrayList _documents = new ArrayList();

    public static DocumentManager Current
    {
        get
        {
            return _current;
        }
    }

    public ArrayList Documents
    {
        get
        {
            return _documents;
        }
    }

    [STAThread()] static void Main()
    {
        // Store the current manager...
        _current = new DocumentManager();

        // Create the first view...
        TextDocumentView view = new TextDocumentView();
        view.Show();

        // Run the application...
        Application.Run();
    }

    public void RegisterDocumentView(TextDocumentView view)
    {
        // Store the view in the list of views...
```

```
        Documents.Add(view);

        // Hook into the "closed" event...
        view.Closed += new EventHandler(ViewClosed);
    }

    private void ViewClosed(object sender, EventArgs e)
    {
        // Remove the sender from our document list...
        Documents.Remove(sender);

        // Have we closed the final window?
        if(Documents.Count == 0)
            Application.Exit();
    }
```

6. Before we can run the application, we have to add a new `Load` event handler to
`TextDocumentView`. Double-click on the form to create an empty handler and add the
following code:

```
private void TextDocumentView_Load(object sender, System.EventArgs e)
{
    // Register...
    DocumentManager.Current.RegisterDocumentView(this);
}
```

7. Next we need to tweak some of the project properties. Right-click on the **TextEditor** project in
Solution Explorer and select **Properties**. Change the `Startup Object` to
`TextEditor.DocumentManager`.

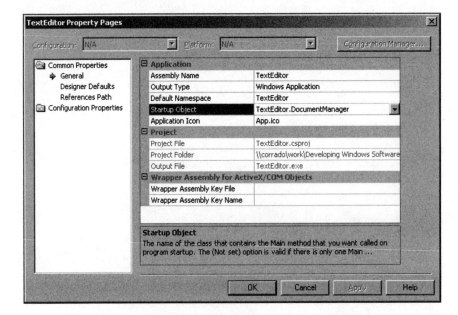

8. In the Designer for `TextDocumentView`, and add a new `MainMenu` control to the form. Rename it to `menuMain`. To the new menu, add a top-level **File** option and call it `menuFile` using the Properties window. Then add a **New Window** option (call this `menuFileNewWindow`) to the submenu of **File**.

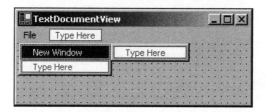

9. Double-click on the **New Window** option to add a `Click` event handler. Add this code:

```
private void menuFileNewWindow_Click(object sender, System.EventArgs e)
{
    CreateNewWindow();
}
```

```
public void CreateNewWindow()
{
    // create and show a new window...
    TextDocumentView view = new TextDocumentView();
    view.Show();
}
```

10. Build and run the project now. You'll be able to open multiple blank document windows by selecting the **File | New Window** option. The application will only close when all of the windows have been closed.

How It Works

By default, when an application starts, .NET needs to find a static method called `Main()` on one of the classes in the application's assembly that it can use as an entry point. Also by default, Visual Studio .NET puts one of these methods in the `Form1` form that is created along with the project. What this `Main()` method does is configure the application so that Windows can present the window to the user and allow interaction. It does this by calling a method on `System.Windows.Forms.Application` called `Run()` and passing in a reference to the first window that should be displayed by the application.

However, for our application, having the `Main()` method in our form class causes a show-stopping problem. If we open several form windows, when the first form window is closed, the application is closed. Imagine that we have ten windows; if we close the window opened first, the other nine will automatically close as well. This obviously isn't what we want.

To get around this problem, we move the `Main()` method into `DocumentManager` instead of the form. That's why we had to change the project properties to configure `DocumentManager` as the startup object. In the `DocumentManager.Main()` method we create a new instance of a `TextDocumentView` object, show it, and then call `Run()` without any parameters. By calling this method with no parameters, we're not associating the method with any specific window.

```
[STAThread ()] static void Main()
{
    _current = new DocumentManager();

    TextDocumentView view = new TextDocumentView();
    view.Show();

    Application.Run();
}
```

Notice that we set `_current` to be a reference to a new `DocumentManager` object. Because `_current` is static, the reference will be globally available throughout the application. In fact, we wrap this field in a property called `Current` that will ultimately provide access to the *same* `DocumentManager` instance from anywhere else in the application code.

```
public static DocumentManager Current
{
    get
    {
        return _current;
    }
}
```

We use this property from within the `Load` event handler of `TextDocumentView` to call the `RegisterDocumentView()` method:

```
private void TextDocumentView_Load(object sender, System.EventArgs e)
{
    DocumentManager.Current.RegisterDocumentView(this);
}
```

The `RegisterDocumentView()` method has two responsibilities. Its first is to add the view to the `_documents` ArrayList (remember that this `ArrayList` is wrapped by the `Documents` property). Its second is to hook into the `Closed` event so that our own `ViewClosed()` method is called when the window is closed. The beauty of this approach is that however the window is closed, we still get to know about it and we don't have to do anything inside the `TextDocumentView` code to "un-register" the window.

```
public void RegisterDocumentView(TextDocumentView view)
{
    Documents.Add(view);

    view.Closed += new EventHandler(ViewClosed);
}
```

So we know that when a `Closed` event is fired, our `ViewClosed()` method will be called, along with any other event handlers that the `TextDocumentView` may also have in place. We use the `Remove()` method on the `_documents ArrayList` to remove the appropriate window from the list. When the number of windows gets to zero, we call `Application.Exit()` to close the application:

```
private void ViewClosed(object sender, EventArgs e)
{
    Documents.Remove(sender);

    if(Documents.Count == 0)
        Application.Exit();
}
```

That's the basic infrastructure of our application in place. Finally, we added a menu option to create a new window, and added an event handler that calls the `CreateNewWindow()` method when this menu option is clicked:

```
public void CreateNewWindow()
{
    TextDocumentView view = new TextDocumentView();
    view.Show();
}
```

Since we registered the window with `DocumentManager` in the `Load` method of `TextDocumentView`, as soon as we call `Show()` from within our new `CreateNewWindow()` method, the new window has been registered.

Note how we've made the event handler call a method that actually performs the functionality we want from the handler. This makes our code more reusable and maintainable, since we can call the `CreateNewWindow()` method from somewhere else in the application rather than having to create another method that does the same thing somewhere else.

Adding File Viewing Functionality

Although we have now implemented the basic structure of our multi-window text editor application, it's not a particularly interesting application since it doesn't present any useful functionality to the user yet. In this section we're going to remedy this by giving the application the ability to display the contents of text files to the user. In the next section we'll go a step further and add the functionality needed to edit and save text to file too.

As we add this functionality, we will at all times need to bear in mind that we are working to the document/view model. Therefore we want to make sure that code that looks after interaction with the GUI is in our view class (`TextDocumentView`), and code that looks after interacting with our data source – files – is in our document class (`TextDocument`).

Obviously we're going to have to add a control that will hold the text from a file so that we can view it (and ultimately edit it). The obvious choice for this would be a multi-line textbox.

To hold the text for the document, we're simply going to need a property that contains the text of the document. To hold the filename of the document, we're going to need another property that will contain the full path to the file. Both of these will need to be on the document rather than the view.

To associate a view class with a document class, we should create a property on the view that gets and sets the document associated with the view (and also sets the text contained by the document too).

We'll also need to create a method to read in and load a text file into the document. Again, note how this method should be in the document rather than the view since it interacts with the data source.

Now that we've got a plan, let's put it into action.

Try It Out – Adding File Viewing Functionality to the Text Editor

In this Try It Out we will add the functionality needed to view text files to our text editor.

1. Open the Designer for `TextDocumentView`. Add a new `TextBox` control to the form. Set the `Name` property of the control to `textDocument`. Clear the `Text` property. Set the `Dock` property to `Fill`, the `ScrollBars` property to `Vertical` and the `MultiLine` property to `True`.

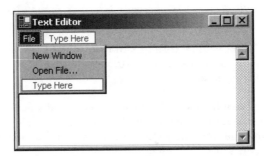

2. Add a new `OpenFileDialog` control to the form and rename it to `dialogOpenFile`. Add a new menu option called **Open File...** under the **File** menu. Set its `Name` property to `menuFileOpen`.

3. Next, open up the Code Editor for the form and add the _document field, the `FileDialogFilter` constant, and the `Document` property:

```
public class TextDocumentView : System.Windows.Forms.Form
{
    private TextDocument _document;

    // const...
    public const string FileDialogFilter =
        "Text Files (*.txt)|*.txt|All Files (*.*)|*.*||";

    public TextDocument Document
    {
        get
```

```
        {
            return _document;
        }
        set
        {
            // Set the document...
            _document = value;

            // Set the text...
            textDocument.Text = _document.Text;
        }
    }
```

4. Double-click on the **File | Open File...** menu item and add the following code to the `Click` event handler:

```
private void menuFileOpenFile_Click(object sender, System.EventArgs e)
{
    OpenDocument();
}
```

5. It's the `OpenDocument()` method's responsibility to display the **Open File** dialog. If the user chooses a file to open, we call the static `Load()` method on `TextDocument` and set the `Document` property to the return value.

```
public void OpenDocument()
{
    // show the dialog...
    dialogOpenFile.Filter = FileDialogFilter;
    if(dialogOpenFile.ShowDialog() == DialogResult.OK)
    {
        // load it...
        Document = TextDocument.Load(dialogOpenFile.FileName);
    }
}
```

6. Open up the Code Editor for `TextDocument`, and import `System.IO` as well as fields to support the `Text` and `Filename` properties, and the properties themselves:

```
using System.IO;

public class TextDocument
{
    // Fields...
    private string _text;
    private string _filename = string.Empty;

    public string Filename
    {
        get
```

```
    {
        return _filename;
    }
    set
    {
        _filename = value;
    }
}

public string Text
{
    get
    {
        return _text;
    }
    set
    {
        // set...
        _text = value;
    }
}
```

7. Finally, add the Load() method to TextDocument:

```
public static TextDocument Load(string filename)
{
    // Create the filestream...
    FileStream stream = null;
    try
    {
        // Open the file...
        stream = new FileStream(filename, FileMode.Open);

        // Create a new document...
        TextDocument document = new TextDocument();
        document.Filename = filename;

        // Read all of the data out...
        StreamReader reader = new StreamReader(stream);
        document.Text = reader.ReadToEnd();

        // Return the new document...
        return document;
    }
    finally
    {
        if(stream != null)
            stream.Close();
    }
}
```

8. Run the project now. Select **File | Open File...** and then choose a text file from your disk:

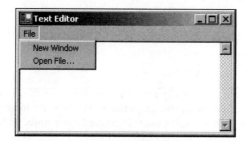

You should see the contents of the document opened in the editor. You will notice that you can edit the contents of the textbox, but there is no way to save the changes that you have made. In the next section we'll add this functionality to the application.

How It Works

We start off by adding a `TextBox` to the form that will hold the text from a text file. We also add an `OpenFileDialog` control that represents the **Open File** dialog box, and a menu option that invokes this dialog box.

Then, inside the `TextDocumentView` class we add a `TextDocument` field to hold the current document, a property to get and set this field (and set the text that it contains):

```
private TextDocument _document;

public TextDocument Document
{
    ...
}
```

We also define a constant that we need to use to filter files in the **Open File** dialog box:

```
public const string FileDialogFilter =
    "Text Files (*.txt)|*.txt|All Files (*.*)|*.*||";
```

The filter is simply a string, separated by | symbols. By Windows convention, we have to give the name of the document, then the file type in parenthesis, for each file type. At the end, **All Files** has to appear. You can comma-separate file types if the document type supports multiple file types. (This happens in cases where the application is able to make a determination of the contents of the file on load.)

The `OpenDocument()` method, called by the event handler for the **Open File...** menu option, actually opens the **Open File** dialog box. We feed the filter string above to the `OpenFileDialog` object, and then when the user clicks **OK** in the dialog box we call the `TextDocument.Load()` method:

```
public void OpenDocument()
{
    // show the dialog...
```

277

```
            dialogOpenFile.Filter = FileDialogFilter;
            if(dialogOpenFile.ShowDialog() == DialogResult.OK)
            {
                // load it...
                Document = TextDocument.Load(dialogOpenFile.FileName);
            }
        }
```

The `Load()` method is where we actually read the text from the file. `Load()` is implemented as a static method, which gives us the interesting design pattern that we can't load a document over one already in memory, as a new instance of `TextDocument` is created each time. In the method we create a `FileStream` object, and use it to open the selected file:

```
        try
        {
            stream = new FileStream(filename, FileMode.Open);
```

Then we create a new `TextDocument` object, and set its `_filename` field to the name of the text file:

```
            TextDocument document = new TextDocument();
            document.Filename = filename;
```

Finally we read the text from the stream using a `StreamReader`, place it in the `_text` field of the `TextDocument` object, and return this object:

```
            StreamReader reader = new StreamReader(stream);
            document.Text = reader.ReadToEnd();

            return document;
        }
```

Note how we've placed the functionality in a `try...finally` block, so that the stream always gets closed when we've finished with it, conserving resources:

```
        finally
        {
            if(stream != null)
                stream.Close();
        }
```

Also note how we have successfully divided up our code so that user interface aspects are dealt with in `TextDocumentView`, and data source aspects (reading files) are dealt with in `TextDocument`. We are therefore implementing the document/view model correctly.

Adding File Save Functionality

The next step is to add the functionality needed to change the text file viewer to a text file editor. In other words, we need to add menu items and functionality that will enable a user to:

❑ Open a new blank text document ready for editing

❑ Save modifications made to an existing text file

❑ Save text into a new text file, allowing the user to name the file

Saving text implies writing it to file. According to the document/view model, we should add this functionality to the document rather than the view.

Giving the user the ability to edit text files and then save them adds a new layer of complexity to our application. We will need to design the application such that the user cannot easily accidentally lose modifications made to text files. Provided that the form is already associated with a text file and the text has been modified since the last save, we will need to prompt the user to save the file in the following situations:

❑ The user attempts to quit the application, or to close the editing window

❑ The user selects File | New File from the menu

❑ The user selects File | Open File... from the menu

We will also therefore need to keep track of whether changes have been made to the text in the first place. To do this, we can make use of the TextChanged event associated with the TextBox on the form, which is fired when the contents of the textbox are modified.

There are other common user actions that we will need to generate the appropriate response for too:

❑ If the user selects the File | Save option and the document is untitled, we have to prompt them for a filename

❑ If the user selects the File | Save option and the current document has a filename associated with it, we do not prompt them for a filename – we just save the file

❑ If the user selects the File | Save As... option, we prompt for a filename whether or not the document already has one

Now that we have a grasp of the problems we need to solve to implement the required functionality, let's look at a possible solution.

Try It Out – Adding File Save Functionality to the Text Editor

In this Try It Out we are going to complete the core functionality for our editor, so that the user can edit files and save the modifications to disk, and even create new text files.

1. Open the Designer for `TextDocumentView`. Add new menu options under the **File** menu for **New File**, **Save** and **Save As....** Call them `menuFileNewFile`, `menuFileSave`, and `menuFileSaveAs` respectively. Before adding some code, add a new `SaveFileDialog` control to the form, and call it `dialogSaveFile`.

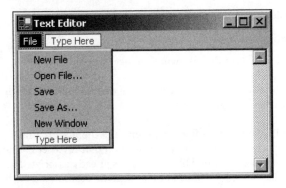

2. Next, open the Editor for `TextDocumentView`. Add the `CheckSaveResult` enumeration, and modify the `Document` property as shown below:

```
public class TextDocumentView : System.Windows.Forms.Form
{
    // Fields...
    private TextDocument _document;

    // Enum...
    public enum CheckSaveResult { Ok, Cancel };

    public TextDocument Document
    {
        get
        {
            return _document;
        }
        set
        {
            // Have we changed it?
            if(_document == value)
                return;

            // Are we going to lose the existing document?
            if(_document != null && Document.IsDirty() == true)
                throw new InvalidOperationException(
                    "The existing document has not been saved.");

            // Set the document...
            _document = value;

            // Set the text...
            textDocument.Text = _document.Text;
        }
    }
}
```

3. In the `TextDocumentView()` constructor, add a call to `NewDocument()` (we'll define this method in a moment):

```
public TextDocumentView()
{
    //
    // Required for Windows Form Designer support
    //
    InitializeComponent();

    // Create a new document...
    NewDocument();
}
```

4. Add the `CheckSave()` method too:

```
public CheckSaveResult CheckSave()
{
    // If we don't have a document, or it's clean, return OK...
    if(Document == null || Document.IsDirty() == false)
        return CheckSaveResult.Ok;

    // Ask the user...
    DialogResult result = MessageBox.Show(this,
        "Do you want to save changes to this document?",
        "Text Editor", MessageBoxButtons.YesNoCancel,
        MessageBoxIcon.Question);
    switch(result)
    {
        case DialogResult.Cancel:
            return CheckSaveResult.Cancel;

        case DialogResult.Yes:
            return SaveDocument();

        case DialogResult.No:
            Document.SetAsClean();
            break;

        default:
            throw new InvalidOperationException();
    }

    // return...
    return CheckSaveResult.Ok;
}
```

5. By double-clicking on the menu items, create event handlers for the new menu items, and then add the code shown below:

```
private void menuFileNewFile_Click(object sender, System.EventArgs e)
{
    NewDocument();
}


private void menuFileSave_Click(object sender, System.EventArgs e)
{
    SaveDocument();
}


private void menuFileSaveAs_Click(object sender, System.EventArgs e)
{
    SaveDocumentAs();
}
```

6. Next, add the `NewDocument()`, `SaveDocument()`, and `SaveDocumentAs()` methods called by the event handlers:

```
public void NewDocument()
{
    // Do we already have a document?
    if(CheckSave() == CheckSaveResult.Cancel)
        return;

    // Create a new document...
    Document = new TextDocument();
}

public CheckSaveResult SaveDocument()
{
    // Do we have a document?
    if(Document == null)
        return CheckSaveResult.Ok;

    // Do we have a filename?
    if(Document.IsUntitled() == true)
        return SaveDocumentAs();

    // Save it...
    Document.Save();

    // Return ok...
    return CheckSaveResult.Ok;
}

public CheckSaveResult SaveDocumentAs()
{
```

```
        // Do we have a document?
        if(Document == null)
            return CheckSaveResult.Ok;

        // Show the dialog...
        dialogSaveFile.Filter = FileDialogFilter;
        if(dialogSaveFile.ShowDialog() != DialogResult.OK)
            return CheckSaveResult.Cancel;

        // Save as...
        Document.Save(dialogSaveFile.FileName);

        // Return ok...
        return CheckSaveResult.Ok;
    }
```

Notice how both of the save methods call `Save()` methods, defined in `TextDocument`; we'll add these methods in a moment.

7. Double-click on the `TextBox` to create a new `TextChanged` event handler. Add this code:

```
private void textDocument_TextChanged(object sender, System.EventArgs e)
{
    Document.Text = textDocument.Text;
}
```

8. Finally, click on the title bar of the form and then click on the events button in the Properties window (it's the one with the lightning image on it). Double-click on the `Closing` event to generate an event handler, and then add this code:

```
protected void TextDocumentView_Closing(object sender,
    System.ComponentModel.CancelEventArgs e)
{
    if(CheckSave() == CheckSaveResult.Cancel)
        e.Cancel = true;
}
```

9. Now open up the Editor for `TextDocument`. Add a flag field `_isDirty` which indicates whether the text has been modified, the associated `IsDirty()` and `SetAsClean()` methods, and the `IsUntitled()` method. Also modify the `Text` property as shown below:

```
public class TextDocument
{
    // fields...
    private string _text;
    private string _filename = string.Empty;
    private bool _isDirty;

    public bool IsDirty()
```

```
   {
      return _isDirty;
   }

   public void SetAsClean()
   {
      // Reset the flag...
      _isDirty = false;
   }

   public bool IsUntitled()
   {
      if(Filename == string.Empty)
         return true;
      else
         return false;
   }

   public string Text
   {
      get
      {
         return _text;
      }
      set
      {
         // Has it changed?
         if(_text != value)
         {
            // Set...
            _text = value;

            // Flag...
            _isDirty = true;
         }
      }
   }
}
```

10. To actually implement the save process, we need to add appropriate methods to the TextDocument class. Add the following Save() methods:

```
public void Save(string filename)
{
   // Set the filename...
   Filename = filename;
   Save();
}

public void Save()
{
   // Do we have a filename?
```

```
            if(IsUntitled() == true)
                throw new InvalidOperationException(
                    "The document cannot be saved as it is untitled.");

            // Save it...
            FileStream stream = null;
            try
            {
                // Create the file...
                stream = new FileStream(Filename, FileMode.Create);

                // Write...
                StreamWriter writer = new StreamWriter(stream);
                writer.Write(Text);

                // Flush...
                writer.Flush();
            }
            finally
            {
                if(stream != null)
                    stream.Close();
            }
        }
```

11. Build and run the application. You'll now not only be able to view files, but edit existing ones and save the modifications, or even create and save new text files.

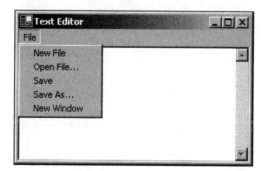

If you edit a document and try to shut the window before saving your changes, you will be prompted to do so by a dialog box:

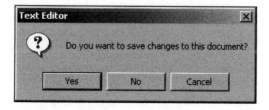

How It Works

We started off by adding some more menu options to our form. These options will ultimately allow the user to open a new blank text file ready for editing, save modifications to an existing file, or save text into a file with a user-specified name. We also added a `SaveFileDialog` control to the form, so that we can use the **Save File** dialog box.

Since we are now interested in not only viewing files, but editing the text and saving the changes, we need to make sure that the user doesn't accidentally lose modifications made to text files. This might happen if, say, the form was closed before a save was made, or if another file is opened in the same window. In these situations we will want to prompt the user to save the existing file before proceeding.

However, we also don't want to prompt the user to save a file that hasn't been modified. Therefore we need to keep track of whether the file has been modified since the last save. Therefore, we introduce a field `_isDirty` to `TextDocument`, which is a flag that indicates whether or not the text has been modified. We also add the `IsDirty()` method, which returns the value of `isDirty`, and `SetAsClean()`, which resets `isDirty` to `false` (indicating that the text has not been modified). The `Text` property of `TextDocument` is modified too, so that setting `_text` to a new value sets the `_isDirty` flag to `true`:

```
set
{
    // has it changed?
    if(_text != value)
    {
        // set...
        _text = value;

        // flag...
        _isDirty = true;
    }
}
```

When the contents of the `TextBox` are modified, the `TextChanged` event handler is called:

```
private void textDocument_TextChanged(object sender, System.EventArgs e)
{
    Document.Text = textDocument.Text;
}
```

As you can see, this updates the `TextDocument.Text` property to contain the new contents of the `TextBox`. As we noted above, this means that the `_isDirty` flag is set to `true` as well.

We make use of the `_isDirty` flag in the `CheckSave()` method, which is called by several other methods to determine if the current document needs to be saved, if we need to prompt the user to save it, or if it doesn't need saving. The method returns a value from the `CheckSaveResult` enumeration defined in `TextDocumentView`; this value can be `Ok` (the file doesn't need to be saved) or `Cancel` (the user may want to save the file):

```
public CheckSaveResult CheckSave()
{
```

In the method, we first check whether there is any file opened, or if any changes have been made to the text. If not, we return Ok, indicating that the file doesn't need to be saved:

```
if(Document == null || Document.IsDirty() == false)
    return CheckSaveResult.Ok;
```

If there is a file open and the text has been modified, we display a message box prompting the user to save if necessary:

```
DialogResult result = MessageBox.Show(this,
    "Do you want to save changes to this document?",
    "Text Editor", MessageBoxButtons.YesNoCancel,
    MessageBoxIcon.Question);
```

Depending on whether the user clicks on the Cancel, Yes, or No button of the message box, we either return a enumeration value of Cancel, call the SaveDocument() method to save the file, or simply reset the _isDirty flag:

```
switch(result)
{
    case DialogResult.Cancel:
        return CheckSaveResult.Cancel;

    case DialogResult.Yes:
        return SaveDocument();

    case DialogResult.No:
        Document.SetAsClean();
        break;

    default:
        throw new InvalidOperationException();
}

// return...
return CheckSaveResult.Ok;
}
```

Let's now turn our attention to what happens when the user clicks one of the New File, Save, and Save As... menu items. In all cases, the appropriate event handler calls another method that actually performs the required action.

The handler for **New File** calls the `NewDocument()` method. This method simply calls `CheckSave()` to see if the form is already associated with a text document. If not, it sets the `Document` property to the value of a blank `TextDocument` object:

```
public void NewDocument()
{
    // do we already have a document?
    if(CheckSave() == CheckSaveResult.Cancel)
        return;

    // create a new document...
    Document = new TextDocument();
}
```

You should note that we also added a few extra lines of code into the `Document` property to double-check that we aren't overwriting a document too.

You may have noted that `NewDocument()` is also called in the `TextDocumentView()` constructor; in other words a newly created form is associated with a blank `TextDocument`.

The **Save** menu item handler calls the `SaveDocument()` method, which simply checks whether there is a `TextDocument` open in the form and whether it has a filename before saving it. The **Save As...** menu item handler calls a similar method called `SaveDocumentAs()` that invokes a **Save File** dialog before saving the document. Both methods are defined in `TextDocumentView`, so to maintain our Document/View model we have them call `Save()` methods on `TextDocument` which actually save the document to file.

There are two `Save()` methods; one takes a filename as an argument, and the other takes no arguments. The version that takes a filename simply sets the `Filename` property of the `TextDocument` before calling the other version of `Save()`:

```
public void Save(string filename)
{
    // set the filename...
    Filename = filename;
    Save();
}
```

In the no-arguments version of `Save()`, we check that `Filename` has been set, before creating a `FileStream` and writing the contents of the `_text` field to file using a `StreamWriter`:

```
try
{
    stream = new FileStream(Filename, FileMode.Create);

    StreamWriter writer = new StreamWriter(stream);
    writer.Write(Text);

    writer.Flush();
}
```

As when we read text in from file, we use a `try...finally` construct in order to make sure that the stream is closed when we're finished with it:

```
finally
{
    if(stream != null)
        stream.Close();
}
```

Finally, we have one last situation to take into account. We want to make sure that the user is prompted to save a modified text file before the window is closed. So we added an event handler for the form `Closing` event:

```
protected void TextDocumentView_Closing(object sender,
    System.ComponentModel.CancelEventArgs e)
{
    if(CheckSave() == CheckSaveResult.Cancel)
        e.Cancel = true;
}
```

The handler calls `CheckSave()` in order to determine whether the document might need saving – if so it postpones the closure of the form.

Navigating Between Windows

We have now added the core functionality for the application. However, there are a few aspects of our application that make it look a little unprofessional. First, once we've opened a file in the editor, it's easy to lose track of which file has been opened since the name of the file is not displayed anywhere on the form. Second, many multi-window applications allow you to navigate between windows by providing a Window menu that lists the open windows. In this section, we'll take care of both of these issues.

Try It Out – Enabling Navigation Between Windows

In this Try It Out we are going to finish off our Text Editor application by giving it a bit of polish. We will add a Window menu that allows you to navigate between the open windows. We will also make it easier for the user to keep track of which text files have been opened in which windows, by making the title of bar of each form display the text file path.

1. Open the Designer for `TextDocumentView` and create a new top-level menu option called Window. Call it `menuWindow`. Underneath this option, create an option with the text Dummy. (Don't worry about the `Name` property for this.)

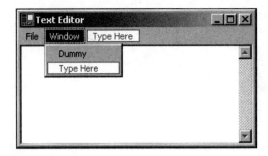

2. Create a new class called `WindowMenuItem`. Make this class extend `System.Windows.Forms.MenuItem`:

```
public class WindowMenuItem : System.Windows.Forms.MenuItem
{
    ...
}
```

3. Delete the existing constructor. Add a `TextDocumentView` field, and add this new constructor:

```
public TextDocumentView View;

public WindowMenuItem(int index, TextDocumentView view)
{
    // Set...
    View = view;
    Text = string.Format("{0} {1}", index, View.ToString());
}
```

4. Next, override the `OnClick()` method:

```
protected override void OnClick(System.EventArgs e)
{
    View.Activate();
}
```

5. Open the Code Editor for `TextDocumentView` and find its constructor. Add this code to hook the `PopUp` event handler of `menuWindow` to the `menuWindow_PopUp()` method:

```
public TextDocumentView()
{
    //
    // Required for Windows Form Designer support
    //
    InitializeComponent();

    // Events...
```

```
    this.menuWindow.Popup += new EventHandler(menuWindow_Popup);

    // Create a new document...
    NewDocument();
}
```

6. Then, add the `menuWindow_PopUp()` method itself:

```
private void menuWindow_Popup(object sender, System.EventArgs e)
{
    // Replace the menu items...
    menuWindow.MenuItems.Clear();

    // Go through each window...
    int ordinal = 1;
    foreach(TextDocumentView view in DocumentManager.Current.Documents)
    {
        // Create the item...
        WindowMenuItem item = new WindowMenuItem(ordinal, view);
        if(view.Equals(this))
            item.Checked = true;

        // Add it...
        menuWindow.MenuItems.Add(item);

        // Next
        ordinal++;
    }
}
```

7. Add the following code to the `Document` property:

```
public TextDocument Document
{
    ...

    set
    {
        ...

        // Set the text...
        textDocument.Text = _document.Text;

        // Update the caption...
        UpdateCaption();
    }
}
```

8. Add the following code to the `SaveDocumentAs()` method:

```
public CheckSaveResult SaveDocumentAs()
{
    // Do we have a document?

    ...

    // Save as...
    Document.Save(dialogSaveFile.FileName);

    // Caption...
    UpdateCaption();

    // Return ok...
    return CheckSaveResult.Ok;
}
```

9. Add the following method to `TextDocumentView`:

```
protected void UpdateCaption()
{
    // what do we want to do?
    this.Text = Document.ToString() + " - Text Editor";
}
```

10. Finally, override the `ToString()` method in `TextDocumentView`:

```
public override string ToString()
{
    if(Document != null)
        return Document.ToString();
    else
        return "(No Document)";
}
```

11. Then open up the Code Editor for `TextDocument` and add another override of the same method:

```
public override string ToString()
{
    if(IsUntitled() == true)
        return "(Untitled)";
    else
        return Filename;
}
```

12. Build and run the project now. You'll be able to select windows using the **Window** menu, and you'll notice that for each window the text file path appears in the form title bar. If you create a new file, it will be initially called **Untitled**.

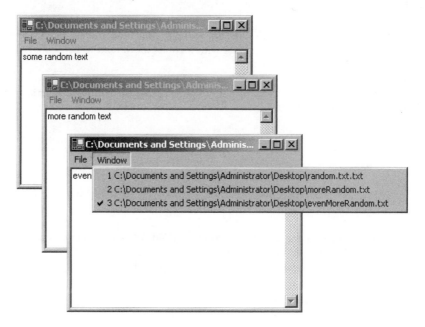

How It Works

Let's start by considering the functionality associated with the **Window** menu. Before a menu "pops up" (or "down", depending on your perspective!) the `PopUp` event is fired. We can use this to recreate the window. In fact, that's precisely what we do. Each time this happens, we clear out all of the items and iterate each of the views in the `Documents` collection of the `DocumentManager`.

Per iteration, we create a new `WindowMenuItem` object and add it to the `MenuItems` collection of the `menuWindow` object:

```
private void menuWindow_Popup(object sender, System.EventArgs e)
{
    menuWindow.MenuItems.Clear();

    int ordinal = 1;
    foreach(TextDocumentView view in
                DocumentManager.Current.Documents)
    {
        WindowMenuItem item = new WindowMenuItem(ordinal, view);
        if(view.Equals(this))
            item.Checked = true;

        menuWindow.MenuItems.Add(item);
```

293

```
        // next
        ordinal++;
      }
   }
```

We also check to see if the view that we're adding to the menu is the current view. If it is, we set the Checked property so that the window appears with a check mark next to it.

WindowMenuItem() is where all of the clever stuff happens. We extend System.Windows.Forms.MenuItem, and in the constructor we use the ToString() method of the view itself to create the text for the item.

```
      public WindowMenuItem(int index, TextDocumentView view)
      {
         // set...
         View = view;
         Text = string.Format("{0} {1}", index, View.ToString());
      }
```

When the user selects a menu item, the Click event is fired. We can detect this and react to it by overriding the OnClick() method defined on the base MenuItem class. As we have a reference to the View object, all we have to do is call Activate() to display the window.

```
      protected override void OnClick(System.EventArgs e)
      {
         View.Activate();
      }
```

Finally, let's consider what we needed to add to make the form title bar display the path to the text file. We added two methods. TextDocument.ToString() derives a string containing the file path, and the UpdateCaption() method uses this method to reset the Text property of the form to the file path string:

```
      protected void UpdateCaption()
      {
         // what do we want to do?
         this.Text = Document.ToString() + " - Text Editor";
      }
```

The UpdateCaption() method gets called twice: in the Document property (when we load a new document), and in the SaveDocumentAs() method (when we save a file with a new name).

Summary

In this chapter we took a look at how to build an application that supports multiple documents being opened at once. We looked at three major design patterns.

The first pattern we looked at was breaking **document** (interaction with the data source) and **view** (GUI) functionality into separate classes. This allows us to create and manipulate documents without specifically requiring a user interface, either because it doesn't make sense to have one (in the case of reusing the classes on the Web), or when you want to roll your own. Separating code according to this document/view model makes our applications more maintainable and reusable.

The second pattern we looked at was how to manage maintaining a list of open documents. We did this by creating a central management class accessible through a shared property and an `ArrayList` containing the documents. We used the multicasting ability of the .NET event model to hook into the `Closed` event so that we could "un-register" the window when it closed.

We also looked at how to code to stop the user from losing work when the windows are closed, new documents are created and opened, or existing documents are opened from disk.

In the next chapter we will discuss how to design and provide help facilities with your Windows applications.

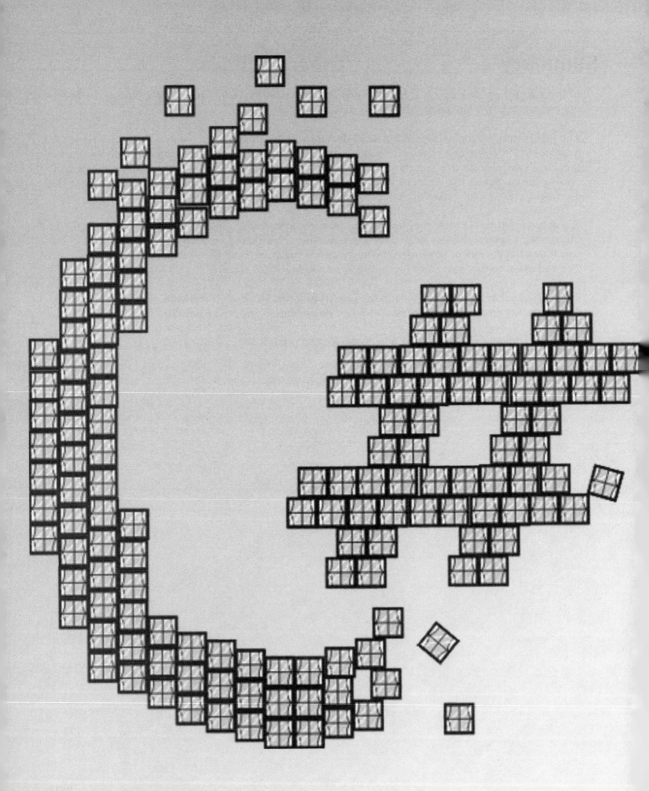

Providing Help

Current software products are complex, and complex products require comprehensive help systems. Even simple applications come with hundreds of pages of documentation, help systems, and online tutorials.

Despite all of this information, sometimes software applications are uninstalled from the end users' systems and left sitting on the shelf because people don't read manuals or use Help. One of the important reasons for this is that the documentation doesn't provide precise practical information on how to use the product. To ensure that the information systems that we develop do not become unusable, we must take care to design easy-to-use help systems that provide useful information and accommodate diversity.

In this chapter, we will teach you design guidelines for creating help systems and then follow that up with an examination of the various help authoring tools available. Finally we will discuss the support provided by the .NET Framework for linking external help systems with Windows applications. In this chapter we will cover:

- ❑ The different types of help authoring tools
- ❑ The fundamentals of the HTML Help workshop
- ❑ How to create effective and usable help systems using HTML Help workshop
- ❑ The support provided by the .NET Framework for integrating help systems with Windows applications
- ❑ The various help-related classes such as `Help` and `HelpProvider` that are part of the `System.Windows.Forms` namespace
- ❑ How to provide help using the `ToolTip` component
- ❑ Examples that show how to hook external help systems into a Windows application

Why Do Users Need a Help System?

The first question that needs to be answered when creating any help system is why users will want to read the information provided in the help. The answer to this question will help us create better help systems that are not only easy to use but also very effective. The following list identifies the four most common reasons why people use help.

❑ **To learn more about the application**
Novices and other users often choose to use help to learn a new application, since help is perceived as part of the application.

❑ **To find specific information**
Many users use help only when they have a specific question or problem. Often, they have tried to do something first on their own and were unsuccessful.

❑ **To explore**
Users sometimes browse the help file just to see what's there, following one topic to the next, gradually tracing a path through the information, and building an understanding of it. Hypertext systems based on HTML are especially compatible with this kind of use.

❑ **For reminders**
Sometimes users refer to help to remind them of something they have forgotten. For example, users frequently look up specific tasks and keyboard shortcuts.

Design Guidelines for Creating Help Systems

Now that we understand the main reasons that user help is required, let's establish some design guidelines for creating our own help systems.

Presentation

The first step in developing our own help system is determining the style guide to be used for online communication. We can do this by examining the in-house style manual to see if it can be used as is or if it needs to be modified to support our requirements.

Once we identify the company's style guide, we then need to figure out the different standard formats to use for the online help. Because online help can convey information using a variety of methods, we need to identify the set of methods to use in our help system. The various commonly used online formats are as follows:

❑ Contents

❑ Main window

❑ Pop-up window

❑ Topic heading and text

❑ Step-by-step instructions

- Tables
- Graphics
- Tooltip
- Status bar help

Navigation

In terms of navigation, the following questions need to be answered:

- How do you expect the user to navigate between different topics?
- How will the user move between sections of the online help?
- How will the user access the Glossary or otherwise obtain information on terminology?
- How will the Index and Contents be displayed or accessed?
- How will the user locate background or related information?
- How will the user exit the online help system?

These and similar questions should be kept in mind while creating navigations within the online help.

Content

Finally, we need to address the content of the help files; after all, we want our help files to be coherent and usable so that users will want to use them.

Writing Conventions and Standards

In order to make the content coherent, online standards should be introduced that include concrete and specific guidelines for writing. These should include standards for developing required topics, the desired syntax for presenting background information, guidelines for presenting step-by-step instructions, definitions, and examples, as well as general online document conventions.

Usability

There are lots of usability questions that arise as you create the files. One of the important questions that needs to be answered is the exasperation problem. For example, users can't find information they need, or a description does not make sense. To solve exasperation problems, we need to know a lot about the work the end users will do with our application. Will they be troubleshooting different system components to solve a problem? What context are they working in? What skills do they have? Answers to these questions will help us design a help system that can meet the requirements of the end users.

Since the user can access the online topics in any order, the topics must be self-contained. Requiring users to scroll through multiple screens to read a topic is guaranteed to frustrate them. The topics should also have relevant links to other topics that are closely related.

Another important thing to be evaluated while designing a help system is to consider the degree to which the help system is integrated with the application's overall support strategy. A well-designed help system is integrated with other support options. For example, a wizard can be linked to a related help topic and a help topic can reference a related topic in another help system. When the help system is properly integrated into the overall performance support strategy, it becomes part of a seamless support interface for the user.

Finally, help systems often suffer because they don't contain the best-matched information, which means that users can't find answers to less obvious questions. One way to anticipate the right questions is by providing context-sensitive help. Users generally expect the help system to know their context, to interpret their request for help in that context, and to understand their questions. Providing context-sensitive help is one of the best design decisions you can make as a help author, because context-sensitive is convenient, saves time and effort, and it is more likely to keep the users from overlooking something important.

Help Authoring Systems

Given that we would like to create a help system for our application, ideally we would like to use an authoring tool to create it with, in order to save us time and give the system a professional feel. Let us now consider the various help authoring mechanisms available.

WinHelp

WinHelp was the original Microsoft Windows help and it allowed us to create help systems similar to HTML help. If you expect a lot of the users of your software to use old versions of Windows, you can afford to create a help system using this. This is not a recommended choice for creating new help systems, as most people today use only HTML-based help files. Help systems created in this system had file suffixes of `.hlp`, `.cnt`, and `.gid`. In the eras of Windows 3.x and Windows 95 (First Edition), the only help system people worked with or even knew about was WinHelp. Problems started with the transition to Windows 95, when developers and users alike had to learn to deal with WinHelp 4.0's separate dialog with the Contents, Index, and Find functions.

HTML Help

In 1997, Microsoft released HTML Help, which became the standard for Windows 98 and 2000. HTML Help allows us to create help systems that stand alone or as part of an application. HTML Help is the type of help system you will see in recent Microsoft products when choosing Help from the main menu. It combines the functionality of WinHelp with the flexibility of HTML and the power of Active X control and scripts. Being based on HTML files, it requires both Windows and Internet Explorer to be present in the user's machine. HTML Help integrates HTML and Microsoft's ActiveX technology with the rich feature set of application help. Using HTML Help, we can deploy the complete navigation help system for an application in a small compressed file.

WebHelp

WebHelp is an exclusive browser-based cross platform help developed by e-Help corporation (http://www.ehelp.com/). It is designed to create online help systems for web-based applications. The main advantage to WebHelp is that it supports virtually all the programming languages and provides online help for Windows, Mac, Linux, and UNIX. It also works with all the browsers including Netscape Navigator and Internet Explorer. WebHelp supports standard HTML as well as all the key help functionalities like table of contents, full-text search, context-sensitive help and more.

JavaHelp

JavaHelp is really a Help delivery system, not a help-authoring tool. It is designed to work with applications written in the Java programming language. It leverages the many benefits of the Java language making it possible to deploy them on multiple platforms as long as the targeted platform has the Java language runtime. Due to the cross-platform nature, Java Help systems can run inside any Java software-enabled browser such as Netscape Navigator or Microsoft Internet Explorer.

OracleHelp

This is also used in conjunction with Java applications and can be used to create help formats for Java- and Oracle-based systems.

A Closer Look at HTML Help

In this section, we will discuss the features of HTML Help to see how it can be used to create HTML Help systems that can be seamlessly integrated with Windows applications.

HTML Help is the standard help system for the Windows platform. HTML Help is a help-authoring tool that provides an easy-to-use graphical design-time environment for creating compiled (.chm) project files, HTML topic files, content files, index files, and so on. Since HTML Help uses HTML for creating the help content files, it allows us to display text and graphics and use hyperlinks to navigate to other documents seamlessly.

Help system authors can use HTML Help to create online help for a software application or to create content for a web site. Apart from allowing authors to create content, the HTML Help workshop also exposes a programmatic interface using the HTML Help API making it possible for developers to program a host application or hook up context-sensitive help to an application. As an information delivery system, HTML Help is suited for a wide range of applications, including software applications, training guides, interactive books, electronic newsletters, and so on.

HTML Help also supports an advanced full-text search interface. Using the search interface, we can not only perform Boolean searches, but also search the results of previous searches so that we can systematically narrow the focus of the search.

Since HTML Help is based upon HTML, we can take full advantage of DHTML (Dynamic HTML) to make our help content more interactive and dynamic. Using HTML Help, we can also define a set of standard styles using cascading style sheet templates that can be consistently applied across all the help topics thereby making it possible to easily control the look and feel of the entire help system.

The HTML Help User Interface

HTML Help presents the information in a "tri-pane" window, with a navigation pane on the left, a content pane on the right, and a toolbar pane at the top. A typical HTML help file looks like the following.

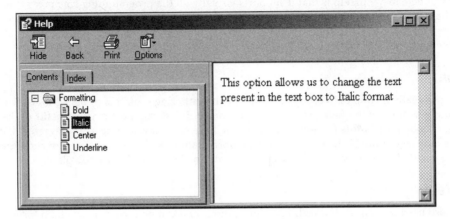

If users navigate through a help system using hyperlinks in the content pane, the table of contents automatically follows links within the help system content, expanding the relevant book and highlighting the topic being displayed in the content pane. This way, users can always keep track of where they are in the help system and will not get lost.

When we create an HTML Help system, we need to combine several individual pieces such as text, graphics, and HTML files together into a help project (`.hhp` file), this manages all the files in the help system. After this help project is compiled, we get a single compiled help file with the extension `.chm` that represents the entire help system.

Even though the types of files appearing on the help system depend on our requirements, we typically will have the following types of files contained in a help project:

- ❑ **HTML topic files** – Topics are sections of information contained in an HTML file.

- ❑ **Graphics and multimedia files** – These contain information about graphics, sound, video, animation, and other multimedia types.

- ❑ **Help project files** – As the name suggests, these files contain information about the name and location of all the files such as topic files, graphic files, index files, and so on. These files normally have the extension `.hhp`.

- ❑ **Content files** – A table of contents allow users to navigate a help file with ease. It presents information in a hierarchical format, using headings and pages. This file is identified by the file extension `.hhc`.

- ❑ **Index files** – An index file can be considered as the group of keyword entries merged together into a single file. These files are saved with the extension `.hhk`.

Now we have understood the theory behind HTML Help, let's begin creating a simple help system using HTML Help Workshop.

Try It Out – HTML Help System Creation using HTML Help Workshop

We will create an HTML Help system by using the HTML Help workshop tool version 1.3, which can be downloaded for free from Microsoft's web site (http://www.microsoft.com/downloads/release.asp?releaseid=33071). The purpose of this example is to give you a good grounding in using the HTML Help workshop tool to create industry-standard HTML Help systems.

1. Select Start | Programs | HTML Help Workshop | HTML Help Workshop from the Start menu.

2. Once you are in HTML Help Workshop editor, select File | New and you will see the following screen.

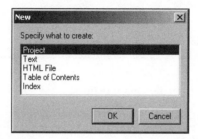

3. Select Project from the above listing and click OK. This will then bring up the following screen:

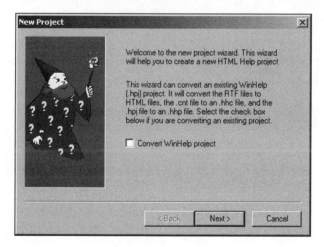

4. Since we want to create a new HTML Help project, we click Next without selecting the checkbox. When you click Next in the above screen, you will get the following screen, which allows you to select the name of the HTML Help project as well as the location in which it will be created. Type the path and file name information in the input box or click the Browse button to select the folder and filename.

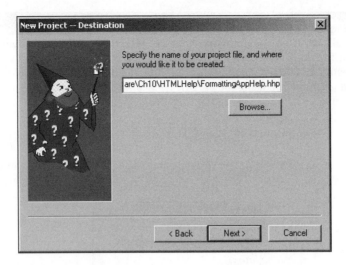

5. Clicking Next brings us the following screen:

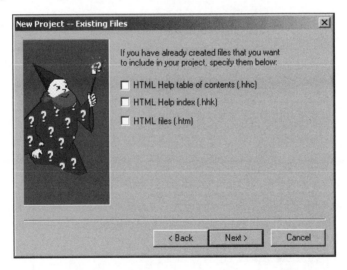

If you already have your help topics in external HTML files, you can add them as part of the help project by checking the checkbox next to HTML files option. In the same way, you can also add an existing content and index file to the help project at this time.

6. Click Next, and as we have no existing files we will get the following screen.

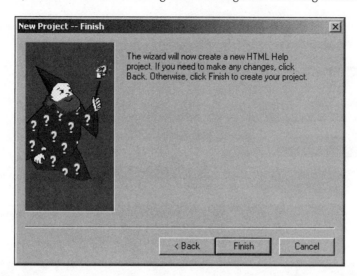

7. Finally when we click Finish, it creates the help project file and adds appropriate links to the project file depending on the options we selected.

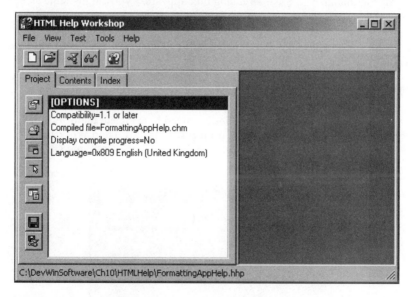

8. Now that we have created the help project, let us add topic files to it. To add a topic file, select File | New | HTML File. Alternately click the New button in the toolbar.

9. Enter the topic title as Bold and click OK.

10. In the HTML template created enter your text for that topic. After adding some content, the HTML file should look like the following.

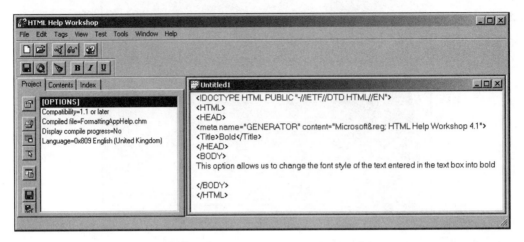

11. Save the contents by either clicking the Save button from the toolbar or by selecting Save from the File menu. The Save as dialog box appears. Type the filename as Bold.htm and save the file in the HTMLHelp project folder.

12. Follow the same steps and create separate topic files named Italic.htm, Underline.htm, and Center.htm. These files are included in the code download for the book from the Wrox web site at http://www.wrox.com. There is also a Formatting.htm file in the download, which is used as the default topic file. We will deal with this later.

13. Now that we have created the topic files, we need to associate them with the appropriate table of contents entries. When we create a project with HTML Help Workshop, by default there isn't a Contents (.hhc) file. Therefore, when you click the Contents tab, it displays the Table Of Contents Not Specified dialog.

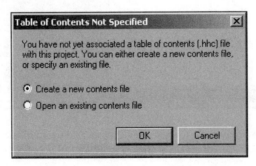

14. If you have an existing contents (.hhc) file that you want to associate with the project, select the appropriate option and then select the file. Since we want to create a new contents file, accept the default option and select OK. Accept the default filename (Table of Contents.hhc) and choose Save.

15. In this step, we will add a heading to the contents file. To add a heading to the contents file, click the Insert a heading button on the left-hand toolbar.

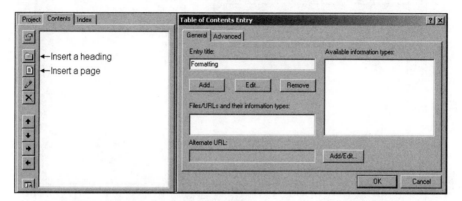

The Table of Contents Entry dialog box appears. Enter the heading title as Formatting and then click Add. Now click Browse and select the Formatting.htm file, click Open, then OK twice. A Formatting heading appears at the top of the contents tab.

16. We will now add topics under the Formatting heading we just created. To perform this, click Insert a page from the left-hand side toolbar. When you first insert a page, it displays a message, asking if you want to insert this page at the top of the hierarchy. Click No and the Table of Contents Entry dialog box displays.

17. Type the page title as Bold. Click Add. The Path or URL dialog box appears. Click Browse and select Bold.htm from the Open dialog box. The completed screen should look like the following. Click OK.

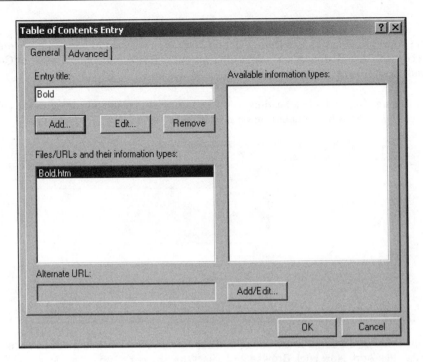

18. Repeat the same steps (steps 16 and 17) and add topics named Center, Italic, and Underline (also associating them with the appropriate HTML files) to the contents file. Remember that these need to be added as separate topics under the formatting header. Your display should then look like the following:

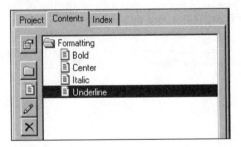

19. In this next step, we will add index entries to the project file. By default, when you create a project, there isn't an index (.hhk) file. Therefore, when you click the Index tab, it displays the Index Not Specified Message. Accept the default option and choose to create a new index file. Accept the default filename then press Save.

20. To create a new index entry, click Insert a keyword entry. The Index Entry dialog box appears. Type the keyword as Bold in the keyword textbox. Click Add and the Path or URL dialog box appears. Click the Browse button and navigate to the directory path of the Bold.htm file and select it. Also enter the title for the keyword entry as Bold. Click OK. After entering all the information, the finished dialog box appears as follows. Click OK.

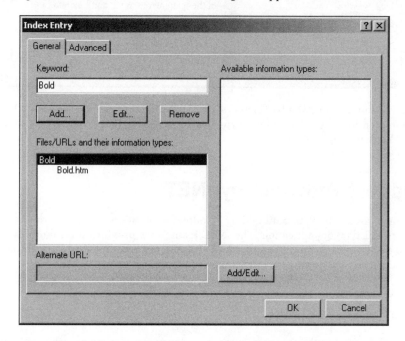

21. Repeat the previous step and add keywords Center, Italic, and Underline to the help project file. When inserting the second entry you will get a dialog asking if you want to insert this entry at the beginning of the index. Click No; this just allows you to sort the entry order.

22. Now we can set the default topic file that appears when running the help file. Select the Project tab and click the Properties icon in the left-hand side toolbar to open up the project Properties window.

23. In the Properties window, in the General tab, you should see the Default file combo box, where you can select (Formatting.htm) any one of the HTML files contained in the project as a default file. This file becomes the default file that is opened whenever the help system is launched.

24. Compile the help project by clicking the Compile button from the toolbar. Select both of the options and press Compile. The file will now be compiled and a log file produced of the process. Compiling this produces a single compressed help file called FormattingAppHelp.chm that looks like the following:

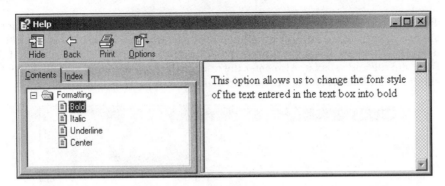

Now that we have understood the basics of creating HTML Help systems using HTML Help Workshop, let us turn our attention to see the support provided by the .NET Framework to use these external help systems in a Windows application.

Help Support Provided by .NET

Obviously, since this is a book about building Windows applications, we are most interested in adding help systems to this type of application. The .NET Framework provides several means for hooking up external help systems into Windows applications. It is mainly accomplished through the classes contained in the `System.Windows.Forms` namespace:

❑   `Help`

❑   `HelpProvider`

Because these classes are in the `System.Windows.Forms` namespace we are unable to create help systems for ASP.NET. Let us take a look at both of these classes in detail.

The Help Class

The `Help` class encapsulates the HTML Help 1.0 engine used in the HTML Help Workshop. We cannot create an instance of the `Help` class as it exposes all its functionalities only by means of static methods. Since the `Help` class encapsulates the HTML Help engine, it can be used to display not only compiled help files but also other files that are in HTML format. The static methods supplied by the `Help` class are as follows:

❑   `ShowHelp()` – As the name of the method suggests, it allows us to display the contents of a help file. This method is overloaded to provide for variations in the display of the help content to the user.

❑   `ShowHelpIndex()` – Allows us to display the complete index of the specified help file.

❑   `ShowPopup()` – Allows us to display pop-up messages.

The HelpProvider Class

Using the `HelpProvider` class, we associate an HTML Help file (`.chm` file) or an HTML file (`.html` file) with a Windows application. Once the initial association is established, we can then use it as a repository of help for the individual controls contained in the windows form. This initial association is required for us to display appropriate help information for different controls.

Using the `HelpProvider` class, we can display the help in a variety of ways:

- ❑ Provide context-sensitive help for controls on Windows Forms
- ❑ Provide context-sensitive help on a dialog box or specific controls on a dialog box
- ❑ Open the specific parts of the help file such as table of contents, index, or search functions while launching the help file
- ❑ Display help information in a pop-up window for specific controls

These steps should be followed when using the `HelpProvider` class to link help systems to individual controls on a form:

1. Firstly, we need to create an instance of the `HelpProvider` class.

2. Then we need to associate an external help file with the `HelpProvider` object by setting the `HelpNamespace` property.

3. Finally we hook up the individual controls to the specific topics of the help file by invoking the `SetHelpNavigator()` method of `HelpProvider` object. To this method, we pass the name of the control and a value from the `HelpNavigator` enumeration. We will discuss the `HelpNavigator` enumeration in a moment. But for this discussion, we will need to understand that it is used to open to the specific parts of the help file.

Using the `HelpProvider` class, we can also optionally display context-sensitive help information in a pop-up window, when the user presses *F1*. To accomplish this, we need to use the `SetHelpString()` method (which allows us to specify the help information to be displayed) of the `HelpProvider` class. To this method, we need to pass the name of the control and the help string to be associated with that control as arguments. At runtime, when the user presses *F1* for help, the help string associated with the `HelpProvider` class is displayed in a pop-up window.

The following table lists the important methods of the `HelpProvider` class.

Method	Description
`GetHelpKeyword()`	Allows us to get the help keyword for the specified control. This method takes the name of the control for which to retrieve the help keyword.

Table continued on following page

Method	Description
GetHelpNavigator()	Allows us to gets the current HelpNavigator setting for the specified control. This method takes the name of the control for which to retrieve the help topic.
GetHelpString()	Allows us to get the contents of the pop-up window for the specified control.
GetShowHelp()	Allows us to get the value indicating if the specified control's help should be displayed. This is useful in situations when you want to dynamically determine the help topic to display for the controls.
SetHelpKeyword()	Allows us to set the help keyword used to retrieve Help when the user invokes Help for the specified control.
SetHelpNavigator()	Allows us to set the Help command to use when retrieving Help from the Help file for the specified control.
SetHelpString()	Allows us to set the Help string associated with the specified control.
SetShowHelp()	This specifies whether help should be displayed for the specified control.

Using the SetHelpXXX() methods (shown in the above list) repeatedly, we can use a single instance of the HelpProvider object to maintain a collection of references to individual controls and their related help content.

The HelpNavigator Enumeration

As the name suggests, this allows us to provide access to the specific elements of the help file. Keep in mind that it is always used in conjunction with Help and HelpProvider classes. The constants defined by the HelpNavigator enumeration are as follows:

Member Name	Description
AssociateIndex	Allows us to specify constants indicating which elements of the Help file to display.
Find	When specified, it allows us to specify that the search page be displayed, when the help system is launched.
Index	Allows us to display the index function of the specified help file with the selected keyword highlighted, when the help system is launched.

Member Name	Description
KeywordIndex	Displays the Index function of the help system, which allows us to specify the keyword to search for in the index function of the help file.
TableOfContents	Allows us to display the TableOfContents function of the specified help file, when the help system is launched.
Topic	Allows us to display the specified topic referenced in the specified help file, when the help system is launched.

Now we will look at examples to understand how to use the help-related classes to hook up an external help system file with a Windows application.

Try It Out – Using HelpProvider to Link to an External Help System

We will use the HTML help file (FormattingAppHelp.chm) we created earlier as the external help system. We will create our Windows application to utilize this external help file. In this example, we will use the HelpProvider and Help classes to accomplish the desired result.

1. Select File | New | Project and create a new Windows Application under Visual C# Projects. Name the project HelpSampleApplication.

2. Rename the default Form1.cs to HelpProviderClassClient.cs and also change the Name property to HelpProviderClassClient. Change the Text property to Formatting Application - HelpProvider Class Client.

3. Drag a Label control onto the form and call it headingLabel, entering the Text to display as Enter the text: Also drag a RichTextBox control onto the form, calling it rtfText.

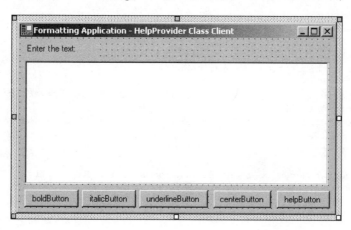

4. Add five button controls to the bottom of the form. Change the Name properties of the Button controls to those indicated in the screenshot.

5. That concludes the visual part of the example and we'll move straight to the code. Double-click the **Bold** button to add the click event handler to the code. Here is the code for the event:

```
private void boldButton_Click(object sender, System.EventArgs e)
{
  Font oldFont;
  Font newFont;

  //Get the font that is being used in the selected text
  oldFont = this.rtfText.SelectionFont;

  //If the font is using bold style now, remove the formatting
  if (oldFont.Bold)
    newFont = new Font(oldFont,oldFont.Style & ~FontStyle.Bold);
  else
    newFont = new Font(oldFont,oldFont.Style | FontStyle.Bold);

  //Insert the new font and return focus to the Richtextbox
  this.rtfText.SelectionFont = newFont;
  this.rtfText.Focus();
}
```

6. Double-click the **Italic** button to add the click event handler to the code. The code for the event handler is the following:

```
private void italicButton_Click(object sender, System.EventArgs e)
{
  Font oldFont;
  Font newFont;

  //Get the font that is being used in the selected text
  oldFont = this.rtfText.SelectionFont;

  //If the font is using Italic style now, remove the formatting
  if (oldFont.Italic)
    newFont = new Font(oldFont,oldFont.Style & ~FontStyle.Italic);
  else
    newFont = new Font(oldFont,oldFont.Style | FontStyle.Italic);

    //Insert the new font and return focus to the Richtextbox
  this.rtfText.SelectionFont = newFont;
  this.rtfText.Focus();
}
```

7. Double-click the Underline button to add the following click event handler to the code:

```
private void underlineButton_Click(object sender, System.EventArgs e)
{
  Font oldFont;
  Font newFont;

  //Get the font that is being used in the selected text
  oldFont = this.rtfText.SelectionFont;

  //If the font is using Underline style now, remove the formatting
  if (oldFont.Underline)
    newFont = new Font(oldFont,oldFont.Style & ~FontStyle.Underline);
  else
    newFont = new Font(oldFont,oldFont.Style | FontStyle.Underline);

    //Insert the new font and return focus to the Richtextbox
  this.rtfText.SelectionFont = newFont;
  this.rtfText.Focus();
}
```

8. Double-click the Center button and add the following code to the click event handler:

```
private void centerButton_Click(object sender, System.EventArgs e)
{
  if (this.rtfText.SelectionAlignment == HorizontalAlignment.Center)
    this.rtfText.SelectionAlignment = HorizontalAlignment.Left;
  else
    this.rtfText.SelectionAlignment = HorizontalAlignment.Center;
  this.rtfText.Focus();
}
```

9. Double-click the Help button to add the following lines of code, remembering to use our own path to the file.

```
private void helpButton_Click(object sender, System.EventArgs e)
{
  Help.ShowHelp(this,
                @"C:\DevWinSoftware\Ch10\HTMLHelp\FormattingAppHelp.chm",
                HelpNavigator.TableOfContents);
}
```

10. Double-click the main form and, in the `HelpProviderClassClient_Load()` event, add the following lines of code. Again remember to use you own path to the external resource.

```
private void HelpProviderClassClient_Load(object sender,
                                          System.EventArgs e)
{
  HelpProvider helpProv = new HelpProvider();
  helpProv.HelpNamespace =
```

```
                   @"C:\DevWinSoftware\Ch10\HTMLHelp\FormattingAppHelp.chm";

    //For the Form level context sensitive help,
    // show the TableOfContents tab
    helpProv.SetHelpNavigator(this,HelpNavigator.TableOfContents);

    //For the individual controls,
    // show the index tab with the appropriate text selected
    helpProv.SetHelpKeyword(boldButton,"Bold");
    helpProv.SetHelpKeyword(italicButton,"Italic");
    helpProv.SetHelpKeyword(underlineButton,"Underline");
    helpProv.SetHelpKeyword(centerButton,"Center");
}
```

11. Now build the solution and run the application by pressing *F5*. It should look like the following. We have entered some sample text to demonstrate its use:

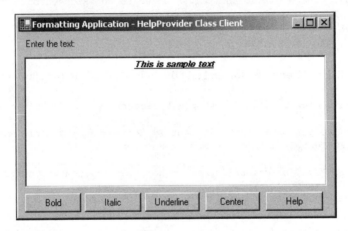

12. When the Bold button is tab-selected, if you press *F1*, you will see the help file opening up with the selected keyword Bold appearing in the Index function of the help system. Click Display to then see the topic:

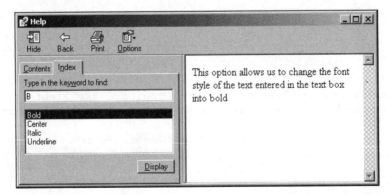

13. When you click on the Help button, you will see the help file opening up with TableOfContents being the selected function but without a selected context.

How It Works

We will cover the way help works in a little while, but let us start our explanation by considering the `Click` event of the Bold button.

```
private void boldButton_Click(object sender, System.EventArgs e)
{
   Font oldFont;
   Font newFont;
```

We start by getting the font, which is being used in the current selection and assigning it to a local variable. Then we check if this selection is already bold using the bitwise ~ operator. If it is, we remove the bold setting; otherwise we add the bold setting. We achieve this by creating a new font using the `oldFont` as the prototype, but add or remove the bold style as needed.

```
//Get the font that is being used in the selected text
oldFont = this.rtfText.SelectionFont;
//If the font is using bold style now, remove the formatting
if (oldFont.Bold)
   newFont = new Font(oldFont,oldFont.Style & ~FontStyle.Bold);
else
   newFont = new Font(oldFont,oldFont.Style | FontStyle.Bold);
```

Finally, we assign the new font to the selection and return focus to the `RichTextBox`.

```
//Insert the new font and return focus to the Richtextbox
this.rtfText.SelectionFont = newFont;
this.rtfText.Focus();
}
```

The code for the click event handlers of the italic and underline buttons is similar to the above, except we deal with either italic or underline font styles, while setting the font.

Let us consider the click event of the Center button.

```
private void centerButton_Click(object sender, System.EventArgs e)
{
```

Here we check the `SelectionAlignment` property to see if the text in the selection is already centered; if it is we make it left aligned and if it isn't we center it.

We do this by checking the `HorizontalAlignment` enumeration.

```
if (this.rtfText.SelectionAlignment == HorizontalAlignment.Center)
  this.rtfText.SelectionAlignment = HorizontalAlignment.Left;
else
  this.rtfText.SelectionAlignment = HorizontalAlignment.Center;
this.rtfText.Focus();
}
```

In the `Form_Load()` event, we hook up the external help file into our application. We start by creating an instance of the `HelpProvider` class.

```
private void HelpProviderClassClient_Load(object sender, System.EventArgs e)
{
  HelpProvider helpProv = new HelpProvider();
```

Then we set the `HelpNamespace` property to the external file that we created.

```
helpProv.HelpNamespace =
    @"C:\DevWinSoftware\Ch10\HTMLHelp\FormattingAppHelp.chm";
```

Once we have set the `HelpNamespace` property to an external file, we can then link that external help file to the individual controls in the form. We also invoke the `SetHelpNavigator()` method to specify that the `TableOfContents` function be displayed when invoking help with the focus on the form.

```
helpProv.SetHelpNavigator(this, HelpNavigator.TableOfContents);
```

In the following lines of code, we specify the keywords to be used for retrieving help when the user invokes help for the specified control.

```
helpProv.SetHelpKeyword(boldButton,"Bold");
helpProv.SetHelpKeyword(italicButton,"Italic");
helpProv.SetHelpKeyword(underlineButton,"Underline");
helpProv.SetHelpKeyword(centerButton,"Center");
}
```

When the user clicks the **Help** button, we invoke the static `ShowHelp()` method to display the contents of the external help file.

```
private void helpButton_Click(object sender, System.EventArgs e)
{
  Help.ShowHelp(this,
                @"D:\FormattingAppHelp.chm",
                HelpNavigator.TableOfContents);
}
```

Displaying Pop-Up Help via a Help Button

If you have used Windows-based software applications before, you have probably come across the Help button (often identified by ?) that is normally found in the right side of the title bar of the form. This kind of help is well suited to cases where we need to display modal dialog boxes. This is due to the inherent nature of the modal dialog boxes, since modal dialog boxes have to be closed before the focus can shift to another window. It is also important to keep in mind that using the Help button requires that Maximize and Minimize buttons not be present in the title bar.

In the previous example, we used the `HelpProvider` class present in the `System.Windows.Forms` namespace. By default, Visual Studio .NET comes bundled with a component (which can be accessed from the toolbox) named `HelpProvider` that encapsulates the functionalities of the `HelpProvider` class. This can be found in the toolbox on the **Windows Forms** tab. In the following example, we will make use of the `HelpProvider` component and take advantage of its easy-to-use Properties window to display pop-up helps in our application.

Try It Out – Displaying Pop-Up Help using the HelpProvider Component

1. Open up the `HelpSampleApplication` project that we used in the previous example.

2. Add a new Windows Form named `HelpProviderComponentClient.cs`. With the focus on the form, press *F4* to display the Properties window of the form. Set the `HelpButton` property to `True`. Also change the `MaximizeBox` and `MinimizeBox` properties to `False`. If you do not set these values, the `HelpButton` property of the form is ignored at run time.

3. To this form, we add the same set of controls that we used for the other form (`HelpProviderClassClient.cs`). We also copy over the `Main()` method and all of the event handlers for all of the controls to this form.

4. Drag and drop a `HelpProvider` component from the **Toolbox** to the Designer. It will sit in the tray at the bottom of the Designer. Look at its Properties window. Remember to use your own path for the `HelpNamespace` property.

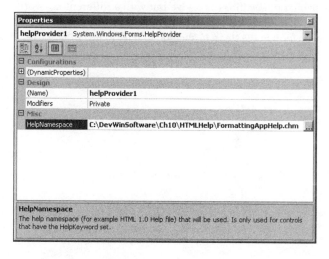

5. In the window, set the `HelpNamespace` property to the `FormattingAppHelp.chm` file that we created earlier using HTML Help workshop.

6. Select the Bold button in the form designer and display its Properties window:

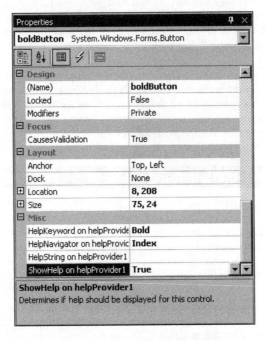

7. Set the `HelpKeyword`, `HelpNavigator`, and `ShowHelp` properties to the values as shown above. These values only appear due to the addition of the `HelpProvider` control on the page.

8. We perform the same steps for the rest of the controls in the form (Center, Italic, and Underline), using same settings as above but with a different keyword.

9. Setup the startup form in the `Main()` method to refer to `HelpProviderComponentClient` form.

10. Press *F5* to run the application. It should look like the following:

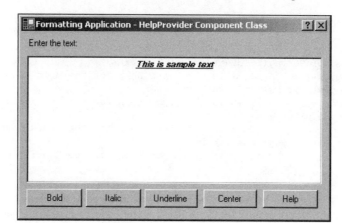

11. If you click the Help button in the title bar, you will see the mouse pointer icon having a help icon attached to it. Then if you click the **Bold** button or any of the other controls, it opens up the help file with the appropriate content highlighted.

Displaying Pop-Up Help as a String

In the previous example, we displayed pop-up help in the form of HTML topic files from an external help system. It is also possible to display pop-up help in a small pop-up window. This is very useful in cases where we want to display short help information without having to launch the external help system. This kind of help differs from a tooltip-based help in that it opens up a small pop-up window; whereas in the tooltip-based help does not open a pop-up window to accomplish this. We will see an example of the tooltip-based help in the later section of this chapter.

Try It Out – Displaying Pop-Up Help as a String using the HelpProvider Class

1. Open up the `HelpSampleApplication` project that we created earlier.

2. Add a new Windows Form and name it `PopUpHelp.cs`.

3. To this form, we add the same set of controls that we used for the other form (`HelpProviderClassClient.cs`). We also copy over all of the event handlers' code (except for the code in the form load event) to this form.

4. Double-click the form and add the following lines of code to the Load event of the form.

```
private void PopUpHelp_Load(object sender, System.EventArgs e)
{
  HelpProvider helpProv = new HelpProvider();
  helpProv.SetHelpString(boldButton,
                         "This is the popup help for the Bold button");
  helpProv.SetHelpString(italicButton,
                         "This is the popup help for the Italic button");
  helpProv.SetHelpString(centerButton,
                         "This is the popup help for the Center button");
  helpProv.SetHelpString(underlineButton,
                         "This is the popup help for the Underline button");
}
```

In the above lines of code, we start by creating an instance of the HelpProvider class. We then invoke the SetHelpString() method of the HelpProvider object to associate appropriate help strings with the individual controls.

5. Reset the startup form in the Main() method to point to PopUpHelp form.

6. In the **Solution Explorer** right-click on the HelpSampleApplication and select **Properties**. Under the Startup Object property set the value as HelpSampleApplication.PopUpHelp.

7. Now run the application by pressing *F5*.

If you press *F1*, with the focus on the **Bold** button, you should see output something that is similar to the following:

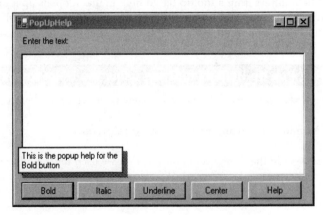

Providing Control Help Using a Tooltip

Another popular and widely used way of providing help information in an application is by using a tooltip. By using tooltips, we can provide a brief description of the control's purpose when the user moves the mouse over the control. This is a familiar behavior that can be seen in all of the Microsoft products. In addition to providing static help information about a control, we can also configure the tooltip to display help information that is created dynamically. For example in a data entry form, the tooltip for a textbox control can be configured to display dynamic help information based on the values the user enters in the other controls in the form. The `ToolTip` class is contained in the `System.Windows.Forms` namespace.

It is possible to use a single `ToolTip` component to provide help for multiple controls. For example, by having a single instance of the `ToolTip` component, we can provide help for a button control, and a label control, and so on. The `ToolTip` component exposes a method named `SetToolTip()`, which allows us to specify the tooltip text displayed for each control on the form. The tooltip component is very flexible in that it can be configured in such a way that there is a delay before the tooltip is shown.

The following table describes the important properties of the `ToolTip` class.

Property	Description
Active	Allows us to get or set a value specifying if the tooltip is currently active
AutoPopDelay	Allows us to get or set the amount of time the tooltip remains active when the mouse pointer is stationary
InitialDelay	Allows us to get or set the initial delay that elapses before the tooltip appears
ShowAlways	Allows us to get or set a value indicating if the tooltip is shown even when the parent control is not active

The following table describes the important methods exposed by the `ToolTip` class.

Method	Description
SetToolTip()	Allows us to associate tooltip text with the specified control
GetToolTip()	Allows us to retrieve the tooltip associated with the specified control
RemoveAll()	Removes all the tooltip text associated with the Tooltip component

Let us take a look at an example application that demonstrates the usage of `ToolTip` component to display help information in a Windows application.

Try It Out – Providing Help Using a Tooltip

In this example, we will make use of the `ToolTip` component to display a tooltip help message.

1. Open up the `HelpSampleApplication` project that we created earlier.

2. Add a new Windows Form and name it `ToolTipHelp.cs`.

3. To this form, add the same set of controls that we used for the other form (`HelpProviderClassClient.cs`). Also copy over all of the event handlers to this form.

4. Drag and drop a `ToolTip` component from the toolbox onto the designer surface of the form.

5. Double-click the form and add the following lines of code to the `Load` event handler of the form.

```
private void ToolTipHelp_Load (object sender, System.EventArgs e)
{
  toolTip1.SetToolTip(boldButton,
                      "Change the font style to bold");
  toolTip1.SetToolTip(italicButton,
                      "Change the font style to Italic");
  toolTip1.SetToolTip(underlineButton,
                      "Change the font style to Underline");
  toolTip1.SetToolTip(centerButton,
                      "Change the font alignment to Center");
  toolTip1.SetToolTip(helpButton,
     "Click here to find more information on this application");
}
```

In the above block of code, we associate a tooltip for the individual controls by invoking the `SetToolTip()` method of the `ToolTip` component. To this method, we pass in the name of the control and the tooltip to be shown for that control as arguments.

6. Change the startup form in the main method to refer to `ToolTipHelp` form.

7. Run the application by pressing *F5*. If you move the mouse over the controls, you will see the tooltip information being displayed.

Summary

We started off this chapter by discussing the need for comprehensive help systems for software applications. We then went on to discuss the design guidelines to be followed while creating effective help systems. We also talked about the different types of Help authoring systems provided by different vendors. After that, we shifted our focus to HTML Help Workshop, the industry-standard help authoring system supplied by Microsoft, and understood the procedures to be followed for creating help systems using HTML Help Workshop.

We then looked at the support provided by the .NET Framework for hooking up external help systems into Windows applications for providing help. While demonstrating this, we looked at the classes supplied by the Framework such as `Help` and `HelpProvider` and so on. Specifically we:

❑ Discussed the properties and methods of the `HelpProvider` class that are necessary to display help information from an external help system

❑ Also looked at the functionalities of the `Help` class to understand how it encapsulates the HTML Help engine

❑ Saw how to utilize the `ToolTip` component to display brief help information about a control's purpose in a Windows Form

In the next chapter we are going to look at the options available to us when we distribute our Windows application.

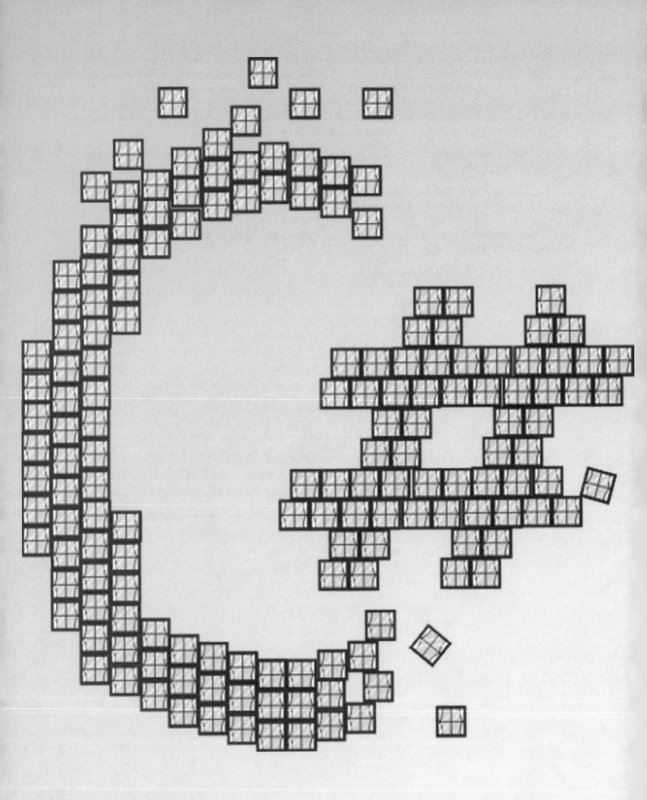

Deploying Windows Applications

In the early days of personal computing, constructing an application that could be installed successfully on another computer was often as simple as compiling an .exe file and copying it to a floppy disk. As applications have become increasingly complex and sophisticated, the number of files needed for a typical installation has grown from a handful of files to several hundreds. This is especially true with Windows applications, which have historically required sophisticated setup programs to copy the correct dynamic link libraries and support files to the end user's computer and to register the applications appropriately with the operating system.

In this chapter, we will discuss the support provided by the .NET Framework for deploying Windows applications to the end user's machine. We will also discuss the different types of deployment options provided by the .NET Framework. Specifically we will:

- ❑ Introduce the fundamentals of deployment
- ❑ Explain how to plan for deployment
- ❑ Discuss the deployment options supported by the .NET Framework
- ❑ Clarify the difference between XCOPY and the Windows Installer
- ❑ Describe the architecture of the Windows Installer
- ❑ Explain the process of packaging up Windows Forms applications using the setup and deployment project types supported by Visual Studio .NET
- ❑ See how to deploy these applications onto the end user's machine

As we cover these aspects of deployment, we will focus on the practical aspects of creating deployment projects in Visual Studio .NET using a number of walkthroughs.

Deployment and Setup

Before we appreciate the processes involved in setting up and deploying applications, we need to understand the difference between setup and deployment. **Deployment** is the process of packaging up the application we have created and installing it in on another machine. A **setup** is an application or process that allows us to package up our application into an easy-to-deploy format.

Deployment in .NET

At one time or another, most computer users have experienced the dark side of installing Windows programs. For example, prior to the .NET era, when you installed a new version of your Windows application, the installation program copied the new version of your DLLs into the system directory and made all the necessary Registry changes. This installation might have potentially had an impact on other applications running on the machine, especially if an existing application was using the shared version of the installed component. If the installed component is backward-compatible with the previous versions, then this is fine, but in many cases it may not be possible to maintain backward compatibility. If you cannot maintain backward compatibility, you will often end up breaking the existing applications as a result of new installations. By using .NET we can try to avoid these problems to an extent because of the built-in support for checking if the files we are trying to replace are used by the other applications in the system.

One of the areas Visual C# .NET was designed to address was the installation shortcomings of Windows applications that relied heavily on COM components. In Visual C# .NET, it is possible to simplify the installation process because Visual C# .NET applications rely on .NET assemblies (which are built on a completely different programming model to COM) for much of their functionality. In addition, Visual Studio .NET applications are compiled as assemblies. To understand how Visual Studio .NET simplifies the deployment process, we need to take a brief look at the structure of the assembly that allows this simplification.

Assemblies contain four elements:

❑ **MSIL (Microsoft Intermediate Language) code** – Language code (C#, VB.NET, and others) is compiled into this intermediate common language that can be understand by the common language runtime (CLR)

❑ **Metadata** – Contains information about the types, methods and other elements defined in the code

❑ **Manifest** – Contains name and version information, a list of included files in the assembly, security information, and so on

❑ **Non-executable content** – Including supporting files and resources

As you can see, assemblies are so comprehensive and self-describing that Visual Studio .NET applications don't need to be registered with the Registry. This means that Visual Studio .NET applications can be installed by simply copying the required files to the target machine that has the .NET Framework installed. This is known as **XCOPY deployment**. However, it is also possible to automate the setup process by making use of the deployment projects that are provided by Visual Studio .NET. Let's now take a closer look at these Windows application deployment options supported by .NET.

Installation Via XCOPY Deployment

Prior to .NET, installing a component required copying the component to the appropriate directories, then making appropriate Registry entries. However, one of the primary goals of the .NET Framework is to simplify the deployment by making possible what is known as XCOPY deployment – in other words, to install the component, all we have to do is copy the assembly into the `bin` directory of the client application, and the application will be able to start using it right away because of the self-describing nature of the assembly. This is possible because compilers in the .NET Framework embed identifiers or metadata into compiled modules and the CLR uses this information to load the appropriate version of the assemblies. The identifiers contain all the information required to load and run modules, and also to locate all the other modules referenced by the assembly. An XCOPY deployment is also called a **zero-impact install** since we are not impacting the machine by configuring the Registry entries and configuring the component. It is also possible to install components into the Global Assembly Cache (GAC) by using the `gacutil` utility.

This zero-impact installation also makes it possible to uninstall a component without affecting the system in any manner. All that is required to complete uninstallation is the removal of the specific files from the specific directory.

Using Visual Studio .NET Installer for Deployment

Even though XCOPY deployment is very simple, it isn't actually desirable for most installation scenarios. Most of the time we will want to allow our users to configure their installation, probably via an installation wizard. For more robust application setup and deployment requirements like this, Visual Studio .NET provides an installer. Visual Studio .NET Installer is built on top of Windows Installer technology, so it takes advantages of all of the features of Windows Installer. So before we dive into a discussion of the Visual Studio .NET installer, it's probably a good idea to take a look at the architecture of Windows Installer first.

Windows Installer Architecture

Windows Installer is a software installation and configuration service that ships with the Windows 2000 and Windows XP operating systems, and is freely available to all Win9x and NT4 platforms. Windows Installer Service maintains a record of information about every application that it installs. The Windows Installer runtime inspects these records during the execution of deployment packages. When you attempt to uninstall the application, Windows Installer checks the records to make sure that no other applications rely on its components before removing them. If it finds that there are other applications using the components it will not uninstall those components.

Windows Installer divides applications into the following three levels:

❑ **Product** – This is something a user can install. For example, MS Word is a product that a user can install.

❑ **Feature** – A product is composed of multiple features. A feature is also the smallest unit of functionality of a product. For example, the AutoCorrect functionality can be considered as a feature of MS Word.

❑ **Component** – A component can be considered as the smallest unit that can be shared across multiple features. It is very important to understand that the component in Windows Installer terms is not the same as the term component in the .NET Framework. A Windows Installer component can be a single file or multiple files that logically belong together. It can be an executable, a dll, or a simple text file. A collection of components can form together to provide a feature and it is also possible for a component to be shared across multiple features. While features are specific to a product and identified by a name unique only within the product, components are global across all products installed on a machine. For example, the spell checker component of MS Word can be shared across all the applications that want to implement spell-checking features.

Information related to a product, such as features and components, are described in a centralized repository known as the **installation database**. The installation database is a file with the extension `.msi` that not only contains information about the features and components of the product but also about the sequence of user interfaces displayed during the installation of the product. Since the Windows Installer is registered as the default application for files with `.msi` extension, the shell automatically invokes it when an `.msi` file is opened by a user. When invoked in this way, the installer reads product information from the installation database file and determines whether the product is already installed. If the product is not yet installed, it launches the product's installation sequence, which is described in the database. If the product is installed, different logic can be invoked, such as to add and remove features, or uninstall the product.

Visual Studio .NET Installer

In addition to the features of Windows Installer, the deployment projects in Visual Studio .NET also provide the following features:

❑ Reading or writing of Registry keys

❑ Allows us to create directories in the Windows file system

❑ Provides a mechanism to register both COM components and .NET components (in the Global Assembly Cache).

❑ Gathering information from the users during installation

❑ Allows us to set launch conditions, such as checking the user name, computer name, current operating system, software application installed, presence of .NET CLR, and so on

❑ Also makes it possible to run a custom setup program or script after the installation is complete

We will take an in-depth look at all the above-mentioned features when we create deployment projects using Visual Studio .NET in the later part of this chapter.

XCOPY or Windows Installer?

As we have seen, XCOPY is ideal for deployment scenarios that are simple and manually executed. Although XCOPY works well for simple scenarios, there are obviously many cases where a more robust deployment solution is required. In those scenarios, it is recommended that we use the Windows Installer technology to install applications. The following advantages of Windows Installer make it an ideal candidate for creating setup and deployments for applications created using the .NET Framework:

❑ If the application installed using Windows Installer is corrupted, the applications can do a self-repair by using the repair feature of Windows Installer packages. In XCOPY-based deployments, we need to manually replace the corrupted component with the newer version.

❑ By using Windows Installer, we can also take advantage of the automatic rollback feature. This not only ensures that the installed components are uninstalled, but also that the machine is brought back to the same stage before the installer started if the installation fails.

❑ Since Windows Installer uses an MSI installation database for storing all of the information, it is possible to get information about what files are copied, and what Registry keys are created.

❑ If you're developing an application that you want to distribute to multiple users (or sell as a package), you need a more convenient, automated approach to deploy them. A manual deployment process such as XCOPY is not desirable and may not work due to the complexity of work involved. However, by using a sophisticated installer technology such as Windows Installer, we can automate the entire installation process, thereby simplifying the deployment.

Deployment Project Templates in Visual Studio .NET

Visual Studio .NET, by default, comes bundled with five types of project templates that can be used to setup and deploy applications created using the .NET Framework. These project templates can be accessed in the same way as any other project in Visual Studio .NET, by using the File | New Project dialog box.

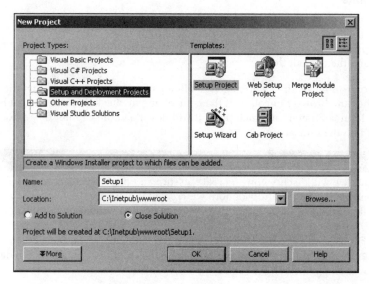

The above figure shows the different setup and deployment project types available in Visual Studio .NET. Let us take a brief look at each of the available project types.

Setup Project Template

The Setup Project template is used to create a standard Windows Installer setup for a Visual Studio .NET application.

Web Setup Project Template

The Web Setup Project template is used to create a Windows Installer setup program that can be used to install a web application onto a virtual directory of a web server.

Merge Module Project Template

Microsoft introduced merge modules as part of the Windows Installer technology to enable a set of files to be packaged up into an easy-to-use file that could be re-used and shared between setup programs that are based on Windows Installer technology. The idea is to package all the files and any other resources that are dependent on each other into the merge module. As you can imagine, this type of project can be very useful for packaging a component and all its dependencies into a single unit, which can then be merged into the setup program of each application that uses the component. During the installation, the merge module component will be installed only if the component is not present in the machine. The merge module Windows Installer package files are identified by the file extension .msm. The latest versions of MSXML (Microsoft XML) Parser are also available in the form merge modules. If your application uses MSXML Parser, you can easily package the merge module into the setup program of your application.

Setup Wizard Template

The Setup Wizard can be used to guide us through the process of creating one of the above setup and deployment project templates.

Cab Project Template

The Cab Project template is used to create a cabinet file (.cab). A cabinet file can contain any number of files, but no installation logic, and is generally used to package components into a single file which can then be deployed on a web server to enable the browser-based clients to download them onto their local machine and then install them.

For example, controls hosted in a web page are often packaged up into a cabinet file and placed in the web server. When the browser encounters the control, it will check that the control isn't already installed in the local computer, at which point it will download the cabinet file, extract the control from it, and install it into the user's computer.

Try It Out – Creating a Windows Installer Project

In this Try It Out, we will discuss how to create a setup and deploy project for the Formatting Application (named HelpSampleApplication) we created in Chapter 10. We will start by adding a Windows Installer project to the solution that contains the C# formatting application project.

   1. Select File | Open | Project and navigate to the path where you have created the HelpSampleApplication. If you did not create the solution, you can download it from the Wrox web site (http://www.wrox.com/).

2. To add a setup project to the solution, select File | Add Project | New Project. In the Add New Project dialog box, select Setup and Deployment Projects and select Setup Project and name the project as HelpSampleApplicationSetup.

3. Right-click on the HelpSampleApplicationSetup project from the Solution Explorer and select Properties. Open up the Configuration Properties tree view and select Build. Click the Configuration Manager button to bring up the Configuration Manager dialog box.

4. Change the Active Solution Configuration setting from Debug to Release for the both the projects to create a release build. Also check the Build option for the setup project. After modification, the dialog box should look like the following screenshot. Click Close.

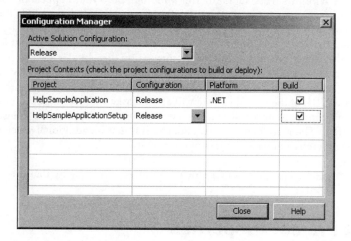

5. In the Build tab, change the Package files option to In setup file. Next, change the Bootstrapper option to Windows Installer BootStrapper. Now change the Compression option to Optimized for speed. Click OK.

How It Works

By setting the configuration settings to Release, we create a release build that can be installed onto the end user's computer. When you are working with a Visual Studio .NET project, by default you will be creating a debug build, that creates the debugging information as part of the project output and the project output is also not optimized for performance. However, before deploying the application, this needs to be changed to the release build, which not only optimizes the project output for performance but also ignores the unnecessary debugging information.

The files that are part of the deployment project can be packaged into any one of the following three formats:

❑ As loose uncompressed files – No compression takes place and the entire program and data files are stored as they are.

❑ In Setup file – When selected, this option merges all the files and compresses them into a MSI file.

❑   In Cabinet file(s) – All files are packaged into one or more cabinet files. The MSI file contains entries about all the project cab files and it uses that information at run time to load and install the cab files. These files will be placed in the same directory as the MSI file.

In our case, since we want to compress all the files into a single MSI file, we selected the option In Setup file.

Next in the BootStrapper property, we set it to Windows Installer Bootstrapper.
A bootstrapper is a program that must be executed before the actual application can be run. When you install the application created using Visual Studio .NET installer, it requires that Windows Installer version 1.5 be present on the target computer. Windows XP operating system is the first operating system that comes bundled with Windows Installer 1.5. If you want to deploy your application on earlier systems, you need to include the bootstrapper as part of the installation program. If you include this option, it increases the file size by about 3MB. Since we want to include the bootstrapper to support earlier systems, we selected that option. However, it is important to note that if you are deploying your application only on Windows XP-based systems, you can safely ignore this option thereby decreasing the size of the final installation program. If we use Web Bootstrapper option, we need to make the bootstrapper available for download over the Web, as it isn't included in the MSI download. When selecting this option, we will be asked to provide the URL of the download, we will also be asked for the application setup directory, but the URL is the more important information. The user installing the application to install the bootstrapper will then use this URL. The main benefit to this approach is that no additional space is required in the installation package thereby reducing the size of the install.

By setting the Compression property to Optimized for speed, we specify that the files will be compressed to install faster.

Deployment Project Properties

Apart from setting the configuration properties for the entire solution, we also need to set the following deployment-specific properties for the deployment project, HelpSampleApplicationSetup. These properties are accessed through the Properties window. The following table discusses some of the important properties that can be set for a deployment project:

Property	Description
AddRemoveProgramsIcon	Specifies the icon to be displayed in the Add/Remove Programs dialog box on the target computer
Author	Allows us to specify the name of the author of the application
Description	Allows us to specify the description that is displayed during the installation
Keywords	Specifies the keywords that can be used to search for an installer in the target machine
DetectNewerInstalledVersion	Allows us to specify if we want to check for the newer versions of the application during the installation

Property	Description
RemovePreviousVersions	Allows us to indicate if we want to remove the previous versions of the application during the installation
Manufacturer	Specifies the name of the manufacturer of the application
ManufacturerUrl	URL of the manufacturer's web site
ProductCode	Specifies a unique identifier (GUID) for the application
ProductName	Name of the product
SupportUrl	URL for the web site that contains support information about the application
Title	Title for the installer
Version	Specifies the version number of the installer

Try It Out – Setting the Deployment Project Properties

Let's now go back to our HelpSampleApplication project and set the deployment project properties.

1. Ensure HelpSampleApplicationSetup project is selected in the Solution Explorer. Select View | Properties Window from the menu.

2. Fill in all the details as shown below:

Property	Value
AddRemoveProgramsIcon	(None)
Author	Wrox Author Team (Or whatever you want)
Description	This is the setup for the HelpSample Application
Keywords	HelpSampleApplication, Wrox
Localization	English (United States)
Manufacturer	Wrox Press
ManufacturerUrl	http://www.wrox.com/
ProductCode	(This will vary)
ProductName	HelpSampleApplicationSetup
RemovePreviousVersions	False

Table continued on following page

Property	Value
SupportUrl	http://www.wrox.com/support/
Title	HelpSampleApplication Setup
UpgradeCode	(This will vary)
Version	1.0.0

Using Setup Editors

Because of the flexibility offered by the deployment projects in Visual Studio .NET, it is very easy for us to specify how and where a solution will be deployed. The bulk of an installer's work is copying files to the right places, so there is a file system configuration editor within the setup editors; however, a setup can also include Registry configuration options, checking for special conditions, and so on. It is also useful to be able to customize the installer's user interface as well. For these reasons, Visual Studio .NET includes a number of setup editors:

- ❑ **File System Editor** – Used to add files and shortcuts, such as Start menu items, to the installation package.

- ❑ **Registry Editor** – Allows us to manipulate Registry entries on the target computer.

- ❑ **File Types Editor** – Allows us to associate file extensions with applications. This is useful in cases if your application uses custom file extensions and you want to associate a specific application with that file extension.

- ❑ **User Interface Editor** – Allows us to configure the dialogs that are shown during the installation.

- ❑ **Custom Actions Editor** – Allows us to start external programs during installs and uninstalls.

- ❑ **Launch Conditions Editor** – Allows us to specify the requirements for our application to be installed on the target computer.

All of these editors can be accessed through the View | Editors menu. Let's now take an in-depth look at all the editors, with examples of how to make use of them.

File System Editor

As the name suggests, this editor allows us to add project output files, assemblies, and other files to the deployment project. Using this editor, we can also specify the directory location where these files will be installed on the end user's computer.

You can open the File System editor by selecting **View | Editor | File System** menu. It looks like the following (We have added the Global Assembly Cache Folder to the display; it is not included by default).

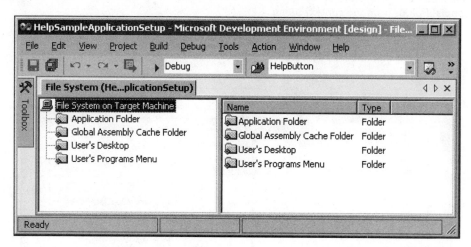

By using any of the predefined folders above, we can choose a destination folder on a target computer without even having to know the actual path to that folder; it is worked out by the installer from the virtual path at installation. Let us take a brief look at each of the above folders and their purposes.

❑ **Application Folder** – Application Folder is normally represented by the path [ProgramFilesFolder][Manufacturer]\[ProductName]. On English systems, by default, the [ProgramFilesFolder] folder resolves to [Drive Name]\Program Files. The names for the Manufacturer and ProductName directories will be taken from the settings that we defined while setting the project properties. It is also possible for the end users to override these settings while installing the application.

❑ **Global Assembly Cache folder** – Allows us to specify the assemblies that need to be installed as shared assemblies on the target computer.

❑ **User's Desktop** – This folder acts as a placeholder for files and folders that should appear on the desktop of the user. The default location of this folder is [DriveName]\Documents and Settings\[UserName]\Desktop, with the username representing the name of the user that performs the installation.

❑ **User's Programs Menu** – This folder acts as a placeholder for entries that should appear on the programs group of the user. The default location of this folder is [DriveName]\Documents and Settings\[UserName]\Start Menu\Programs, with the username representing the name of the user that performs the installation.

Apart from the above four folders, we can also add custom folders from a predefined list of folders to the File System editor. To display the list of special folders that can be added to the File System editor, Right-click on the File System on Target Machine folder from the File System editor and then select Add Special Folder from the context menu:

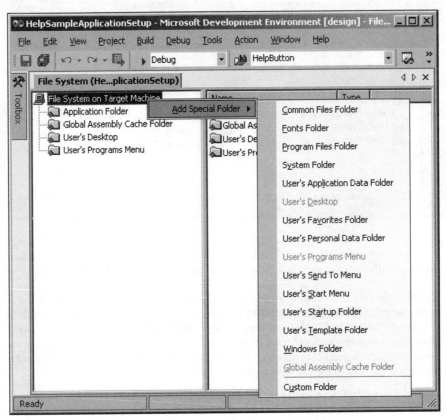

Adding Items to Special Folders

Using the File System editor, we can add any of the following four items as shown in the following screenshot to the special folders:

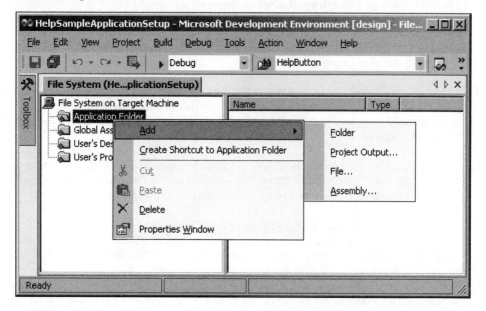

❑ **Folder** – Allows us to create a folder on the target machine in the specified directory.

❑ **Project Output** – Allows us to specify where the output of one or more projects (.dll or .exe files) in the solution will be deployed on a target computer. It also adds all the dependencies to the folder.

❑ **File** – Using this option, we can also deploy loose (zero compression) files to a target computer. It can be very useful for deploying help files, such as Readme.txt.

❑ **Assembly** – Allows us to specify the assemblies that need to be added. When this option is selected, it adds all the referenced assemblies as well.

Try It Out – Adding Files to the Setup Project

Let's now add files to our HelpSampleApplicationSetup setup project.

1. The first step in creating a setup is specifying what files you want to be copied to the target computer, using the File System editor. Select the Application Folder directory and then add the primary output of the HelpSampleApplication to the installer using the Project | Add | Project Output menu. Select Primary Output in the Add Project Output Group dialog box.

2. When you press OK in the dialog box, the primary output of the HelpSampleApplication project will be added to the Application Folder in the File System Editor. At the same time, it also adds the dependencies to the installer project. Since the HelpSampleApplication requires the .NET runtime, you will see that being automatically added to the installer project, as a result of which the merge module for the .NET runtime dotnetfxredist_x86_enu.msm becomes visible in the Solution Explorer. This merge module includes all files for the .NET runtime. If the .NET runtime is not already installed on the target system, it will be installed along with our application.

3. In our case, since we require that the .NET runtime be already present on the target machine, we will exclude this file from the package. We do this by selecting the file dotnetfxredist_x86_enu.msm and then setting the Exclude property to True through the Properties window.

4. Now, we will add the additional folders and files. Right-click on Application Folder in the File System editor and select Add | Folder. Name the created folder Support. This folder will be used as a placeholder where all the supporting files for the application are stored.

5. Right-click on the Support folder and select Add | File and add `readme.rtf`, `license.rtf`, `Readme.txt`, `splashscreen.bmp`, and `wroxlogobitmap.bmp` files to the Support folder. You can download all these files from http://www.wrox.com/.

6. Since we want the `Readme.txt` file to be available as an individual file to allow the end user to read that information before the installation, we will have this file as a loose file (uncompressed) in the installer package. To do this, select `Readme.txt` file from the Support folder and select View | Properties Window. Change the `PackageAs` property to `vsdpaLoose`. The setting `vsdpaDefault` packages the overall application and we override it with this new setting.

7. In this step, we will add the provision for the users to create a shortcut to the HelpSampleApplication in their desktop. As we said already, this requires the shortcut to be added to the User's Desktop folder. To add the shortcut, right-click on the Primary output from HelpSampleApplication (Active) item in the Application Folder and select Create Shortcut to Primary output from HelpSampleApplication (Active) from the context menu. Rename the shortcut to Formatting Application. Drag and drop this shortcut to the User's Desktop folder. However, we want this shortcut to be installed only if the user wants to install it. Therefore, set the Condition property of the User's Desktop folder to SHORTCUTDEMO. This ensures that the shortcut will be installed only if this condition is set to True. In the later part of this chapter (when we look at the User Interface Design editor), we will create a dialog box where this property can be set.

8. Since we also want to make the program available from the Start | Programs menu, we will add a shortcut to the User's Program Menu folder. To add the shortcut, create another shortcut as before, renaming it again to Formatting Application. Drag and drop this shortcut to the User's Programs Menu folder. This time we always want this shortcut to install so we don't alter the Condition property.

Registry Editor

This editor allows us to manage the Registry settings in the target computer where the application will be installed. By default, the registry editor displays the standard Windows Registry keys such as HKEY_CLASSES_ROOT, HKEY_CURRENT_USER, HKEY_LOCAL_MACHINE, and HKEY_USERS. Using the Registry Editor, it is also possible to add custom Registry keys under any of the above keys. Selecting View | Editor | Registry from the menu displays the following Registry Editor.

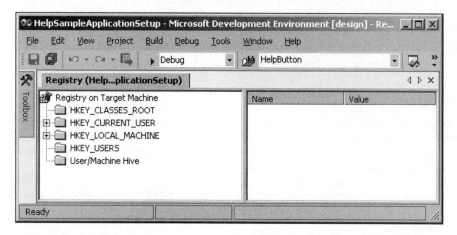

To add additional information to the Registry that your application requires at run time, you can use either HKEY_LOCAL_MACHINE\Software\[Manufacturer] or HKEY_CURRENT_USER\Software\[Manufacturer]. It is a good practice to add the application-specific information under the value specified in the Manufacturer property. Prior to Windows XP there was a distinct difference between the hive and non-hive Registry structure, and the Registry Editor provides a consistent interface to the Registry structure in all Windows operating systems.

File Types Editor

The File Types editor allows us to set up file associations on the target computer. This is accomplished by assigning an application to a file extension, so that double-clicking the file will launch the correct application. Once the initial association is done, the extension and the file type description will appear in the file types list in Windows Explorer. This is very useful if your application uses custom file types that require a separate external application to be launched.

The following table describes the important properties associated with the File Types editor.

Property	Description
Name	Allows us to specify the name used in the file types editor to identify a particular file type
Command	This property can be used to set the executable file that should be launched when the user opens a file with this type

Table continued on following page

Property	Description
Description	Provides the description for the file type
Extensions	Allows us to specify the file extensions with which the executable should be registered
Icon	Specifies an icon to be displayed for the file type
MIME	Specifies one or more MIME types to be associated with the selected file type
Verb	With this property, we can specify the verbs such as open, edit, and play that are used to invoke the selected action for the file type.

Custom Actions Editor

This editor allows us to link to another program, which can then be launched at the end of the installation. To create a custom action, we need to create a .dll or .exe that performs the custom action and then add it to the deployment project. It is also important to note that the custom actions can be launched only at the end of the installation.

These custom actions can be associated with any one of the following four installation outcomes:

❑ Install

❑ Commit

❑ Rollback

❑ Uninstall

For example, if you want to launch a specific external program after installing the application, you can accomplish this by associating that external program with the Install node.

Launch Conditions Editor

Using this editor, we can specify conditions that must be met in order for the setup to run. If the user tries to install the application on a system that does not meet the launch condition, the setup will not run. While setting the launch condition, it is also possible for us to specify that searches be performed on the target computer in order to determine the existence of a particular file, Registry key, or a component, and so on.

As you can see from the following screenshot, this editor has two sections to specify the requirements:

❑ Search Target Machine – This section allows us to specify the kind of search that needs to be performed on the target computer. This may include searching for a specific file, registry key, and so on.

❏   Launch Conditions – This allows you to define the conditions that need to be met to allow the application setup to be launched. One is already defined for the setup application.

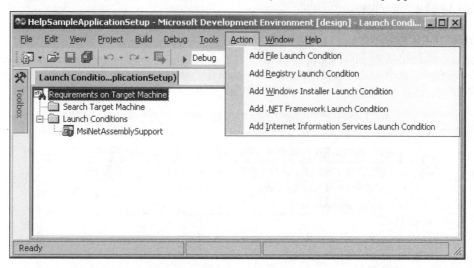

The screenshot above also shows some of the launch conditions that can be defined using the Action menu.

Condition	Purpose
File Launch	Used to search for installed files on the target system
Registry Launch	To search for Registry keys before the start of the installation
Windows Installer Launch	To search for Windows Installer files
.NET Framework Launch	To check for the existence of the .NET Framework on the target computer
Internet Information Services Launch	To check for the installed version of IIS

Try It Out – Adding a Launch Condition to the Installer Package

While adding the primary output of the HelpSampleApplication project to the installer, we excluded the .NET runtime file (dotnetfxredist_x86_enu.msm) from the installer package. Since we did not include the .NET runtime with the installer package, we will check for the existence of the .NET runtime on the target computer by using the .NET Framework launch condition.

1.   Open the Launch Conditions editor by selecting View | Editor | Launch Conditions.

2.   Add a launch condition using Action | Add .NET Framework Launch Condition. Set the Name property to CHECKDOTNETCONDITION.

343

Now that we have set the .NET Framework launch condition, if the user tries to run the installation without having the .NET Framework installed, the installation will not run. An error message will be displayed and the installation will quit.

User Interface Editor

As indicated by the name, this editor permits us to specify the sequence of user interface dialogs that are displayed during the installation of the application on the target computer. We will see an example of this in action when we look at configuring these dialog boxes in the later part of this chapter.

As you can see from the following diagram, the user interface editor consists of two different high-level installation modes.

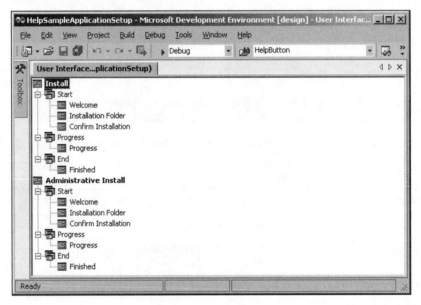

❑ **Install** – The Install section lists all the dialog boxes that will be displayed when the end user runs the installer.

❑ **Administrative Install** – This section lists all the dialog boxes that will be displayed when a system administrator uploads the installer to a network location.

The predefined dialog boxes present in the **Install** and **Administrative Install** sections can be further subdivided into the following three categories.

❑ **Start** dialog boxes – The dialog boxes in this category are displayed before the installation begins.

❑ **Progress** dialog box – Allows us to provide the users with feedback on the progress of the installation.

❑ **End** dialog boxes – Displays that the installation has successfully completed. It can also be used to allow the users to look at the `Readme` file or launch the application.

It is easy to rearrange the dialog boxes by dragging and dropping them onto proper locations. The above-mentioned set of default dialog boxes will always show up in the installation sequence of the application even if we have not configured these dialog boxes ourselves.

Try It Out – Configuring the Default Installation Dialogs

Let's configure the properties of the default installation dialogs for HelpSampleApplicationSetup.

1. Select the Welcome dialog and then select View | Properties Window to display its Properties window. Set the `BannerBitmap` property to `wroxlogobitmap.bmp` by clicking Browse. In the `ComboBox`, navigate to the Application Folder\Support (where we already placed all the support files). Also set the `CopyrightWarning` and `WelcomeText` properties to appropriate values that suit your requirements.

2. Since we want the logo bitmap to be displayed on all of the default dialogs, set the `BannerBitMap` property to `wroxlogobitmap.bmp` in the Installation Folder, Confirm Installation, Progress, and Finished dialog boxes as well.

How to Add Additional Custom Dialogs

In the last exercise, we configured the properties of the default dialogs. The default dialogs are very flexible and can form the core foundation for many of the simple installations. However, there are times where you may want to customize the installation sequence to support your application's requirements. We can accomplish this by adding a new set of dialog boxes by using the Add Dialog menu. Select Start from the User Interface editor and then choose Action | Add Dialog menu: you will see the following dialog box being displayed.

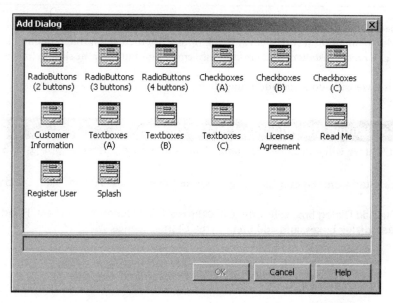

From the above set of dialog boxes, we can choose the dialog box we want to add to our installation sequence. The following table briefly discusses the usage of these dialog boxes and the dialogs already present by default.

Window Type	Purpose
Welcome	Allows us to display an introductory window that can display text information from the `CopyrightWarning` and `WelcomeText` properties.
Customer Information	Allows us to display a window that requires customer information such as name, organization name, and so on. We can also force the user to enter a serial number and perform simple validations using this dialog box.
License Agreement	Allows us to display licensing information to the users that requires them to agree to the licensing conditions. This licensing information is obtained from an external file, which is linked to this dialog through the `LicenseFile` property that can be assigned a Rich Text Format (`.rtf`) file.
Read Me	Displays information from the `.rtf` file specified by the `ReadmeFile` property.
Register User	Allows the users to complete the installation by asking them to register the installation. It displays a **Register Now** button that can either be used to launch an external executable or take them to a web site. We specify the information about the external application and the arguments to be passed to them through `Executable` and `Arguments` properties respectively.
Splash	Displayed at the beginning of the install to display the company logo that can be set through the `SplashBitmap` property.

As you can see, the Windows Installer is very restricted in that we can't design custom windows and add them to the deployment project. However, by adopting a standard approach defined by Windows Installer, we can create installers that are not only consistent but are also simple to use.

In this exercise, we will add some additional dialog boxes to our installation sequence by using the Add Dialog menu.

Try It Out – Configuring the Additional Install Dialogs

In this Try It Out we will add some additional dialogs to our HelpSampleApplicationSetup project.

1. Select Start from the user interface editor and then choose Action | Add Dialog menu.

2. In the Add Dialog box, select the Checkboxes (A), License Agreement, Read Me, and Splash dialog boxes, and add them to the Start sequence.

3. Drag and drop the dialog boxes to arrange them in their proper sequence as displayed in the following screenshot.

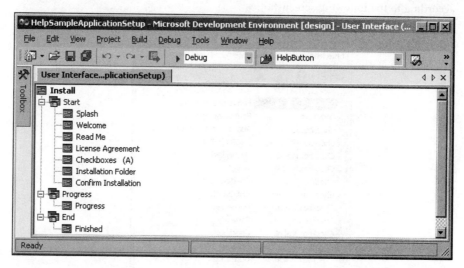

4. Since we want the Wrox logo bitmap to be displayed on all of these additional default dialogs apart from the Splash dialog, let us set the `BannerBitMap` property to `wroxlogobitmap.bmp`. For the Splash dialog change the `BannerBitMap` property to `splashscreen.bmp`.

5. Select the License Agreement dialog box and view its Properties window. Change the `LicenseFile` property to `license.rtf`.

6. Select the Read Me dialog box and view its Properties window. Change the `ReadMeFile` property to `readme.rtf`.

7. We use the Checkboxes (A) dialog box to ask the user if the demo shortcut we placed in the user's desktop folder should be installed or not. Modify the properties of this dialog box according to the following screenshot:

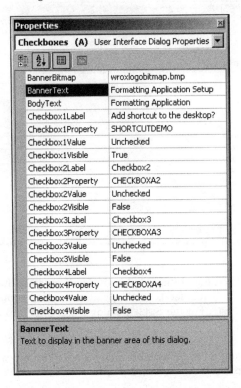

Keep in mind that we set the `CheckBox1Property` to `SHORTCUTDEMO`. This value is the same as the `Condition` property that we set for the **User's Desktop** folder in the File System editor. During installation if the user selects this checkbox, the value of the `SHORTCUTDEMO` condition will be set to `True`, as a result of which the shortcut will be installed to the user's desktop. If the user does not select this checkbox, the `SHORTCUTDEMO` condition will be set to `False` and the shortcut will not be installed. In the above window, we also set the `Visible` property for the rest of the checkboxes to `False` to prevent them from being displayed.

Building the Installer Package

Once we have configured all the editors and set all the options for our setup project, it's pretty easy to build the installer project. So let's do that for our HelpSampleApplicationSetup project.

1. Select Build | Build Solution from the menu to create the MSI installer package.

2. Once the installer is successfully built, you will see the following files in the `Release` directory of your installer project directory.

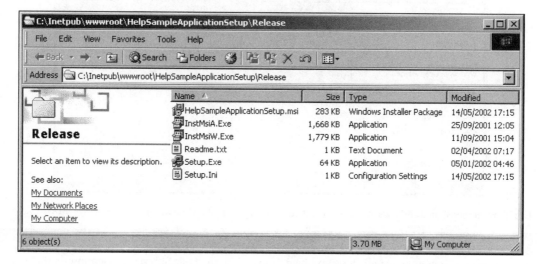

3. In the above picture, you can see that the `Readme.txt` file alone appearing as a single file. This is due to the `PackageAs` property setting (`vsdpaLoose`) that we made while configuring the File System editor. In addition, you can also see two variants of Windows Installers; one version (`InstMsiA.exe`) for Windows 98/ME; another version (`InstMsiW.exe`) for Windows NT/2000/XP.

Installing the Application

To install an application, you can now use any one of the following options.

❑ Double-click on either `.msi` file or `Setup.exe` file from Windows Explorer to start the installation. That `.msi` file launches the `Setup.exe` to start the actual setup process.

❑   Right-click on the `.msi` file and then choose Install from the context menu (shown in the screenshot below).

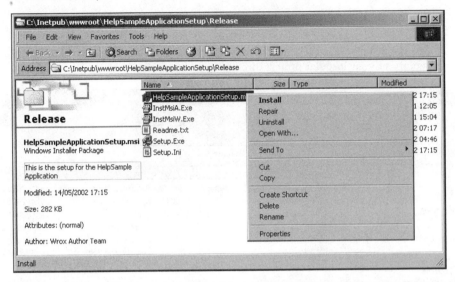

The above screenshot also shows that it is possible to Repair or Uninstall the application from Windows Explorer.

Try It Out – Installing the Application

Now let us go through the actual steps involved in installing the HelpSampleApplication on the end user's computer. Let's start the installation by double-clicking the `HelpSampleApplicationSetup.msi` file from the Windows Explorer. You will see the following steps as you go through the installation.

1.   The first dialog to be seen is the splash dialog, which will appear after a popup window that states Preparing to install. This dialog box displays the bitmap that we specified using the SplashBitmap property.

2. The next dialog that is displayed is the Welcome dialog box. Since we set the BannerBitMap property to the Wrox logo, we see that being displayed in the dialog box.

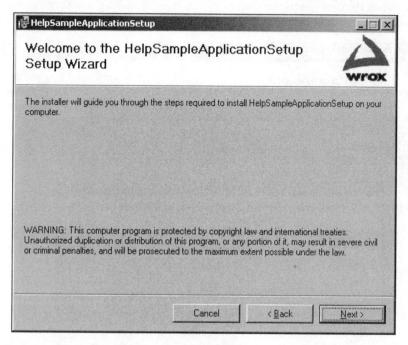

3. The Readme dialog displays the contents of the readme.rtf file that we specified using the ReadMeFile property.

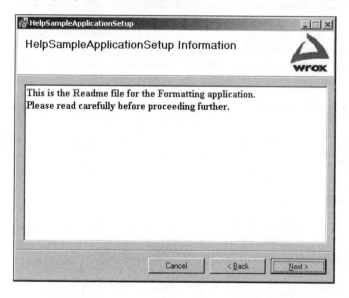

4. The License Agreement dialog displays the contents of the `license.rtf` file that we specified using the `LicenseFile` property. The Next button in the dialog box is enabled only when the user selects the I Agree option thereby making sure that the user agrees to the licensing terms and conditions.

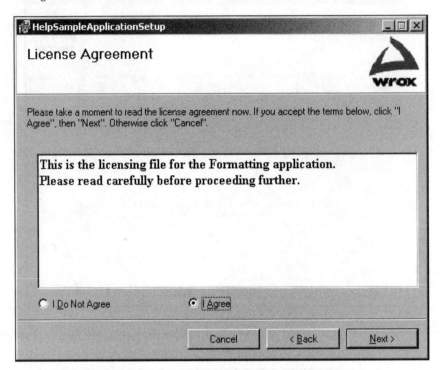

5. The next dialog box asks the users if they want a shortcut to the application to be installed in their desktop or not. When the user checks the checkbox, the condition `SHORTCUTDEMO` is set to `true`, as a result of which a shortcut to the application is installed on the user's desktop.

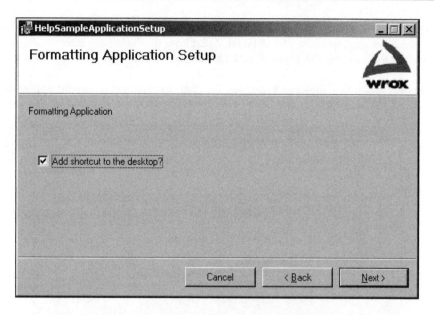

6. The shortcut checkbox dialog box is followed by the Select Installation Folder dialog, which displays the path to the installation folder where the application will be installed. It also provides the users with an option to change the installation folder, if required. Using this dialog box, we can also specify if we want to install the application only for ourselves or we want to make this application available to everyone that will be using this computer. In addition, we can also find out how much of disk space is required for installing the application by clicking the Disk Cost button.

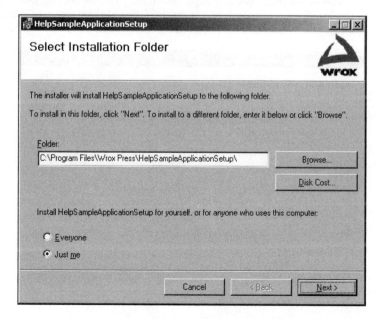

7. Next we get a pop-up dialog box that helps us identify the suitable drive (that has enough space) in which the application can be installed. Apart from displaying the amount of disk space required for installing the application, it also displays the free space available on each drive.

8. The next dialog box allows us to provide the final confirmation before the application install can proceed. Clicking Next button on this dialog box installs the application on the user's computer.

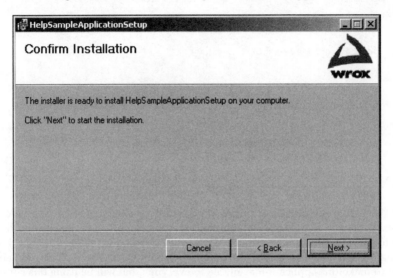

9. When the Next button is pressed in the Confirm Installation dialog box, the installation starts, and the progress of the installation is displayed in the Progress dialog box through a progress bar. Once the installation is complete, we get the following Installation Complete dialog box, which shows that the installation has been successfully completed.

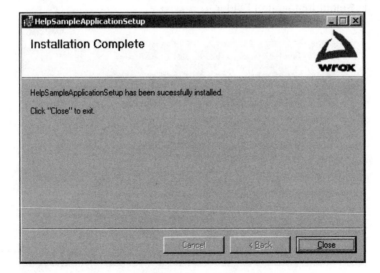

10. If there is any problem with the installation and it does not complete properly, then an error message is displayed.

Uninstalling and Repairing the Application

Now that we have successfully installed the application, let us see what it takes to uninstall the application from the end user's computer. The process of uninstalling the application is very simple. It just requires us to open up the Add/Remove Programs window by going to Start | Control Panel and then double-clicking the Add/Remove Programs icon. As a result, you get the following window.

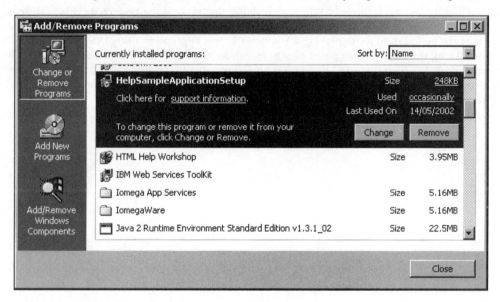

To uninstall the application, all we have to do is to click the Remove button and a confirmation dialog box (asking us to confirm the uninstall process) appears. If you click Yes, the uninstall process begins and the application is completely removed. It is also possible to uninstall the application by right-clicking on the HelpSampleApplicationSetup.msi from the Windows Explorer, and selecting Uninstall from the context menu.

When you right-click on the HelpSampleApplicationSetup.msi file from the Windows Explorer, you can also see the Repair option in the context menu. This is very useful in situations where you have accidentally deleted any of the application-related files from the machine and you want to repair the application so that it is brought back to its original state.

Summary

In this chapter, we have discussed the different aspects of deployment for a Windows Forms application. We considered the fundamentals of deployment and then went on to discuss the different types of deployments supported by .NET. Specifically we covered:

❑ XCOPY deployment

❑ Windows Installer-based deployment

We then highlighted the features of Windows Installer that make it the preferred choice for deploying Windows Forms applications. After discussing deployment methods, we then walked through the procedures to be followed for deploying a Windows Forms application using the Visual Studio .NET Installer. Along the way, we also noted how to customize the installation sequence by making use of the various editors. We then discussed the steps involved in actually installing the application on the end user's computer. Finally, we covered how to uninstall the application by using the Add/Remove Programs dialog box.

Index

Symbol

A

B

S

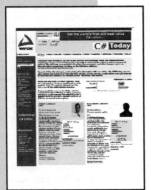

wrox

Programmer to Programmer™

Registration Code: | 737X2Z9P9031KO01 |

Wrox writes books for you. Any suggestions, or ideas about how you want
information given in your ideal book will be studied by our team.
Your comments are always valued at Wrox.

Free phone in USA 800-USE-WROX
Fax (312) 893 8001

UK Tel.: (0121) 687 4100   Fax: (0121) 687 4101

Developing C# Windows Software – Registration Card

Name _____

Address _____

_____

_____

City _____ State/Region _____

Country _____ Postcode/Zip _____

E-Mail _____

Occupation _____

How did you hear about this book?

❏ Book review (name) _____

❏ Advertisement (name) _____

❏ Recommendation _____

❏ Catalog _____

❏ Other _____

Where did you buy this book?

❏ Bookstore (name) _____ City _____

❏ Computer store (name) _____

❏ Mail order _____

❏ Other _____

What influenced you in the purchase of this book?

❏ Cover Design   ❏ Contents   ❏ Other (please specify):

_____

How did you rate the overall content of this book?

❏ Excellent   ❏ Good   ❏ Average   ❏ Poor

What did you find most useful about this book? _____

_____

What did you find least useful about this book? _____

_____

Please add any additional comments. _____

_____

What other subjects will you buy a computer book on soon?

_____

What is the best computer book you have used this year?

_____

Note: This information will only be used to keep you updated
about new Wrox Press titles and will not be used for
any other purpose or passed to any other third party.

Check here if you DO NOT want to receive support for this book ▮

wrox

Programmer to Programmer™

Note: If you post the bounce back card below in the UK, please send it to:

Wrox Press Limited, Arden House, 1102 Warwick Road,
Acocks Green, Birmingham B27 6HB. UK.

Computer Book Publishers